D0378042

GLOBALIZATION: WHAT'S NEW

A COUNCIL ON FOREIGN RELATIONS BOOK

GLOBALIZATION: WHAT'S NEW

EDITED BY MICHAEL M. WEINSTEIN

COLUMBIA UNIVERSITY PRESS   NEW YORK

COLUMBIA UNIVERSITY PRESS
Publishers Since 1893
NEW YORK, CHICHESTER, WEST SUSSEX

Copyright © 2005 Columbia University Press
All rights Reserved

Library of Congress Cataloging-in-Publication Data
Globalization : what's new / edited by Michael M. Weinstein.
p.   cm.
"A Council on Foreign Relations book"—Half t.p.
Includes bibliographical references and index.
ISBN 0–231–13458–4 (cloth : alk. paper)—ISBN 0–231–13459–2 (pbk. : alk. paper)
1. International trade.   2. International economic relations.   3. Globalization.
I. Weinstein, Michael M.

HF 1379.G594 2005
337—dc22
2004058290

Columbia University Press books are printed on permanent and durable acid-free paper
Printed in the United States of America

c 10 9 8 7 6 5 4 3 2 1
p 10 9 8 7 6 5 4 3 2 1

References to Internet Web Sites (URLs) were accurate at the time of writing. Neither the contributors, the editor, nor Columbia University Press is responsible for Web sites that may have expired or changed since the articles were prepared

ACKNOWLEDGMENTS

THIS BOOK OWES ITS EXISTENCE to Leslie H. Gelb, President Emeritus of the Council on Foreign Relations, who dreamed of a book that would strip away journalistic drivel on globalization to bring the careful insights of experts before interested laypeople. He helped me launch this book as one of the first projects of the Council's Maurice R. Greenberg Center for Geoeconomic Studies, which I had the privilege to serve as its first director.

I thank Karl Weber for expert editing, helping to make these chapters accessible to nonexpert readers.

TABLE OF CONTENTS

DISCLAIMER

FOUNDED IN 1921, the Council on Foreign on Foreign Relations is an independent, national membership organization and a nonpartisan center for scholars dedicated to producing and disseminating ideas so that individual and corporate members, as well as policymakers, journalists, students, and interested citizens in the United States and other countries, can better understand the world and the foreign policy choices facing the United States and other governments. The Council does this by convening meetings; conducting a wide-ranging Studies program; publishing *Foreign Affairs*, the preeminent journal covering international affairs and U.S. foreign policy; maintaining a diverse membership; sponsoring Independent Task Forces; and providing up-to-date information about the world and U.S. foreign policy on the Council's website, www.cfr.org.

THE COUNCIL TAKES NO INSTITUTIONAL POSITION ON POLICY ISSUES AND HAS NO AFFILIATION WITH THE U.S. GOVERNMENT. ALL STATEMENTS OF FACT AND EXPRESSIONS OF OPINION CONTAINED IN ITS PUBLICATIONS ARE THE SOLE RESPONSIBILITY OF THE AUTHOR OR AUTHORS.

GLOBALIZATION: WHAT'S NEW

1

Introduction

MICHAEL M. WEINSTEIN

G LOBALIZATION IS a slippery term that lends itself to abuse. Pundits argue about its consequences in part because they make up its meaning to suit their needs. For some, the spectacular economic growth of China and India proves that globalization works to cure poverty. For others, China and India have grown precisely because they've chosen policies that spit in the face of West-prescribed globalization. This volume's primary mission is to create received wisdom—an agreed upon base of information.

To achieve that goal, I asked the country's leading authorities to answer the same question: What's New? They take their best shot at addressing what an interested layperson needs to know to understand current international economic relationships. The guts of this volume lie in the early chapters. They rivet on the facts, describing the world that is—what's new in trade, capital flows, and immigration. The goal is to illuminate, not proselytize. Later chapters delve deeper into cause-and-effect: for example, David Dollar's fact-filled chapter traces the impact of globalization on poverty and living standards in poor countries as well as in the United States. The final chapters devote more attention to policy options and issues of global governance.

The authors are economists living in the United States. Restricting attention to the United States might seem oddly narrow for a book about global matters. I hope you find that the loss of generality is more than offset by what's gained in focus. Narrowing the authors to economists meant that some issues get short shrift. Take the issue of culture. Critics of globalization, especially protesters marching in the streets of Seattle and Davos during recent trade convocations, hold globalization responsible for trampling indigenous culture. France works to protect French filmmakers. Canada seeks protection for home-grown magazines. Is this an important issue? You bet. Yet no chapter devotes much attention to the matter, in part because economists have so far provided few concrete insights into the matter. Jagdish Bhagwati, a colleague at the Council on Foreign Relations, has written a new book that seeks to remedy that oversight. This volume also skips over issues of democracy. Here too, the Council on Foreign Relations seeks to plug the gap by issuing a volume, by Morton H. Halperin, Joseph T. Siegle, and myself, tracing the relationship of democracy to development. Because the volume focuses on what's new and not on shopworn debates, many policy issues (for example, should industrialized countries block imports from countries with "lax" labor standards) are mostly overlooked. And though every economic voice could not be captured in a single volume, the authors range from globalization's most fact-based cheerleader (David Dollar) to its most influential critic (Joseph E. Stiglitz)—with many other authors in between (Jeffrey D. Sachs and Dani Rodrik).

I'm four paragraphs into the introduction about globalization and I've yet to define the term. And I won't. I've left that task to each author to define the term as befits the subject. In general, globalization refers to a process—an evolution of closer economic integration by way of increased trade, foreign investment, and immigration. To others, like Joseph E. Stiglitz in this volume, the term also refers to government and institutional policy. I doubt the reader will choke over the lack of a common definition, because all authors agree on the basics.

They agree, for example, that globalization isn't new. Trade, capital flows, and immigration flourished in the years before World War I, but globalization collapsed between the world wars, and recovered only slowly thereafter. Indeed, it was not until the 1980s that capital flows would return to levels that prevailed prior to World War I. But over the past 20 years or so, economic integration has soared. Trade, measured in relation to world income, has nearly doubled to 18 percent from 10 percent at the dawn of World War I. At the same time, capital flows as a percentage of world income has soared to nearly 20 percent from under 10 percent during the early part of the twentieth century. Nearly 10 percent of the world's population has migrated from one country to another.

The authors also agree that the shape of globalization has changed dramatically over the past 15 or 20 years. The late nineteenth-century version of globalization was a rich nation's play toy. Poor countries mostly hid behind high tariff walls and other barriers. But since about 1980, poor countries, led first by China, have opened their borders, dismantling layers of tariff and non-tariff trade barriers. India, Mexico, Thailand, and others followed China's lead. Some countries opened up because of plummeting transportation costs, which made trade feasible. Others, like China and India opened up because of explicit policy.

With the spread of globalization beyond rich countries has come a massive change in the nature of international economic relations. Twenty-five years ago, poor countries exported minerals and food. Now, they export manufactured products—clothes from Bangladesh, refrigerators from Latin America, music devices from Asia. The Third World has emerged as a serious manufacturing competitor to the Western industrialized powers. The authors point to the important development of production networks—where production plants for, say, automobiles do little more than assemble parts made around the globe. But what comes across in the chapters is the subtlety of globalization. Few simple generalities hold sway. Most economists agree that trade promotes growth in exporting and importing countries, but they are not as sure about capital flows—which do good and bad. Immigration holds enormous promise to help rich and poor countries alike, but also poses immense political difficulties. Everyone wants to reap the benefits of globalized markets, preserve local rules and regulations, and foster democratic control over policy. But, as several authors point out, such three-way goals are mutually impossible. Indeed, three authors in this volume present impossible "trinities" or "trilemmas"—a veritable trifecta of trilemmas—whereby they demonstrate the logical impossibility of achieving unfettered international cooperation while preserving complete control over internal economic rules and regulations. Compromises are necessary, leaving important grounds for policy debate.

The first three chapters go to the heart of "what's new," with a "just give me the facts" approach. They tackle the three key ingredients of international economic relationship: goods, capital, and labor. Douglas A. Irwin of Dartmouth College identifies the important changes in the trade patterns. Charles W. Calomiris of Columbia does the same for capital flows and George J. Borjas of Harvard discusses cross-border movements of people. The next several chapters engage the reader in analysis—what's been the impact of the trends documented in the first three chapters. David Dollar traces the impact of globalization on wage and inequality in poor countries and the United States. Jeffrey A. Frankel analyzes the impact on the environment. William Easterly turns the question around, analyzing the impact of foreign aid on development and globalization. Jeffrey D. Sachs puts the power of policy in perspective, identifying overpowering factors that largely determine the fate of many poor economies no matter what policies are pulled from the economist's playbook. Finally, Dani Rodrik and Joseph E. Stiglitz turn to issues of global governance—what happens when global markets burgeon but global governance remains inchoate.

Below I summarize the major findings of each author, leaving the rich morsels to a close reading of the chapters.

Douglas A. Irwin tackles trade, which is the least controversial component of globalization; economists generally agree that trade promotes growth for exporters and importers. As documented in the volume, no society that closed itself off to trade managed to generate higher living standards over the last several decades of the twentieth century. Not one.

But the trade-leads-to-growth story is old. What's new? First, says, Irwin, there's shear volume. Over the past 20 years, production around the world rose by about 30 percent. But trade goods and services rose 80 percent. Increased trade brought specialization, lower production costs and, therefore, higher living standards. In recent years, shriveling costs of acquiring information have created opportunities for trade. New Yorkers can find out about the features of a product made in India as easily as they can find out about a product made across town.

Second, composition. Service-sector exports have soared as agriculture and mining exports have shrunk. These trends reflect in part the fact that as people grow richer they consume less food and more services. In the United States, services now account for about two-thirds of production and about a half of all trade. But there's also been something new and important over the recent past that's altered the worldwide landscape of production and trade. Technological change and precipitous reduction in transportation costs have focused manufacturers on vertical specialization and outsourcing. A typical automobile plant, for example, produces less than 40 percent of the components of each car on site. The majority of these components are built in specialized plants around the world, leaving the plant to do little more than assemble parts. For typical products in the modern world, specialized components are produced in high-wage countries and then sent to low-wage countries for assembly. In that way, the new world of specialization has reconfigured economic production in rich and poor countries alike. It has also cut prices, as production gravitates to the low-cost centers. Swapping components back and forth until assembly into final products distorts the public's perception of the importance of trade. Almost 60 percent of the recorded value of U.S. imports from Mexico consists of components manufactured in the United States. In other words, American is importing mostly from itself.

Technological change, including the growth of the Internet, has reshaped trade another way—boosting trade in services by making previously non-tradable services now tradable. Computer programs can be written in India and shipped to the United States instantly at very little cost. Radiological services can be outsourced to foreign medical centers.

Irwin notes the birth of the World Trade Organization in 1995. It not only oversees agreements governing trade in goods, but also trade in services, investment and intellectual property. Compared to its predecessor, the WTO also provides a more muscular mechanism for resolving trade disputes—a key to keeping trading lanes unfettered. The dispute-resolution system has already handled a series of controversial issues—including the European Union's ban on hormone-treated beef, a dispute that hinges on the conformity of domestic health regulations with international trade rules that say such regulations need a scientific basis.

Irwin disposes of the public perception that trade creates or destroys jobs. In recent decades, central banks around the world have come to assume responsibility for controlling economic performance, in effect attempting to keep economies near full employment despite the ups and downs of trade flows. Trade, then, does not much affect how many jobs exist but does determine where they exist—whether in the corn fields of Iowa or the aircraft factories in Washington.

Irwin points to important recent changes in regional trade balances. Asia accounts for more of the world's trade; Africa and the Middle East account for less. China's share of world exports shot to 4 percent in 2000 from under 1 percent in 1980. Reversing three centuries of practice, the United States traded more across the Pacific Ocean by the mid 1990s than it traded across the Atlantic Ocean.

Irwin makes the interesting point that in some respects trade has become less important of late. Sectors where trade matters most—manufacturing, agriculture, mining—are shrinking as a percentage of total economic activity. And sectors where trade matters least—health care and other service sectors—are growing. So trade-dependent sectors are shrinking. But, as noted above, trade accounts for an increasing percentage of economic activity. How are those two trends simultaneously possible? Irwin points out that sectors dependent on trade, like automobile manufacturing, are becoming increasingly, and massively, dependent on trade even as the entire sector falls in size relative to the overall economy. For example, the fraction of manufactured goods in the United States that is exported rose to 40 percent in 2000 from 15 percent in 1970.

Charles W. Calomiris addresses the second component leg of globalization, the movement of capital flows to emerging markets—economies whose governments have adopted policies of privatization, trade liberalization, and deregulation. Here the economics profession is raucously split. On one side are those that argue economies big and small ought to open themselves up to foreign capital. Others preach caution. This is an age-old debate. What's new is the actual dynamics of modern capital markets, requiring fresh thinking about policy.

Calomiris first cites evidence on recent capital flows. He shows that international capital flows were high and rising prior to World War I, fell dramatically thereafter, and reached the previous high levels only in recent years. But the form of capital flows changed along with the volume. Prior to World War I, capital flows, dominated by Great Britain's supply, mostly went from developed to developing countries and increasingly took the form of loans to private-sector borrowers. But after World War II, capital was supplied by a larger and more diverse group of nations, and it consisted of equity and direct investment, as well as bond issues. Pointing to shrunken differences in interest rates among countries, Calomiris concludes that international capital markets grew much more integrated over the past 40 or so years. He points to another important trend of the past several decades—the increasing willingness of foreign investors to send capital to low-income countries. As recently as the 1970s, more capital left these countries than came in. By the 1980s, the so-called developing countries began to attract capital and by the early 1990s absorbed large amounts of capital.

Direct foreign investment increased eightfold during the 1990s, bringing modern technology and skilled personnel to poor countries. Foreign investors in banking and other sectors also injected competition into otherwise protected markets. But, Calomiris concedes, some studies of the period find that the foreign capital packed little economic wallop in emerging markets. Weighing all the evidence from recent years, he finds that foreign direct investment boosts emerging markets but other types of capital flows, namely loans, pose serious short-term risks.

The source of much of that risk is currency depreciation. In an oft-repeated cycle, giddy lenders first pour money into an emerging market, then turn skittish—fleeing at the first sign of economic or financial distress. Their desperate attempt to convert local assets into dollars drives the value of the local currency down. But the depreciation of the local currency triggers a destructive wave of bankruptcies. Domestic borrowers—including, ominously, domestic banks—scramble to come up with more local currency to repay their dollar-denominated foreign loans. This chain of events has come to be known as the "twin crises"—capital flows out of countries in financial trouble, like Indonesia, Russia, and Argentina, leading to a collapse of the country's exchange rate and its banking system.

Calomiris's major point is that "twin crises" are new. Take the decades prior to World War I, an earlier period of globalization. In those years, foreign capital flowed into countries under financial stress, mitigating financial crises. Why the difference? Calomiris's answer: the gold standard—the commitment to a fixed valued of domestic currency, defined in terms of gold, and the ironclad commitment to set the nation's money supply to whatever level is needed to keep the value of the currency at the pre-set level. When financial crisis struck, driving the value of the local currency down, foreign capital would rush in, betting that currency values would return to traditional levels. In the bygone era, foreign capital mitigated pressure on interest rates and exchange rates because investors knew that fluctuations would be temporary. Compare that to the modern world, where capital takes flight at the flimsiest signs of financial trouble, toppling countries like bowling pins.

Calomiris thereby offers a startlingly pointed story about what's new in the world economy. He then turns to the debate over the role of short-term capital in modern financial crises. He notes that countries that rely on short-term capital flows—Mexico and East Asia in the 1990s—fall prey to financial crisis. That fact invites the presumption that short-term borrowing is the root of all financial evil: foreign investors panic at the slightest whiff of problem because no one wants to be last in line for a country's meager dollar reserves. Even good economies can be brought down by creditor panic. Here's the basis for having an intermediary like the International Monetary Fund coordinate withdrawals of foreign creditors, removing the urge by any one of them to flea before the others. But Calomiris offer an equally plausible alternative story. When crisis looms, for whatever reason, countries attract only those investors willing to make a short-term bet at very high promised rates of return. In this version of the story, short-term borrowing serves as a symptom of problems, not their cause.

Calomiris tries to resolve this debate by, again, turning to history. He returns to the observation that twin crises were rare before World War I—even though capital flowed freely across borders, economic shocks were prevalent and currency rates were fixed. So, he concludes, the modern instability cannot be traced to capital mobility, fixed exchange rates or economic shocks. The source of the problem must lie with something new to modern markets. His candidates? He focuses on rejection of fixed exchange rates and the role of government institutions, namely the International Monetary Fund, in bailing out creditors. For him, explicit and implicit government-provided subsidies drive capital to crisis-prone countries, driving their debt burdens to imprudent levels. Capital flows in the modern world do cause financial ship wrecks because poor countries follow bad policies and international financial institutions reward bad behavior.

Calomiris concludes that financial instability is not inherent to global capital markets. Indeed, in bygone eras, capital flows mitigated economic crises. And though he recognizes the case for limiting the most crisis-prone component of twin crises—short-term loans denominated in foreign currencies, especially those going to domestic banks—he points out that such control often do not work and often invite corruption. Citing Latin America in 1980s, countries that imposed capital controls performed no better than countries that rejected controls.

George J. Borjas tackles the third, and last, component of immigration. It might not seem to be a natural fit for an examination of globalization. But trade and immigration can play similar economic roles. Whether the United

States imports tomatoes from Mexico or imports Mexicans to work in California tomato fields, the effective supply of low-wage workers and tomatoes rises. Put aside, for the purposes of this volume, the important issues of politics and culture. Is the economic case for opening the country's borders to immigration as compelling as the case for opening borders to trade?

No, says George Borjas. Under current circumstance, there are good economic reasons for welcoming imports but restricting immigration.

First, the facts as they apply to the United States. The number of legal immigrants has soared, rising from about a quarter million people a year in the 1950s to about a million a year by the 1990s. The percentage of the population which is foreign born has risen to about 10 percent today from about 5 percent in the 1970s. There has also been a substantial rise in illegal immigration—perhaps 10 million residents in the United States, of which about half may be from Mexico.

The composition of immigration has shifted heavily toward uneducated workers from poor countries. Before 1965, national origin dominated the composition of immigrants, with more than two-thirds coming from developed countries like Germany and the United Kingdom. After 1965, by act of Congress, family reunification came to dominate, drawing immigrants from mostly from poor countries. Latin American and Asia now account for more than two-thirds of legal immigrants. Less than 10 percent of recent immigrants are driven by employer's needs. Immigrants concentrate in a handful of states—California, New York, Texas, Florida, Illinois and New Jersey. The rest of the country has been relatively unaffected by recent waves of legal and illegal immigration.

Borjas makes the important point that the economic performance of immigrants has been falling steeply. Fifty years ago or so, immigrants and native American were equally likely to be high school dropouts; immigrants earned more than natives. Today, immigrants are almost four times more likely to have dropped out of high school and earn about 25 percent less. Young immigrants in the late 1960s earned about 13 percent less than native workers of the same age. Thirty years later, the immigrants had nearly caught up. But immigrants who arrived in the late 1980s started more than 20 percent behind native workers and the gap has actually grown since their arrival.

In the 1980s and early 1990s, he shows, immigration increased the supply of workers who are high-school dropouts by over 20 percent. He cites evidence that this shift in the labor force toward unskilled workers reduced the average wage of high school dropouts (about $20,000 a year) by about $1,000, or 5 percent. But he reminds the reader that the 5 percent figure may exaggerate the impact once the interaction between trade and immigration is taken into account, If low-wage workers had not emigrated to the United States, some of the products (clothing, for example) that those workers would have made abroad would have flowed here instead. The impact on domestic workers might have been largely the same.

Immigrants create demand for the products produced by native workers and native-owned businesses. By driving down labor costs, they reduce the price of products bought by native workers. But they also reduce wages of workers with similar skills. So on net, what are the impacts? Borjas cites recent evidence showing that though the net impact on the economy is positive, the magnitude of the impact is indeed very small—probably less than $10 billion a year, or less than $50 per native American. But immigration shifts about $150 billion a year from the pockets of unskilled workers who compete with immigrants for jobs to the pockets of consumers who pay less for the products that immigrants produce. Borjas concludes that recent immigration does not affect the size of the American economy, but it does create winners and losers—shifting income away from native low-wage workers.

Borjas suggests that assimilation can be a mixed blessing. Rapid assimilation militates against the creation of a poor underclass, with all the ugly social consequences so implied. But the economic benefit of immigrants derives almost entirely from the fact that they are different from natives—in the United States, they provide unskilled labor, a scarce resource. Assimilation, in this sense, dilutes the economic benefit of immigration. Borjas suspects that the benefits of assimilation outweigh its costs.

Indeed, ethnic differences persist over time, even as they weaken. By the late 1990s, Canadian immigrants earned 120 percent more than Mexican immigrants. If historical patterns repeat themselves, Canadian descendants of today's immigrants will, by 2100, out-earn their Mexican counterparts by 25 percent. But Borjas's chilling anxiety is that assimilation is slowing, so that today's low-wage immigrants may never find escape hatches up the high-tech job ladders of tomorrow's economy. The widening gap between high- and low-wage jobs suggests that future opportunities for low-wage workers—the starting place for an increasing share of immigrants—are worsening.

The implications for the social fabric of America could prove profound. Milton Friedman has observed that a country could largely drop its immigration rules, inviting anyone in, were there no welfare system. People would relocate here only if they could find employment, and if an employer voluntarily hired an immigrant it must mean that the immigrant added more value to the economy than he or she consumed by way of wages. On this score, Borjas documents a disturbing trend. In 1970, immigrants were less likely to receive cash and other types of welfare benefits than native workers, but by the end of the last century the pattern was reversed (20 percent of immigrants versus 13 percent for natives). Borjas cites evidence that in California in the mid 1990s, public support for immigrants cost state and local taxpayers about $1,200 per household per year. In New Jersey, support for immigrants cost taxpayers less than $230 per household. For the nation, the tax bill was only around $200 per year. Overall, Borjas looks at immigrants imposing about $20 billion in transfers (taxpayers to immigrants) and a net economic gain nationally of about $10 billion. By any measure, these are very small numbers.

Borjas's data tell a consistent story. Measured in the aggregate, immigration has not made much of a dent on the $11 trillion U.S. economy. Yet distributional trends remain disturbing. The 1996 welfare law cracked down on welfare for natives and even more so for immigrants. But states can offer their own welfare benefits to immigrants. Borjas cites numbers showing that while caseloads for domestic families have plummeted since the mid 1990s, the drop in welfare participation by immigrants has been relatively small. Borjas worries that the eventual drain on federal taxpayers could become substantial.

David Dollar addresses how globalization has affected rich and poor countries alike. Heightened globalization over the past 20 years or so helps explain, he says, three trends: unprecedented reductions in worldwide poverty; a modest reduction in worldwide inequality, reversing a 200-year trend; and lower wage rates of low-skilled labor in rich countries.

First, by one way of making the calculation, poor countries have grown faster than rich countries since 1980. Weighting the data from countries based on population—in effect, counting data from the United States as only about one-fifth as important as data from China—per capita incomes in the richest 25 countries in 1980 grew over the next 17 years by an annual average of less than 2 percent. By contrast, per capita incomes in the poorest 25 countries in 1980 grew by an annual average of about 4 percent over the same period. If, instead, China and India are counted the same as any other poor country, then the averages tell a very different story: average growth of the poorest countries falls to about zero. However, some small poor countries, including Bangladesh, Uganda, and Vietnam, did rack up impressive growth rates.

Second, the number of poor people has fallen steeply, the first such decline in recorded history. Growth and poverty are linked, Dollar points out, so poverty, as defined by countries themselves, fell steeply in fast-growing poor countries. He cites evidence that there were about 1.5 billion people in 1980 living on less than one dollar a day. Perhaps 60 percent of them lived in two countries alone, China and India. In those two countries alone poverty (at the dollar-a-day standard) fell to 650 million from 1 billion between 1978 and 1998—driving the poverty rate to under 30 percent from over 60 percent during the same period. Poverty also fell in Bangladesh, Indonesia, and Vietnam, countries with high growth rates. But, he estimates, poverty in Sub-Saharan Africa, where growth lagged, probably rose by about 170 million after 1980. The reductions in poverty in Asia more than outweighed the rise in poverty Africa, driving poverty worldwide down by at least 200 million since 1980. Dollar points out that these declines in poverty reversed the trend of at least the previous 20 years.

Third, global inequality—differences between high- and low-income people around the world—has declined "modestly," reversing a 200-year-old trend. Inequality rose for a century and a half after 1820 largely because rich western countries grew faster than poor countries. But the pattern reversed after 1980, easing inequality down. In effect, slow growth in Africa increased inequality. But the impact was slightly offset by faster growth in China, Asia, and other low-income Asian countries.

Fourth, wages rose faster in countries that he labels globalizers—countries that opened their economies to international competition.

Fifth, Dollar argues that globalization has not in general fueled inequality within countries. Indeed, inequality did not, as is generally presumed, rise within individual countries—so the worldwide reductions in inequality since 1980 are almost entirely due to differential growth rates between rich and poor countries cited above. Specifically, the growth of the poorest individuals in societies generally rose at about the same rate as incomes overall in society. Uganda and Vietnam are examples of countries that opened up their borders to trade and investment, yet reduced the gap between rich and poor.

Within countries, Dollar concedes, trade did help skilled workers in globalizing countries more than unskilled workers. Thus, trade increases inequality among wage earners. He cites evidence published by him and others that immigration of low-skilled labor into the United States and imports of products made by low-wage labor abroad have reduced wages of such workers by about 5 percent. But trade's downward pressure on the wages of low-skilled workers is of limited importance to people living in poor countries—the vast majority of whom live on farms and do not earn wages. And by increasing competition, trade ends to reduce the gap in earnings between men and women.

The link between globalization and poverty reduction goes well beyond mere statistical correlation. He finds clear historical evidence of causation. He reviews explicit policy changes—policies that fostered economic integration—undertaken by China, India, Vietnam, and Uganda to make the case that pro-integration policies produced growth and growth reduced poverty. As a final, stunning piece of evidence he notes that there is not a single case of a country that closed its borders and has higher living standards today, compared to the rest of the world, than it did 40 years ago.

Dollar gives credence to the call, repeated elsewhere in this volume, for encouraging greater movement of workers from poor to rich economies. The movement would raise wages and remittances in poor countries while easing labor shortages in industrialized countries. He points to the fact that the world's population increases by 83 million people every year, 82 million of whom in poor countries.

Jeffrey A. Frankel offers three rebuttals to the accusation that globalization degrades the world's environment. First, environmentally conscious consumers around the world now work together—for example, by pressuring governments to adopt labels that tell consumers which goods are environmentally friendly and by pressuring corporations to adopt environmental codes of conduct. Second, multilateral organizations are moving to adopt environmentally friendly multilateral rules. Third, globalization makes citizens richer; and richer citizens, the data show, demand more environmental cleanup from government.

Frankel observes that every society faces the task of finding the right balance between creating material wealth and cleaning up the environment. Some factors, like trade, affect pollution because they affect economic growth—the more an economy produces, the more it pollutes. Other factors, like regulation, affect the amount of pollution an economy creates at any given level of production. The distinction matters. The environment can be protected from the first set of factors only by sacrificing economic growth. But the second set of factors can be managed without smothering growth.

Frankel then reviews the evidence on threats, real and imagined, to the environment. First, he shows that growth—whether trade induced or not—generally helps the environment. He cites evidence on the "Environmental Kuznets Curve," a statistical relationship that finds for some pollutants that as countries grow they begin to adopt environmentally friendly policies. London's air is cleaner today than it was in the pea-soup fog days of the 1950s. Also, economic growth steers economies away from manufacturing and toward non-polluting services. But, Frankel notes, the Kuznets effect isn't strong enough to make growth a cure-all for the environment.

Another alleged threat, say critics of globalization, comes from a "race to the bottom." This phrase refers to the claims that countries will dumb down environmental regulations to cut costs and thereby become more internationally competitive. A related claim has some countries moving to become pollution havens as a way of attracting foreign capital and jobs. But Frankel points to research (both his own and others') that shows no such pattern of regulatory meltdown. Environmental rules turn about to impose rather minor costs in international trade. No surprise, then, that most U.S. trade takes place with countries whose living standards are comparable to that of the United States, not with poor countries with low wages and lax regulatory standards.

Frankel proceeds to identify ways that globalization helps the environment. For example, increased trade and investment provoke technological and managerial innovation. After making all due statistical adjustments, the data shows that openness to trade and investment promotes environmental protection.

Not everything about the globalized economy bodes well for the environment. Frankel focuses on what he calls an impossible trinity—an analytical construction that reappears in several chapters of this volume. Every country wants to grow as fast as possible, a goal fostered by globalization. Every country wants a clean environment. And every country wants national sovereignty—national control over policies. Frankel's impossible trinity says that these three goals are incompatible. In this precise sense, globalization can force environmental compromises. For example, a society that wants to push growth to the max will not want to throw up barriers to foreign investors. But that is exactly what environmental rules do. Yet, Frankel reminds the reader that nations cannot protect the environment by looking inward. Protecting the global environment requires every country to pitch in, presumably coordinated through rule-setting organizations like the World Trade Organization. Said another way, tight environmental protection requires more globalization and less national sovereignty. Such trade-offs cannot be avoided.

As positive examples of international rule-setting, Frankel points to sophisticated multilateral agreements like the Montreal accord on the release of ozone-depleting gases. He makes the case that even the arch villain of many environmental advocates, the World Trade Organization (WTO), has become environmentally friendly in recent years, ruling that countries may impose environmental protections even when those protections unintentionally reduce trade flows.

In Frankel's account, trade and investment induce growth and, therefore, increase pollution. But to control pollution by reducing growth is to cancel the poor world's only ticket out of poverty. Besides, growth can be the environment's best friend—inducing environmental-improving innovation, shifting economic output from manufacturing to services, triggering demands for environmental cleanup and fostering international cooperation.

William Easterly examines one form of global economic integration, foreign aid. He accuses donor countries of gross misuse. They fork over billions of dollars to alleviate desperate poverty and hunger. But they fail miserably. Donor countries now spend more than $1 billion a year to lift fewer than 300,000 people out of extreme poverty—spending a whopping $3,500 a year to raise a person's income to a grand total of $365 a year, the World Bank's poverty standard. He shows that funneling scraps of aid to a typical family in a poor country can involve taking months, if not years, to prepare hundreds of pages of forms.

Grant applications refer to P.R.S.C., P.R.G.F., C.D.F., OD 8.60, OP 4.01, C.A.S., HIPC, PERS, FIMS, I.D.G., W.F.P., A.D.B., Unctad, F.A.O., D.F.I.D., I.L.O., U.N.H.C.R., D.A.G. and M.T.E.F. and read like a cruel joke. And what did the decade of bureaucratic bungling get the starving children? Perhaps eight cents per day.

Easterly accuses donor countries of conspiring in recent years to create a "Byzantine" bureaucracy that delivers aid at an "excruciatingly" slow pace. Failure thrives because no one holds aid agencies to account for their performance. Indeed, the agencies themselves avoid blame by forming what Easterly labels a "Cartel of Good Intention," which amounts to a conspiracy to blame someone else for repeated failures. Everyone walks away unscathed—everyone except the poor.

Easterly accuses aid agencies of strategic errors. They cooperate rather than compete, immunizing each from criticism. They define success in self-serving fashion, primarily by measuring by toting up money dispensed. Donors rely on their own agencies to funnel aid, trampling institutions of the poor countries. Easterly documents the recent explosion of stand-alone projects (57 in Honduras alone) in countries with threadbare administrative capacity.

Aid agencies, Easterly charges, too often pursue goals oblivious to the needs of the poor. Aid, he shows, flows to countries that vote with the donor in the United Nations or to countries that were the donor's former colonies. He accuses aid agencies of violating the sovereignty and dignity of recipient countries, taking over the application processes that are supposed to be done locally. He points out that the aid cartel in effect forces poor countries to engage in a level of central planning that not even rich countries could hope to pull off.

But Easterly's most pointed criticism is the system's inability to correct mistakes. He cites reports for Kenya in the 1990s and 2000 that repeat the same, failed ideas that had appeared in its reports for the past 20 years. Kenya received 21 loans from the World Bank and International Monetary Fund as of 2000 despite an unblemished record of failure each and every time.

Jeffrey D. Sachs examines why some poor countries have grown while others stagnate during the past two decades of heightened economic integration. Some experts, he points out, attribute growth in large part to economic institutions, including property rights, open borders, and prudent fiscal and monetary policies. But Sachs' review of the data emphasizes geography and national science and technology policies.

Sachs lumps countries into two camps. Core countries generate economic growth on their own. Non-core countries depend on links to core countries to grow. Economists, he points out, gravitate to endogenous growth models, the notion that growth in advanced countries flows from self-reinforcing cycles of rising incomes and technical innovation. But Sachs says that such ideas apply to only about two dozen advanced countries in North America, Western Europe, and East Asia. The rest of the world borrows the technology of the advanced countries—by importing capital and consumer goods, welcoming foreign investors and skilled workers, and tapping the developed world's scientific knowledge and scientists.

Sachs carefully reviews data on growth from 75 countries between 1980 and 1998. He concludes that technology-induced growth in underdeveloped countries depends on several key factors:

The first is the need for low-cost ways to transport goods to major markets—primarily ready access to coasts. Second, and less obvious, is a common ecological zone with advanced countries, because Western technology works best when used in the ecological zone from which it is derived. Agricultural, medical and construction technologies, for example, are often suited to specific climates, diseases, or materials. Ecological-specific technology contributes to the ability of countries in temperate ecological zones to outpace countries in tropical ecological zones. The third factor comprises the institutions that protect intellectual and other private property rights and promote trade. Fourth comes scientific research and development. Government support for science, Sachs argues, explains the relative success of Korea, Israel, Singapore, and Taiwan. Fifth, and finally, is the size of domestic economy, because small economies located far from major markets have limited opportunities to achieve trade-induced growth. This, says Sachs, strengthens the argument for regional economic integration.

Sachs' point is that good institutions aren't good enough. The drag of bad geography can overwhelm the best governed nations. He estimates that a geographically isolated country in a malarial zone will grow 3 percentage points a year slower than an equally well governed country without those disadvantages. That difference is nothing short of gigantic—the difference between zero growth and a doubling of income over a period of about 20 years.

Sachs draws two major implications. First, in the modern world of science-driven growth, the world's scientific community needs to address the specific agricultural, health, and other ecological needs of poor countries. Second, non-core countries need to pursue a science-based strategy that will move them, like Korea and Taiwan, to self-reinforcing growth of core countries.

Joseph E. Stiglitz, like Dani Rodrik to follow, addresses governance. He says globalization—a term he uses to refer to not only private behavior but also government policies—has been "oversold." First, he accuses the policies of international financial institutions and major industrialized powers of squelching growth in poor countries and of misshaping global economic integration by setting trade and investment rules that serve primarily the needs of special interests in wealthy donor countries. For evidence, he points to dismal growth rates stretching from Latin America to the former Soviet Union during the past 15 years or so—rates far below those during pre-globalization days of the 1950s, 1960s and 1970s.

Second, Stiglitz attacks the West for trampling democracy. He cites examples where policies imposed by the IMF in exchange for bailout funds toppled elected officials, where the West pressured countries to strip politicians of control over central bank (monetary) policy, and where investors, by threatening to withhold capital, forced voters to think twice before siding with anti-market politicians. Economic policies imposed on Asia during the financial crises of 1997 and 1998 by the International Monetary Fund (IMF) extended far beyond those needed to manage the current crisis, running roughshod over domestic political autonomy. Stiglitz cites a systematic pattern, ranging from drug patents to tariff reductions, where international policies favor the industrialized West. He makes the point that economists possess no technocratic blueprint for economic development. Korea, India, and China prove that globalization can provide economic wallop. But each of these countries violated central tenants of the Washington consensus—the mix of privatization, deregulation ,and stabilization preached by Western powers. Economic policymaking requires judgment, and the only defensible judgments are those made by democratic processes. Policies rendered by the WTO and other international agencies reflect no such democratic will. Stiglitz proposes a series of reforms designed to bring more democratic control to international economic policies, breaking the chokehold of special interests.

Third, Stiglitz points out that the policies he associates with the IMF and Western donors create turmoil, and turmoil undermines the trust that comes with repeated cooperative relations. He also finds little sensitivity among major international economic institutions to the need of crisis-stricken countries to set policies that protect ethnic and cultural diversity. Stiglitz rejects the notion that globalization should be stopped to preserve indigenous culture. He also rejects the opposite notion that McDonalds should be allowed to trample anything in sight.

Stiglitz seeks to control the pace and extent of globalization and restrict the mandate of supranational organizations, a middle ground in the debate over globalization. He also backs a policy designed to to pump up the purchasing power of poor countries by creating international financial reserves and handing over a disproportionate share to the poor. But perhaps his most important recommendation is to create global public goods—a cleaner environment, attack on terrorists, or vaccines against communicable diseases like AIDS—with money generated by new taxes on natural resources and financial transactions.

Dani Rodrik, like Stiglitz, addresses fundamental flaws in the governance of the global economy, warning against heading in an "untenable direction: global markets without global governance." But he takes the issue in a different direction. Here's the nub of the argument.

Under the postwar Bretton Woods institutions, economic integration among countries was held in check, leaving room for nations to set their own economic course. Trade accords excluded agriculture, services, and other sectors under threat from catastrophic foreign competition. Nations imposed controls on the flow of capital. The elbow room provided by these restrictions allowed Japan, China, Sweden, Germany, the United States, and Korea to create radically different market-based economies. Then sometime in the 1980s, countries veered toward complete economic integration. The United States pressured developing countries to eliminate all trade and investment barriers. Rodrik regards this choice as unnatural, forcing countries to sacrifice too much local control. He calls instead for exploring "feasible globalizations," by which he means choices about economic integration that leave room for nations to make economic policy independent of their neighbors.

Rodrik's argument comes in three parts. First, markets evolve within specific cultural contexts. Second, cultures give rise to different market forms and institutions. China's uses Township and Village Enterprises to protect local entrepreneurs within a system that provides few explicit legal protections. Russia, by contrast, passed lots of property laws in the 1990s, but few are properly enforced. Third, institutions reflect history and cultural values and cannot be stitched together in arbitrary ways. Japan puts firms in charge of providing lifetime employment and other social protections, and puts banks in charge of watching over these powerful firms. The United States, by contrast, keeps shareholders and managers in check with vigorous enforcement of the antitrust laws.

Such institutional diversity limits the amount of trade and investment that can take place across borders. It's harder to enforce contracts in foreign countries. It's harder to conduct business in foreign countries with different regulatory regimes. The only way to create truly integrated markets—the policy promoted by the West and international financial institutions like the International Monetary Fund—is to wipe away institutional variation. In that sense, full integration strips voters of their ability to set basic rules. There goes democracy at the level of the nation state. In a fully integrated world, economic and financial rules apply worldwide so democracy—the power of the governed to set the rules—can only be wielded at the global level: global governance for global commerce. But global governance means the end to the nation state as a politically autonomous entity.

Rodrik's argument is that no matter how you mix and match, there's simply no way to achieve democratic control, national states, and full integration—his version of the trilemma that Frankel and Calomiris pose earlier in the volume. As Rodrik explains, the world could sacrifice the nation state and move to global governance. Or it could sacrifice democracy, imposing rules and laws for the purpose of achieving full economic integration. Or, as Rodrik prefers, the world could turn back from its recent rush to integrate, moving back to the Bretton Woods notion of limited integration—enough to achieve economic benefits but not enough to wipe away national sovereignty.

Rodrik's pithy conclusion: full integration is feasible, but not desirable. Global government is desirable, but not feasible. The best choice is to cut back on integration, choosing a "thin'" version of globalization, reinventing Bretton Woods for the modern world.

Rodrik then addresses the kind of globalization that would indeed reap the biggest economic dividends. Trade improves living standards by shipping goods from countries where prices are relatively low to countries where prices are relatively high. The bigger the gap in prices, the larger the economic gains to consumers from trade. Immigration, by contrast to trade, raises living standards by moving workers from where their wages are low to where they are high. Here the larger the wage gap, the larger the potential gains from immigration. Rodrik shows that price differential on goods rarely exceeds 2 to 1. But differential in wages for similarly skilled workers can exceed 10 to 1. Using standard economic estimates, he draws the conclusion that the benefits from freer flow of people across borders can yield economic gains 25 times larger than those that flow from promoting freer flow of goods and capital. He advocates temporary work visas that would allow skilled and unskilled workers from poor countries to work for three to five years in rich countries—yielding, he estimates, at least $200 billion a year in higher income for citizens of poor countries. Such measure provide a much smarter choice path toward further economic integration than measures that Rodrik deems threatening to local democratic control.

Beyond these generalizations drawn from each chapter is the rich evidence and engaging analysis that each author provides. Bon Voyage.

2

Trade and Globalization

DOUGLAS A. IRWIN

THE PAST QUARTER CENTURY has witnessed a rapid expansion of world trade, with international commerce now touching nearly every corner of the globe. This expansion of trade—along with increased capital flows, travel, migration, and other contacts between countries—is one of the most pronounced and significant features of the phenomenon known as globalization.

The increasing importance of international trade is strikingly illustrated in the case of the United States. At one time, international trade was a relatively unimportant element of the U.S. economy, with its large domestic market and internal free trade. Today, the situation is dramatically different: the United States imports toys from China, clothing from Costa Rica, and steel from Germany; it exports aircraft from Washington, wheat from Kansas, and machinery from Illinois. Hardly a sector of the economy or a region of the country remains unaffected by international markets, some for better and some for worse. No wonder the rapid growth of trade has triggered an intense debate over its impact on the U.S. economy and over the future direction of U.S. trade policy.

In this chapter, I'll set out the basic facts regarding the changes in international trade over the past few decades, with particular focus on the United States. Then I'll consider various explanations for the expansion of trade. Finally, I'll briefly discuss why the trade-related aspects of globalization have triggered such controversy, as exemplified by popular protests against the World Trade Organization (WTO).

THE GROWTH IN TRADE

Figure 2.1 provides a dramatic illustration of the growth in world trade over the past decade and a half. Since World War II, the volume of world trade

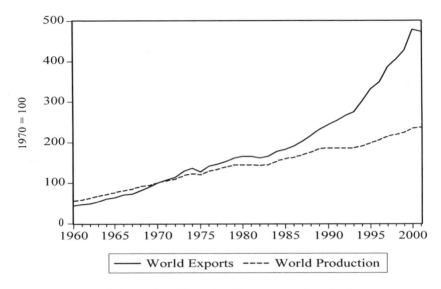

FIGURE 2.1 *Volume of world merchandise exports and production, 1960–2001*
Source: World Trade Organization

in merchandise goods has expanded more rapidly than global production of such goods. But since the mid-1980s, the relative growth in trade has accelerated sharply. While world production of merchandise increased about 27 percent during the 1990s, world exports of merchandise increased more than 80 percent.

Manufactured goods dominate world trade. In 2000, over three quarters of world exports consisted of manufactured products. Conversely, the share of trade accounted for by agricultural and mineral products has declined over time, falling from 35 percent (in 1970) to 22 percent (in 2002). Several factors explain this changing composition of trade. As incomes rise, the share of spending devoted to food tends to fall, while the share of spending devoted to manufactured goods and services tends to rise. In addition, trade in agricultural products has been stifled by high trade barriers as many countries attempt to protect domestic farmers from foreign competition. Finally, changes in production techniques—notably the rise of vertical specialization and outsourcing, to be examined shortly—have encouraged trade in manufactured goods.

While the volume of trade has skyrocketed, the regional pattern of trade has remained fairly stable. As table 2.1 indicates, the share of world exports coming from the Americas and Western Europe was essentially the same in 2000 as in 1980. The most important development in the Americas was the increasing importance of Mexico, which accounted for 2.6 percent of world exports in 2000,

TABLE 2.1 *Regional Shares of World Exports*

	1980	1990	2000
North America	14.4	15.2	16.6
Latin America	5.4	4.3	5.6
Western Europe	40.0	47.6	38.4
Eastern Europe	7.7	3.0	4.3
Africa	6.0	3.0	2.3
Middle East	10.5	3.9	4.1
Asia	15.9	23.0	28.7

Source: World Trade Organization

an increase from 0.9 percent of world exports in 1980. Liberalization of Mexican trade policy, in particular the North American Free Trade Agreement (NAFTA) of 1995, is largely responsible for this development.

The biggest regional changes have been the rising share of Asia in world trade and the declining shares of Africa and the Middle East. The share of world exports originating in Asia jumped from about 16 percent in 1980 to nearly 30 percent in 2000. China's emergence as a world exporter has been especially dramatic. In 1978, China began opening its economy to world markets. As a result, China's share of world exports exploded from 0.9 percent in 1980 to 3.9 percent in 2000.[1] Asia's rising importance in international trade has been spurred by rapid economic growth and policy moves toward freer trade. As a result, by the mid-1980s the United States began trading more across the Pacific Ocean than across the Atlantic Ocean, altering a three-century-old trade pattern and signaling a shift in the world's economic center of gravity.

Trends in the United States illustrate some of the complexities that underlie the increase in world trade. Figure 2.2 shows exports of goods and services as a share of gross domestic product (GDP) for the United States from 1970 to 2001. (Exports and imports tend to track one another because international trade is a two-way street: imports from other countries are paid for by exports.) You can see that the rise in the trade-to-GDP ratio has not been uniform over time. The ratio was quite low in the 1960s, then jumped twice in response to the oil price shocks of 1973 and 1979. In both cases, the higher cost of U.S. fuel imports required an increase in exports to pay for them. (And in both instances, the growth in exports was facilitated by a depreciation in the foreign exchange value of the dollar). The import ratio continued to climb through the 1980s and 1990s,

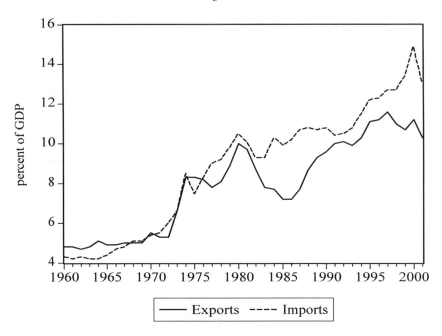

FIGURE 2.2   *U.S. exports and imports of goods and services*
as a percent of GDP, 1960–2001
Source: Council of Economic Advisors (2002), table B-1

but the export ratio has exhibited more variation and appears to be more sensitive to fluctuations in the value of the dollar.[2]

The rise in both ratios since the mid-1980s seems to imply that trade is now a more important part of the U.S. economy than in the past. But in one respect, trade is *less* important for the economy overall. This is because the sectors that produce traded merchandise—specifically, agriculture, mining, and manufacturing—have become a smaller part of the economy. Between 1960 and 2000, the contribution from these three sectors to total current dollar GDP fell from 34 percent to 19 percent, and civilian employment in these sectors fell from 40 percent of the labor force in 1960 to just 16 percent in 2000.

Meanwhile, spending and employment in the service sectors—such as health care, housing, government, education, finance, and others—were growing. Since these sectors tend to be less affected by international trade, trade may be considered less important in that it directly affects fewer workers and a smaller part of the economy today than a few decades ago.

However, there are two qualifying factors. First, for those sectors engaged in trade, international trade is vastly more important now than in the recent past. This is seen most strikingly by comparing merchandise exports as a share

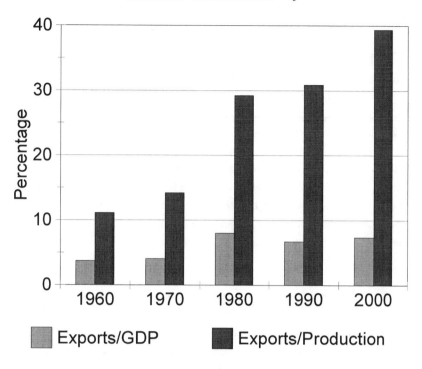

FIGURE 2.3   *U.S. merchandise exports as a percent of*
GDP and merchandise production
Source: Irwin (2002), p. 9

of merchandise production rather than merchandise exports as a share of total GDP. As figure 2.3 shows, while merchandise exports as a share of GDP have remained relatively stable, merchandise exports as a share of merchandise production jumped from nearly 15 percent in 1970 to over 40 percent in 2000. Unlike several decades ago, today every producer or worker in the traded goods sector of the economy must somehow deal with international competition.

Second, although services are often thought to be uninvolved in trade, trade in services is now growing rapidly. U.S. service exports—especially in such cases as telecommunications, transportation, finance, and insurance—now amount to more than 40 percent of merchandise exports. Because government barriers to trade in services are just now beginning to be addressed in international negotiations, the potential for further expansion of trade in this area is large.

The service sector is increasingly exposed to international competition because of foreign investment flows and changes in technology. Foreign direct investments have opened up the service sector to international competition even for services that are not directly tradable. For example, U.S. banks have made direct investments abroad that give them a presence in foreign markets, and foreign banks maintain a presence in the U.S. market through similar investments. American universities have established campuses in Europe and Asia to service demand for business education. And Pret a Manger, a London-based fresh food store, is rapidly openly branches throughout Manhattan.

Furthermore, changes in technology, such as the Internet, have made previously nontradable services now tradable. For example, software programming can now be done in India and shipped to the United States instantly and electronically. Telephone service centers can also be located abroad thanks to the falling costs of telecommunications. Medical data can now be interpreted and processed overseas as well. Such developments intensify competition in pockets of the economy that were once subject only to domestic competition, resulting in better service and lower prices for consumers.

TRADE AND THE FRAGMENTATION OF PRODUCTION

A key driving force behind the recent rapid growth in trade in both goods and services is technical change that allows the fragmentation of production. Two parallel trends are involved: vertical specialization and outsourcing.

Vertical specialization refers to companies' purchasing of intermediate goods and components on the market rather than producing them internally. The automobile industry provides a notable example. A half century ago, Ford's River Rouge plant in Dearborn, Michigan, represented the state of the art in car-making. It was a huge integrated complex in which raw material inputs (such as iron ore and coal) entered one end of the factory, and a finished automobile came out the other end. Today, automobile plants produce few of their own parts on site. Instead, they generally assemble various components produced elsewhere by specialized firms.

The sourcing of these components has become increasingly internationalized. For one particular car produced by an American manufacturer, for example, 30 percent of the car's value can be attributed to its assembly in Korea, 17.5 percent to components from Japan, 7.5 percent to design from Germany, 4 percent to parts from Taiwan and Singapore, 2.5 percent to advertising and marketing services from Britain, and 1.5 percent to data processing in Ireland. In the end, just 37 percent of the production value of this "American" car comes from the United States.[3] All the rest is part of international trade.

The related phenomenon of outsourcing occurs when part of the production process that used to be done domestically is shifted to another country. Outsourcing has been an important feature of the consumer electronics and textile and apparel industries. These industries produce certain designs or components in the United States (circuit boards, textile fabric) with skilled labor, then ship the components to countries with low labor costs (Mexico, East Asia, or the Caribbean) for assembly. Finally, they re-ship the assembled components (televisions, clothing) back to the United States, sometimes for final processing. Because of outsourcing, nearly a third of U.S. imports from Canada, Mexico, and the Caribbean Basin consists of motor vehicles, televisions, and apparel.

Vertical specialization and outsourcing have several important implications. Both reflect greater specialization in the production process, and therefore both should produce efficiency gains. These gains give rise to increased trade, although there is no corresponding increase in production. For example, the increase in automobile trade between the United States and Canada doesn't mean that more cars are being built, just that parts and components that used to be produced domestically are now being traded across borders. The outsourcing of radiological services by hospitals to Indian doctors does not necessarily mean that more x-rays will be taken, but that the cost of providing existing medical services will fall.

This could help explain why world trade has grown much more rapidly than world production.[4] It also means that the increase in recorded trade is somewhat misleading. Every time a component is shipped across a border, it's recorded by customs officials as an export or an import. When components are repeatedly shipped across borders at different stages of production, the official recorded value of trade rises with each crossing, although the final goods output doesn't increase. This inflates the value of trade relative to production.

Outsourcing can make trade statistics misleading in another way. A non-negligible portion of the value of U.S. imports is simply the value of U.S. exports of domestically produced components that are shipped abroad for further processing or assembly and then returned to the United States before sale or export. For example, about 60 percent of U.S. auto exports to Canada are engines and parts, whereas 75 percent of U.S. auto imports from Canada are finished cars and trucks. The value of those finished car imports embodies the previous exports of engines and parts.

To illustrate further, imports that incorporate U.S.-made components are often given duty-free or reduced duty treatment under the "production sharing" provision of the tariff code. In 1998, imports entering the United States under the production-sharing provision amounted to $74 billion, or 8.2 percent of total merchandise imports. The value of U.S.-produced components in these imports was $25 billion, or 34 percent of the total value of imports entered under this provision.

This aspect is a particularly striking in the case of U.S. trade with Mexico. In 1998, the United States imported $93 billion of goods from Mexico. Of this, $27 billion (36 percent) entered under the production-sharing provision, and $14 billion represented the U.S. content of these imports. Thus, 57 percent of the value of imported goods that entered under the production-sharing provision actually reflects the value of U.S.-made components.[5]

What has caused the rise of vertical specialization and outsourcing? Changing technology and reduced transportation and communications costs have clearly played a leading role. But so has government policy. For example, trade in automobiles and parts across the U.S.-Canada border really did not begin to flourish until a 1965 agreement eliminated tariffs on such products. The North American Free Trade Agreement and the Caribbean Basin Initiative, along with the "production sharing" provision of the tariff code, have also promoted and significantly deepened cross-border integration in North America and the Caribbean Basin, enabling firms to subcontract some operations to neighboring countries.

This outsourcing explosion is also related to the prominent role that multinational firms play in international trade. Multinational firms have a global reach that allows them to coordinate production and distribution across many countries, and shift their activities depending on changing cost or demand conditions. A significant part of U.S. trade is simply the exchange of goods between affiliated units of a multinational company: in 2000, such "intra-firm" transactions accounted for 30 percent of U.S. exports of goods and 36 percent of U.S. imports of goods. However, this share has actually fallen in recent years, which reflects not the declining importance of multinationals but their increasing tendency to subcontract activities to firms in which they do not have an ownership stake.[6]

LIMITS TO GLOBAL INTEGRATION

The rapid growth in trade is certainly driving the trend toward global integration. Many people believe that manufacturing can be done anywhere in the world, and that this increasingly holds true for services as well.

Yet the world remains far from perfectly integrated. The United States may be more integrated with the rest of the world than has been the case in the recent past, but we are far from the point at which trade between, say, New York and Rio de Janeiro might be conducted as easily as trade between New York and Los Angeles. About 85 percent of what is consumed in the United States is produced in the United States.

Economist Jeffrey Frankel (2001) uses the following comparison to illustrate how far the world is from perfect trade integration. If Americans were equally likely to purchase goods and services from foreign producers as from domestic producers, then the U.S. import-to-GDP ratio should equal the non-U.S. share of world GDP. In other words, Americans would spend about 75 percent of their money on imports, since 75 percent is roughly the non-U.S. share of world GDP. Since the actual current trade share is only about 12 percent, Frankel concludes that we are only about one sixth of the way to a point at which "it would literally be true that Americans did business as easily across the globe as across the country."

Thus, within-country trade dominates between-country trade by an order of magnitude, suggesting that there is a strong "home-bias" in the pattern of trade. What forces inhibit economic integration? Economists have identified an important "border" effect on trade—that is, the mere presence of a national border significantly impedes trade. For example, despite the free trade agreement between the United States and Canada, trade among Canadian provinces and among U.S. states is roughly ten times greater than trade *between* the provinces and the states.[7] Trade is further diminished when countries do not share a common currency, a common language, a common legal system, and so on. Each of these border effects raises the cost of exchange between markets and acts as a brake on global integration.

Hence the counter-intuitive conclusion: If we focus not on how far global integration has progressed in the past few decades but on how far it has to go to achieve full integration, we're impressed by how *little* integration there is.

Furthermore, because the internationalization of markets has been largely driven by pro-trade government policies, the current trend toward globalization is clearly reversible. Such a reversal has happened before. In the interwar period of 1919 to 1939, governments sought to restrict international trade, capital flows, and labor migration, employing measures such as the Smoot-Hawley tariff in the United States. These anti-trade policies worked as intended. Not until after World War II did world trade recover from the dual blows of the Great Depression and the protectionist trade policies of the 1930s, and the world economy suffered as a result.

Does such a sharp reversal of trade policies appear likely today? No—but it didn't appear likely in 1913, either.[8]

TRADE POLICY AND THE GROWTH OF TRADE

We've seen that vertical specialization and outsourcing have helped stimulate international trade in recent years. Other changes in technology and government policy have also played a role, weakening the effect of factors that previously inhibited trade, such as transportation costs, transactions costs, and government policies.

An earlier expansion of international trade in the late nineteenth century was propelled by a significant decline in shipping costs. We have apparently not experienced a comparable cost reduction in this era. However, transportation has remained inexpensive while becoming faster and more efficient. Containerization, bulk shipping, and other innovations have cut loading times. The rise of air transport has reduced delivery times, bringing an ever-growing variety of perishable goods (cut flowers from Central America, lobsters from Maine) into world commerce. Today, about 20 percent of U.S. imports and nearly a third of U.S. exports travel by air.[9]

The Internet and changes in global telecommunications have also facilitated the expansion of trade. Other transactions costs are harder to quantify, but also potentially important. The costs of acquiring information, for example, can limit the extent of market integration. A century ago, before the age of mass communications, learning about distant markets was far more difficult than today. Producers are now more likely to have better information about local tastes and demands than in the past, which makes them able to service demand in those markets more effectively. Conversely, consumers formerly had good information only about locally produced goods, but now they are likely to be equally well informed about the products of foreign firms.

Another leading force behind the expansion of trade has been the decline in import barriers maintained by governments. Tariffs, import quotas, and exchange controls imposed during the interwar period have been relaxed in the decades since World War II. Average tariffs on manufactured goods dropped from roughly 40 percent after the war to less than 5 percent in most developing countries over the postwar period. Furthermore, whole geographic areas, such as Western Europe and North America, have abolished customs duties and become free trade areas. Although a few stubborn trade restrictions designed to protect domestic producers from foreign competition remain in place, overall trade barriers have fallen substantially in the last half-century.

Global trade agreements have contributed significantly to the reduction of trade barriers. After World War II, the United States and other leading countries negotiated the General Agreement on Tariffs and Trade (GATT), establishing a code of commercial conduct for its signatories. Article I of the GATT sets out the rule of nondiscrimination among signatories, codified in the most-favored nation (MFN) clause. The GATT also prescribes conditions under which countries may raise trade barriers to protect domestic industries, such as through the imposition of tariffs to counteract dumping and foreign subsidies.

The GATT has also sponsored several efforts to reduce tariffs and other trade restrictions. The two most important of these were the Tokyo Round in 1979 and the Uruguay Round in 1994. Under the Tokyo Round agreements, tariffs on manufactured products in industrialized countries were cut by one-third. Under the Uruguay Round agreements, developed countries reduced average tariffs on industrial products (excluding petroleum) from 6.3 percent to 3.8 percent. The remaining tariffs are highly variable—relatively low on sophisticated manufactured goods, substantially higher on labor-intensive manufactured goods. Developing countries reduced their tariffs by 20 percent on average, bringing average tariffs in those countries down from 15.3 percent to 12.3 percent. The Uruguay Round also included agreements to liberalize trade in agricultural products, eliminate the multi-fiber arrangement which limited trade in textiles and apparel, open up trade in services, and liberalize rules on foreign investments related to trade.[10]

The multilateral initiatives of the GATT have been supplemented with regional and bilateral agreements that reduce trade barriers. In 1995, the North American Free Trade Agreement (NAFTA) phased out tariffs on trade among the United States, Canada, and Mexico. North American trade has swelled as a result. The European Union (EU), originally formed as a six-nation customs union in 1958, now includes 15 member states that do not impose tariffs on each other's goods, with another 13 countries in eastern and southern Europe now joining the fold. Regional trade arrangements in Latin America, Asia, and Africa are also in place.

The relative political and economic merits of multilateral and regional trade agreements have been hotly debated. Proponents of multilateral agreements argue that trade liberalization among WTO members will generate the broadest economic benefits. They point out that the so-called free trade agreements at the bilateral or regional level are really preferential trade arrangements that violate the nondiscrimination provision of the GATT. Such agreements, they say, may divert trade from its natural course, possibly reducing overall economic efficiency.

In response, proponents of regional initiatives argue that they are not exclusionary but can expand to include new members; for example, the Free Trade Area in the Americas initiative aims to expand NAFTA to include the entire Western hemisphere. They argue that there is little evidence of trade diversion as a result of regional agreements, and they suggest that such agreements can stimulate multilateral negotiations or serve as a template for them by extending trade rules to new areas, such as services.

Finally, unilateral tariff reductions have been critically important in stimulating international trade.[11] Several countries, including New Zealand, Mexico, South Korea, and India, have undertaken independent trade reforms, with China providing the single most dramatic example. In 1978, China abolished its state monopoly on exports and imports and began liberalizing its foreign exchange controls. Import tariffs were cut from an average of nearly 60 percent in the early 1980s to less than 20 percent by the late 1990s. As a result, the ratio of exports to GDP climbed from under 10 percent in the late 1970s to nearly 40 percent by 2000. The country also began to welcome foreign investment.

China's opening to the world economy has had a dramatic impact on international markets. China now produces one-third of the world's suitcases and handbags, a quarter of the world's toys, and one-eighth of the world's clothing.

The World Trade Organization

In 1995, as a result of the Uruguay Round, the GATT became the World Trade Organization (WTO), the most important multilateral body concerned with trade policy. The WTO is something more, but not much more, than the GATT. While the GATT was simply an intergovernmental agreement overseen by a small secretariat, the WTO is an international organization with more than 140 member countries. Like the GATT, however, the WTO has virtually no independent authority. The power to make trade policy resides with member governments, not with the WTO. The Director-General (DG) of the WTO has no policymaking role and cannot comment directly on member-country policies. Mike Moore, a recent DG of the WTO, recently likened the organization to a car with 140 handbrakes and just one accelerator.

The scope of the WTO is nevertheless broader than that of the GATT because it oversees multilateral agreements not just relating to goods, but also services, investment, and intellectual property. The WTO provides a forum for consultations and negotiations on trade matters, assists with the interpretation of the legal texts, arranges for the arbitration of disputes, and conducts fact-finding surveillance reviews of member country's policies. But the WTO itself lacks the power to force countries to obey trade agreements or to comply with its rulings, and as an institution, the WTO is extremely small, particularly in comparison to the World Bank or the International Monetary Fund.

What most distinguishes the WTO from the GATT, aside from the new agreements, is the dispute settlement process. The original GATT agreement made little provision for settling disputes between member countries. When conflicts arose in the early years of the GATT, an informal and ad hoc process was developed to help resolve them through negotiation. The WTO now has a dispute settlement mechanism that largely formalized GATT practices. But it also strengthened the process by providing for specific time tables to expedite cases and, perhaps most importantly, by preventing countries from blocking the establishment of a panel or the adoption of a panel report. For example, the GATT always operated by consensus, meaning that unanimity was required for most decisions. As a result, a country that was accused of violating GATT rules could simply block the establishment of a panel by withholding its ascent. This procedure hampered the effective enforcement of GATT rules. Under the WTO, the default has changed. The creation of a panel and the adoption of its report is now subject to a "negative consensus" rule in which they automatically go forward unless there is a consensus not to do so.

How does the new dispute settlement mechanism work? Countries may file "violation" complaints, alleging that specific rules (such as nondiscrimination) have been violated, or "nonviolation" complaints, alleging that a government action "nullifies or impairs" a previous concession even if no specific rule has been broken. If initial consultations to resolve the dispute are not successful, a three-member panel is appointed to determine whether there has been a violation of WTO rules. If it concludes that there has been a violation, the panel suggests that the policy in question be brought into conformity with the rules, but generally leaves it to the parties themselves to work out a solution. The panel decision can be appealed to an Appellate Body, which rules on matters of law and legal interpretation in the panel report.

As under the GATT, if the policy in question is found to violate the rules, the country can bring its policy into conformity with the rules, or keep the policy in place and offer compensation (lower tariffs) on other goods exported from the complaining country, which then has the option of accepting or rejecting the compensation offer. If neither has been implemented, the complaining country can seek authorization to "suspend the application to the Member concerned of concessions or other obligations in the covered agreements." In other words, the complainant can retaliate by withdrawing previous tariff "concessions" to the country that has chosen not to comply with the finding. Such retaliations occur infrequently because most disputes are settled through negotiations.

Since 1995, there have been a number of highly controversial WTO disputes. A recent, high profile case authorized the United States to retaliate against the European Union's ban on hormone-treated beef. This dispute concerned the ability of the WTO to rule on domestic health and safety regulations. The European Union argued the ban did not discriminate against trade and was allowed under the "precautionary" principle of safety first. The United States argued that there was no scientific basis to the ban, and the WTO panel agreed.

GLOBAL TRADE AND PUBLIC OPINION

The growth in world trade has produced rapid economic change for participating countries. With this change has come intense debate over the benefits and costs of trade and controversy over the future direction of trade policy.

While most people in the United States and the developed world appear to favor a system of open trade, there are concerns about the equity of trade policies and the outcomes they generate. As a result, groups of highly visible, vocal opponents to the current system, and particularly the WTO, have emerged.

The University of Maryland's Program on International Policy Attitudes (PIPA) monitors the views of Americans on trade policy. Its surveys find strong support for globalization in general as having significant benefits for the U.S. economy. However, Americans are divided about the role of trade. In a January 2004 poll, 53 percent say that government should actively support trade or allow it to continue, while 43 percent say that government should slow down or stop trade. The same poll revealed that 36 percent of Americans think that the growth in trade is positive for the United States, 38 percent believe equally positive and negative, and 23 percent negative.

Americans seem to support trade agreements. When asked if the United States should lower its trade barriers if other countries agree to lower theirs, 67 percent responded favorably. However, a majority of respondents have serious reservations about the effects of trade on workers, income inequality, the environment, and on labor standards in other countries. In surveys, they indicate unease with the emphasis on commercial interests in trade negotiations; they favor placing greater stress on protecting workers and the environment and introducing measures to enhance labor standards abroad.[12]

Among these pragmatic concerns is the fear that foreign competition harms important domestic industries and their workers. It is true that foreign competition can destroy jobs in import competing sectors. In most developed countries, particularly those of the European Union and Japan, domestic agricultural producers receive high levels of government support to protect them from ruinous import competition. Other industries, like the American steel industry, have sought protection for fear that subsidized foreign competition would drive them out of business.

However, trade does not destroy jobs overall. Jobs are created by exports and by foreign investment flows. Fear that NAFTA, for example, would create a "sucking sound" of U.S. jobs being siphoned off to Mexico did not materialize as the unemployment rate fell to low levels in the 1990s. However, because trade dislocation can be very disruptive (although most employment turnover is not trade related), provisions are made in U.S. law and WTO rules to allow industries to petition the government for tariffs or other assistance to counter foreign subsidies or dumping that injures domestic producers or temporary injury resulting from imports. Trade adjustment assistance is also available for workers who have been harmed by foreign competition.

Another public concern is that imports of cheap foreign goods from China and Mexico may depress the wages of relatively unskilled American workers, worsening income inequality. Is this concern valid? The evidence is mixed. Economists have found that the wage premium commanded by workers with valuable skills has risen in recent decades, but evidence linking this increased wage inequality to international trade rather than technological change has not been strong. In any case, the appropriate remedy is not to stifle trade or technological change but to improve worker education and investment in skills.

Yet another pragmatic issue is the effect of free trade between countries with different labor and environmental standards. In the debate over NAFTA, for example, many worried that the lower standards in Mexico would attract American investment and multinational firms eager to escape the high wages and costly standards in the United States. They claimed that migration of industries to Mexico would harm the environment, exploit foreign workers, hollow out the U.S. economy, and lead to a "race to the bottom" in standards, forcing the United States to relax its policies protecting workers and the environment in order to retain businesses.

However, economists have noted that, as an empirical matter, the costs of environmental compliance are not a major factor in industry location. There is little evidence of a race to the bottom. In fact, trade liberalization may actually enhance Mexico's environment by raising incomes and forcing protected, capital-intensive "dirty" industries to modernize or go out of business. And far from exploiting workers, multinational corporations tend to pay higher wages than previously existed in the local labor markets.

In short, although there are many justifiable concerns about wealth, poverty, and the environment in relation to the world economy, it is not clear that trade is part of the problem—or that trade restrictions are part of the solution.[13] Properly managed, the expansion of trade should be able to produce many economic and noneconomic benefits for those in both the developed and developing world.

Nonetheless, globalization continues to be a target of political attacks. In particular, the WTO has been the target of intense criticism from across the political spectrum, as illustrated by the violent protests in Seattle (1999). Antiglobalization critics charge that the WTO is an anti-democratic institution with the interests of corporations, not workers, at its heart. Environmental critics believe that WTO rulings have undercut domestic environmental regulations. Economic nationalists charge that the WTO undermines the sovereign right of countries to protect their important domestic industries.

The more extreme charges against the WTO have little validity. The WTO pursues liberalization only to the extent that its member countries desire that objective. A few WTO rulings have faulted various national environmental regulations, but usually because those policies discriminate against foreign firms or products in some way. And while world trade rules do, in principle, restrict a country's trade policy choices, the relatively toothless WTO cannot prevent countries from violating the rules if they so choose.

Still, as economic ties between countries become closer and the rules set at the WTO become more pervasive, the likelihood of more disputes and greater conflict between countries will grow. We can expect the WTO to remain at the center of the controversy over trade and globalization for many years to come.

NOTES

1. Previously, other East Asian countries began gaining prominence in world trade: Japan in the 1960s, Korea in the 1970s, and others (such as Taiwan and Malaysia) in the 1980s.
2. In particular, the appreciation of the dollar in the early 1980s reduced the ratio of exports to GDP, while the depreciation of the dollar in the late 1980s led its subsequent rise.
3. This example comes from the World Trade Organization's *Annual Report* in 1998.
4. According to Hummels, Ishii, and Yi (2001), vertical specialization accounts for about a third of the increase in world trade since 1970.
5. These official figures significantly understate the magnitude of production sharing in U.S. trade. A majority of imports from Canada and Mexico incorporate U.S.-made parts but no longer enter the United States under the production-sharing provisions of the tariff code because they are already eligible for duty-free treatment under the North American Free Trade Agreement (NAFTA). See Irwin (2002), pp. 13–16.
6. See Zeile (1997).
7. See Helliwell (1998).
8. For a discussion of globalization over the past century, see Bordo, Eichengreen, and Irwin (1999).
9. Of course, saving time is equivalent to saving money. According to one estimate, each day of shipping time saved is worth 0.5 percent of the value of the products. Over the past fifty years, faster methods of transport have had the same effect as a reduction in tariffs from 20 percent to 5 percent. See Hummels (2000).
10. See Irwin (2002), pp. 179ff.
11. See the studies in Bhagwati (2002).
12. See Kull (2004) and Scheve and Slaughter (2001).
13. These and other pragmatic concerns are addressed in Irwin (2002).

REFERENCES

Bhagwati, Jagdish. 2002. *Going Alone: The Case for Relaxed Reciprocity in Trade.* Cambridge: MIT Press.

Bordo, Michael, Barry Eichengreen, and Douglas Irwin. 1999. "Is Globalization Today Really Different From Globalization a Hundred Years Ago?" *Brookings Trade Forum, 1999.* Washington, D.C.: The Brookings Institution.

Council of Economic Advisers. 2002. *Economic Report of the President.* Washington, D.C.: GPO, February.

Frankel, Jeffrey. 2001. "Assessing the Efficiency Gains from Further Liberalization." *Efficiency, Equity and Legitimacy: The Multilateral Trading System at the Millennium.* Edited by R. Porter, P. Sauve, A. Subramanian, and A. Zampetti. Washington, D.C.: Brookings Institution Press.

Helliwell, John F. 1998. *How Much Do National Borders Matter?* Washington, D.C.: Brookings Institution Press.

Hummels, David. 2000. "Time as a Trade Barrier." Working Paper, Purdue University, October.

Hummels, David, Jun Ishii, and Kei Mu Yi. 2001. "The Nature and Growth of Vertical Specialization in World Trade." *Journal of International Economics* 54 (June): 75–96.

Irwin, Douglas A. 2002. *Free Trade under Fire.* Princeton: Princeton University Press.

Krugman, Paul. 1996. *Pop Internationalism.* Cambridge: MIT Press, 1996.

Kull, Stephen. 2004. *Americans on Globalization, Trade, and Farm Subsidies.* University of Maryland, Program on International Policy Attitudes, January 22.

Moore, Mike. 2003. *A World Without Walls.* New York: Cambridge University Press.

Scheve, Kenneth F., and Matthew J. Slaughter. 2001. *Worker Perceptions and Pressures in the Global Economy.* Washington, D.C.: Institute for International Economics, March.

World Trade Organization. *Annual Report 2002.* Geneva: WTO, 2002.

Zeile, William J. 1997. "U.S. Intrafirm Trade in Goods." *Survey of Current Business* 77 (February): 23–38.

3

Capital Flows, Financial Crises, and Public Policy

CHARLES W. CALOMIRIS

IN THIS CHAPTER, I'll lay out the principal facts and controversies surrounding international flows of capital and their attendant risks. I'll review the perspectives of economic historians and economists on the implications of capital mobility, both during the first wave of globalization (prior to World War I) and during the recent wave (since 1980). I'll emphasize changes over time—especially political changes—that have weakened the case for unfettered capital mobility and have made capital flows more controversial among economists today than in the past. Attention focuses on the role of foreign investment in emerging markets—developing economies whose governments have recently chosen the path of privatization, trade liberalization, and deregulation as a formula for promoting progress.

I'll address several key questions, including:

- How have international capital flows changed in quantity and quality over time?
- How and when can capital flows serve as an engine of growth for emerging markets?
- How great are the risks of accessing foreign capital relative to the rewards from doing so?
- Are there identifiable circumstances that improve or worsen the risk/reward tradeoff?
- Might limits on foreign capital flows sometimes be desirable?
- How can the problems associated with capital flows be reduced through improvements in exchange rate policy, monetary policy, fiscal policy, or bank regulatory policy?

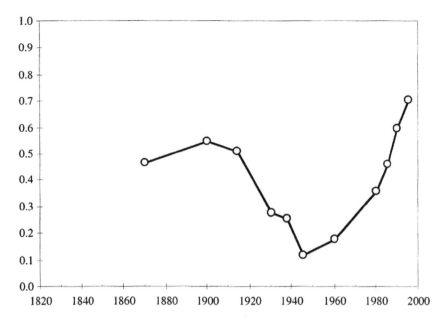

FIGURE 3.1 *International investment as a fraction of GDP since 1870*
Source: Obstfeld and Taylor (2003)

THE CHANGING QUANTITY AND FORM OF INTERNATIONAL CAPITAL FLOWS

Figure 3.1 summarizes the quantity of international investment as a fraction of world GDP since 1870. Capital flows were at high and rising levels relative to GDP in the pre–World War I era, but fell dramatically during World War I, the interwar period, and World War II. Capital flows grew slowly in the immediate post–World War II period, and have accelerated over time. Capital flows relative to GDP reached new all-time highs in recent years.

The form of capital flows has changed over time, as well. Prior to World War I, flows took the form of debt securities. Stock and direct investment were small components of total flows. In this sense, there has been substantial technological progress in international capital flows over time, since it is more difficult to convince distant investors to hold risky equity investments in foreign firms (more on this below). In the pre–World War I era, flows from Great Britain (the primary source of international capital) increasingly were absorbed by private rather than government users, especially when the destination of the capital flow was in North America, South America, and Africa (table 3.1).

TABLE 3.1   *Capital "Created and Called" By Great Britain's*
Capital Market, 1865–1914

Percentage of Total by Continent Receiving Capital Inflow, and by User Type

	1865–1869	1885–1889	1910–1914	1865–1914
North America (%)	18.0	24.3	41.0	33.5
Government (%)	1.9	3.5	7.5	28.5
Private (%)	16.1	20.8	33.4	5.0
S.America / Carib. (%)	16.0	34.5	22.0	19.9
Government (%)	10.4	12.2	7.1	7.2
Private (%)	5.5	22.3	14.9	12.8
Asia (%)	24.9	9.6	12.3	14.0
Government (%)	1.9	6.0	6.1	8.3
Private (%)	23.0	3.7	6.1	5.7
Australia and Pacific (%)	11.1	18.2	9.7	11.7
Government (%)	9.3	14.6	8.1	8.9
Private (%)	1.8	3.6	1.7	2.8
Europe (%)	18.9	7.9	9.3	11.1
Government (%)	6.0	4.1	6.1	7.2
Private (%)	13.0	3.8	3.2	3.9
Africa (%)	11.1	5.4	5.8	9.8
Government (%)	9.6	3.4	2.1	5.2
Private (%)	1.5	2.0	3.8	4.6
Total Flows (Million U.K.P.S.)	193.3	207.7	919.7	3,668.6

Source: Davis and Huttenback (1988), pp. 48–49, Davis and Gallman (2001), p.70

Capital outflows from the main suppliers of capital were sometimes very large as a fraction of their domestic savings in the pre–World War I era, and Great Britain, the wealthiest country with the most developed capital market of that era, was the dominant supplier of international capital. Great Britain invested a rising proportion of its domestic savings abroad prior to World War I (table 3.2), and that proportion reached 53.3 percent in the years 1910–1913. In contrast, in the post–World War II era, the net suppliers of capital have been a more diverse group, including Japan and China, which have maintained large current account deficits (capital account surpluses).

The size of capital inflows relative to GDP has varied greatly across countries, as shown in table 3.3, and those patterns have changed over time, reflecting both

TABLE 3.2 *Foreign Investment as a Percentage of Domestic Savings*
(at current prices)

	UNITED KINGDOM	GERMANY	FRANCE
1850–54	−12.3	NA	−20.1
1855–59	−30.2	NA	21.6
1860–64	−21.5	−1.4	24.8
1865–69	−32.2	−3.4	25.9
1870–74	38.0	−7.3	29.0
1875–79	16.2	−13.1	18.7
1880–84	33.2	18.3	−1.1
1885–89	46.5	19.3	11.3
1890–94	35.3	12.6	10.0
1895–99	20.7	11.5	23.0
1900–04	11.2	9.0	16.1
1905–09	42.7	7.6	22.0
1910–13	53.3	7.3	12.5

Source: O'Rourke and Williamson (2000), p. 209.

changes over time in countries' needs for foreign capital, and changes in market perceptions of the relative desirability of investing in different countries.

The changing amount of international capital flows reflects changes in rules governing both trade and capital mobility, as well as wartime disruptions. Trade rules are important, since future net commodity exports are the means of repaying foreign capital investments. In recent years, and prior to World War I, the greater extent of free trade, and the relative freedom with which capital was allowed to flow, are reflected in the smaller interest rate differentials between countries, in contrast to the period 1914–1959 (table 3.4). Small interest rate differentials indicate that, at least for sovereign and large corporate borrowers with access to global debt markets, world capital markets have become much more integrated since 1960.

In the past 30 years, an important change has been the increasing willingness of foreign investors to send capital to emerging market economies, in particular. Table 3.5 shows that, in the 1970s, net international capital inflows were only positive for developed economies as a group, and developing countries as a group experienced large net outflows of portfolio capital. As the financial "plumbing" of global capital markets improved, and as emerging market economies increasingly privatized their industry and liberalized their trade, they too

TABLE 3.3 *Size of Capital Flows, Measured By Absolute Value of Current Account as a Percentage of National Income*

(Annual Average Percentages for Selected Periods)							
PERIOD	ARG	AUS	CAN	DNK	FIN	FRA	DEU	ITA
1870–1889	18.7	9.7	7.2	1.8	6.2	2.9	1.9	1.2
1890–1913	6.2	6.3	7.6	2.7	5.9	2.3	1.4	1.9
1914–1918	2.7	7.6	3.5	5.4	14.2	3.1	—	11.7
1919–1926	4.9	8.8	2.3	1.2	3.9	11.7	2.2	4.3
1927–1931	3.7	2.8	3.6	0.7	2.9	3.7	1.8	1.5
1932–1939	1.6	3.7	1.6	0.8	2.9	2.5	0.4	0.7
1940–1946	4.8	7.1	6.5	2.4	6.9	1.8	—	3.4
1947–1959	3.1	3.4	2.3	1.4	1.4	1.5	2.0	1.4
1960–1973	1.0	2.3	1.2	1.9	1.7	0.6	1.0	2.1
1974–1989	1.9	3.6	1.7	3.2	2.4	0.8	2.1	1.3
1989–1996	2.0	4.5	4.0	1.8	5.1	0.7	2.7	1.6

PERIOD	JPN	NLD	NOR	ESP	SWE	GBR	USA	ALL
1870–1889	0.5	6.0	1.6	1.0	3.1	4.5	1.5	4.0
1890–1913	2.2	5.3	4.1	1.4	2.3	4.5	0.8	3.7
1914–1918	6.6	—	4.3	3.3	6.3	2.9	3.5	5.8
1919–1926	2.1	—	6.9	2.7	2.0	2.9	1.7	3.9
1927–1931	0.6	0.4	1.9	1.8	1.6	2.0	0.8	2.7
1932–1939	1.1	1.8	1.3	1.2	1.5	1.1	0.6	1.5
1940–1946	1.0	—	4.9	1.3	1.9	7.3	1.0	3.9
1947–1959	1.3	3.8	3.1	2.3	1.1	1.2	0.6	2.0
1960–1973	1.0	1.3	2.4	1.2	0.7	0.8	0.5	1.3
1974–1989	1.8	3.0	2.9	3.2	2.0	2.6	1.2	2.6
1989–1996	2.1	3.0	2.9	3.2	2.0	2.6	1.2	2.6

Source: Obstfeld and Taylor (2003), Table 2.3, p. 54

TABLE 3.4 *Real Interest Rate Parity Since 1870*

	AUS	BEL	CAN	FRA	DEU	ITA	NLD	SWE	GBR	StDev
Average Interest Rate Differential Relative to U.S., Percent Per Annum										
1870–1889	4.5	3.8	4.3	4.8	1.6	1.8	3.3	3.2	3.3	4.2
1890–1913	2.8	4.1	2.1	4.2	2.4	1.8	2.8	2.6	1.8	3.4
1914–1918	7.9	—	1.3	—	0.7	11.0	5.8	8.3	6.2	(9.1)
1919–1926	3.5	34.1	2.2	13.5	6.1	9.4	4.2	5.8	4.6	20.2
1927–1931	2.9	7.6	1.1	6.6	2.9	4.8	1.7	1.8	1.3	6.0
1932–1939	3.3	3.3	1.2	10.7	2.6	4.7	3.8	3.4	3.0	6.5
1940–1946	3.3	10.7	3.2	—	—	38.5	5.5	5.2	3.9	(22.3)
1947–1959	4.4	3.3	1.8	4.5	4.5	4.4	4.2	3.0	2.1	6.0
1960–1973	1.3	1.3	1.0	0.9	1.8	2.0	1.7	1.4	1.3	1.6
1974–1989	1.9	2.4	1.2	1.5	2.4	2.2	2.3	1.8	3.2	3.7
1990–1996	3.6	2.7	2.2	2.6	1.5	3.2	1.6	1.9	1.1	1.8

Source: Obstfeld and Taylor (2003), Table 2.3, p. 54.

became important destinations for portfolio capital flows. By the 1980s, developing countries became important net absorbers of capital, and by the early 1990s, developing countries were absorbing large and growing amounts of capital.

The Benefits of Foreign Capital

Many poor countries remain poor because they lack legal and political infrastructures needed for creation of wealth and, therefore, for growth. (see Beim and Calomiris 2001 for a review). But poor countries also lack capital, for a host of reasons. Low existing wealth and poor corporate governance protections for outsiders constrain the available supply of home-grown equity finance, while weak legal institutions and ineffective creditor protections constrain bank lending.

The problem is worsened by the phenomenon known as "financial repression"—active taxation of the financial sector through a variety of mechanisms. These include direct taxation of financial transactions, bank "reserve taxation" (government rules that require banks to lend a portion of depositors' money to the government for free), government mandates that force banks to lend to government-favored parties on concessionary terms, and barriers to entry in banking that constrain the supply of credit to benefit particular financial institutions.

TABLE 3.5   *Annual Average Flows of Investment for*
Industrial and Developing Countries, 1973–1996

	INDUSTRIAL COUNTRIES		DEVELOPING COUNTRIES	
	Direct Investment	*Portfolio Investment*	*Direct Investment*	*Portfolio Investment*
Gross Outflows				
1973–78	28.6	11.8	0.4	5.5
1979–82	46.9	35.0	1.1	17.8
1983–88	88.2	126.5	2.3	−5.1
1989–92	201.3	274.6	10.4	10.3
1993–96	259.6	436.4	19.2	19.2
Gross Inflows				
1973–78	17.9	24.4	5.0	1.3
1979–82	36.6	51.0	14.6	3.1
1983–88	69.3	139.1	15.5	4.0
1989–92	141.9	343.0	37.8	27.5
1993–96	173.0	549.9	106.4	95.9
Net Inflows				
1973–78	−10.7	12.6	4.6	−4.2
1979–82	−10.3	16.0	13.5	−14.7
1983–88	−18.9	12.6	13.2	9.1
1989–92	−59.4	68.4	27.3	17.2
1993–96	−86.6	113.5	87.2	76.7

Source: International Monetary Fund (1998), pp. 6–7.

Thus, for many emerging market economies, foreign capital offers a potentially important means for jump-starting economic growth.

THE RISKS ATTACHED TO FOREIGN CAPITAL

There are, however, significant disadvantages to using foreign capital rather than local financing.

Local banks should be better able to screen and monitor local risks than foreign banks, and local sources of capital are more willing to write contracts in local currency. By contrast, foreign suppliers of capital incur higher costs of information about and control over the users of funds.

Furthermore, foreign suppliers of capital typically insist on being insulated from fluctuations in the value of currencies in emerging markets. Regulations in developed countries (such as pension laws in the United States) also constrain the ability of foreign investment to be denominated in local currency.

The scarcity of domestic capital and foreigners' demands to denominate claims in their own, "hard," currencies have created an unprecedented degree of risk in financing development in emerging markets. When debt is denominated in local dollars, the domestic central bank can rescue debtors, either directly (by paying their debts for them) or indirectly (by printing money, generating inflation and thereby reducing the real value of loans and other debt). Not so with debts denominated in hard currency. The cost of debt service for local borrowers will rise if their country's exchange rate depreciates.

No wonder, historically, most emerging markets have relied on domestic capital where possible.[1] But the absence of domestic sources of capital gives many of today's emerging markets little choice.

Dependence on foreign capital can be quite risky for emerging markets. The greatest risk is the danger of a financial collapse coinciding with a large fall in the value of the domestic currency (depreciation). Here is how such a collapse typically unfolds.

When the local currency depreciates—say, because foreigners sell the currency out of fear that the country is headed for financial collapse—the amount of local currency needed to pay off debt of a given dollar amount rises. If the depreciation is dramatic, it can trigger financial distress because debtors will be unable to pay the promised amounts in hard currency, even if their domestic-denominated cash flows remain strong. Also, interest rates on foreign loans rise at the first sign of financial problems because lenders demand higher rates to compensate for the higher risk of default.

What's worse, depreciations tend to occur at times of weak or declining domestic economic growth. Thus, while the currency is plummeting, debtors are often suffering both reduced earnings and higher debt service costs due to depreciation. The financial distress of debtors and the rising interest rates further aggravate both the decline in growth and the currency depreciation. In severe financial crises in emerging markets, it is not only currencies that tumble; real GDP plunges too.

The domestic financial system often collapses alongside the currency. As banks fail, credit availability for local borrowers dries up, and the increased fiscal burden on the government (which typically protects failed banks' depositors from loss and also bails out failed banks) puts further pressure on the local currency, because of the need to print money to pay government bills.[2]

WHO BEARS THE RISK?

The risk of private and public sector default in emerging markets associated with exchange rate and banking crises is borne in part by foreign lenders. That risk is passed along to borrowers, in the form of higher interest rates on foreign loans.

However, some of the risk is usually borne by others. Foreign exchange risk (which contributes to default risk on hard currency–denominated debts issued by borrowers in emerging markets) may be borne by speculators in foreign exchange markets. They may sell exchange rate protection to emerging market borrowers in the form of various derivatives contracts that allow local borrowers to transfer the risk of exchange rate depreciation to the exchange rate speculator. These transactions include exchange rate futures, forwards, swaps, and options of various kinds. The cost of transferring that risk appears in the form of the forward exchange rate premium, a gauge of the cost of insurance against exchange rate changes.

A local bank may also bear foreign exchange risk. Such a bank can borrow short-term funds in dollars from foreign lenders, and then re-lend them in local currency to domestic borrowers. In this case, the bank acts as an intermediary of foreign exchange risk by placing itself between domestic currency borrowers and foreign currency lenders. If currency collapse occurs, then the local bank will suffer losses to its net worth from currency depreciation (both because of losses from pure exchange risk, and because of higher loan losses due to the increased real debt burdens of its borrowers). When banks act as intermediaries of exchange rate risk, they concentrate even more risk in the domestic financial system. That can lead to severe collapse of banking sectors in emerging markets.

Finally, local or foreign governments may bear a significant share of default risk to the extent that governments come to the assistance of local borrowers or financial institutions when they suffer losses during exchange rate collapses. In scores of episodes over the past two decades, this sort of policy has created enormous contingent liabilities, which can even bankrupt governments. In recent years, government costs in many cases (including Chile in 1983, Mexico in 1995, Korea, Thailand, and Indonesia in 1997), have exceeded an astounding 20 percent of GDP.

RISK AND THE COMPOSITION OF CAPITAL INFLOWS

In the post-1980 world of massive global capital flows, the *composition* of capital inflows can be just as important for risk as their *level*.

One concern is the potential volatility of capital flows, especially the like-lihood that capital inflows will suddenly reverse at the onset of trouble—the so-called "sudden stop" problem. Sudden stops can create immediate financial distress for firms whose debts fail to roll over, forcing them to come up with money to pay back creditors. Sudden stops also put pressure on the exchange rate as the supply of foreign currency available in the market dries up, driving up rates on foreign loans. Table 3.6, from Calvo and Reinhart (2000), shows that many financial crises in emerging markets have witnessed enormous sud-den reversals of net private capital inflows. The danger is especially great when financial flows predominantly take the form of short-term debt.

Short-term loans have the option to flee at maturity, and capital flight can exacerbate financial crises. That fact has led some to argue, rather naively, that the solution to the sudden stop problem is for emerging markets to avoid rely-ing on short-term dollar-denominated debts for their financing. But it is worth remembering that it is not a coincidence that risky economies borrow more at short term. They may have no other choice. In risky financial circumstances,

TABLE 3.6 *Selected Large Reversals in Net Private Capital Flow*

Episode	Reversal (as a percent of GDP)
Argentina 1982–83	20
Argentina 1994–95	4
Chile 1981–83	7
Chile[1] 1990–91	8
Ecuador 1995–96	19
Hungary 1995–96	7
Indonesia 1996–97	5
Malaysia[1] 1993–94	15
Mexico 1981–83	12
Mexico 1993–95	6
Philippines 1996–97	7
South Korea 1996–97	11
Thailand 1996–1997	26
Turkey 1993–1994	10
Venezuela 1992–94	9

Source: Calvo and Reinhart (2000), p. 181.
[1]*Reversal owing to the introduction of controls on capital inflows.*

foreign lenders will extend only short-term debt denominated in foreign currencies. Indeed, there is empirical evidence that the reliance on short-term debt rises when the macroeconomic environment becomes riskier.[3]

In high-risk circumstances, by structuring foreigners' claims on emerging markets as short-term, dollar-denominated debt, borrowers economize on the cost of accessing foreign capital. That is so for two reasons. First, short-term debt gives holders the option to redeem the debt quickly and exit if the economic circumstances in emerging markets sour. The value of that option increases as the possibility of a financial collapse increases. Effectively, short-term debt is a senior (first) claim on revenues, which implies a lower required yield at the time the loan is made.

Second, structuring the debt as short-term claims raises the probability that the government will bear part or all of the risk of default on those claims, reducing debt service costs of borrowers. Since the sudden redemption of a large amount of short-term debt can create a financial crisis, a massive contraction of credit, and financial distress throughout the economy, financing with short-term debt may make government intervention more likely precisely because it makes the absence of intervention more costly. Expected government intervention helps to reduce the interest rate charged for the debt at the time it is issued.

When foreign capital takes a form other than short-term dollar-denominated debt—such as long-term debt, publicly traded equity investment, foreign direct investment, or foreign entry into the local banking system—the potential for a financial crisis is mitigated. Because equity offerings of corporations held in financial portfolios (portfolio equity) and foreign direct investment do not entail fixed foreign currency–denominated claims on firms, declines in firms' equity values or in the values of foreign direct investments do not imply rising real debt burdens. And unlike debt, equity investments do not mature. These factors lessen the short-term pressures on emerging markets.

Still, capital flight is not confined to short-term debt obligations. First of all, in the context of emerging markets, long-term debt may not be very different in effective maturity from short-term debt. When interest rates are high, the proportion of the market value of debt that is coming due in the near term can be high, even when the date of final maturity of the debt is many years in the future. Furthermore, what is called long-term debt often has limited maturity.[4] Second, the appetite for the publicly traded equity of emerging markets is extremely sensitive to increases in risk, which complicates the valuation of equity. Sudden collapses in equity values and the drying up of the market for new equity flotations raise financing costs for publicly traded firms.

Foreign direct investment can also exit through the repatriation of profits or sale of the assets. Yet, foreign direct investment has been shown to be one of the most stable forms of capital inflow to emerging markets. Tables 3.7 and 3.8 show that even during the emerging market crises of the mid-to-late 1990s, foreign direct investment did not flee emerging markets. In fact, it continued to grow, both absolutely and as a proportion of total inflows.[5] But foreign direct investors are choosy. The ability of a poor country to rely on foreign direct investment depends on convincing lenders that its economy won't collapse (Ito and Krueger 2000, p. 4).

Krugman (2000) points out that, to some extent, the recent robustness of foreign direct investment in the face of crises in emerging markets reflects the demise of government-protected local producers—"crony capitalists" favored with subsidies and other benefits. After financial collapse, government money to support cronies dries up or the political structure is overturned. Only then can efficient foreign owners prosper.

Several studies have found that foreign direct investment is responsive to the institutional climates of recipient emerging markets. Wei (2000) and Wei and Wu (2002) show that corruption acts like a tax, discouraging foreign direct investment in emerging markets. To the extent that crises improve the institutional environment in emerging markets (that is, loosen the hold of crony capitalists,

TABLE 3.7   *Net Private Capital Flows to Emerging Markets, 1990–2000*

	FOREIGN DIRECT INVESTMENT	PORTFOLIO FLOWS	BANK LOANS	TOTAL FLOWS
1990	18.4	17.4	11.9	47.7
1991	31.3	36.9	55.6	123.8
1992	35.5	53.0	28.5	116.9
1993	56.7	81.6	−14.0	124.3
1994	80.9	109.9	−49.5	141.3
1995	96.9	42.6	49.5	189.0
1996	120.4	85.0	18.7	224.2
1997	144.9	43.3	−62.1	126.2
1998	148.7	23.8	−127.2	45.2
1999	153.4	53.7	−135.6	71.5
2000	146.0	58.3	−172.1	32.2

Source: International Monetary Fund, International Capital Markets: Developments, Prospects, and Key Policy Issues, 1999 and 2001.

TABLE 3.8 *Capital Inflows Relative to GDP and Their Volatility,*
By Type of Claim and By Recipient, 1975–1997

	MEAN	MEDIAN	COEFFICIENT OF VARIATION
Total Inflows/GDP			
Industrial Countries	4.53	3.12	1.40
Emerging Countries	1.68	1.09	7.19
Africa	1.84	0.92	9.79
Asia	2.40	0.99	2.19
Eastern Europe	1.48	1.25	2.39
Middle East	1.71	1.26	2.54
Latin America	1.17	1.20	4.81
Debt/GDP			
Industrial Countries	3.80	2.54	1.53
Emerging Countries	0.76	0.70	20.61
Africa	1.56	0.82	9.66
Asia	1.29	0.56	2.83
Eastern Europe	1.07	0.68	3.61
Middle East	1.48	0.66	3.60
Latin America	−1.15	0.74	−20.19
Portfolio Equity/GDP			
Industrial Countries	0.24	0.00	4.77
Emerging Countries	0.02	0.00	16.27
Africa	0.01	0.00	18.91
Asia	0.10	0.00	4.40
Eastern Europe	0.05	0.00	3.73
Middle East	−0.10	0.00	−8.51
Latin America	0.03	0.00	5.05
FOREIGN DIRECT INVESTMENT/GDP			
Industrial Countries	0.54	0.17	2.88
Emerging Countries	0.23	0.07	12.14
Africa	0.13	0.00	22.24
Asia	0.67	0.07	3.04
Eastern Europe	0.50	0.05	2.46
Middle East	0.34	0.10	4.85
Latin America	0.07	0.22	47.69

Source: Edwards (2001), Table 1.

reduce corruption, and improve the rule of law, as the evidence in Kaminsky and Schmukler 2002 suggests they do), crises will also tend to remove prior barriers that limited foreign direct investment.

Changes in the extent of corruption contribute significantly to long-run changes in the availability of foreign direct investment. Crisis-induced reforms create hard to reverse positive changes in corporate ownership and governance in post-crisis emerging markets, which encourage lasting increases in foreign direct investment. Such gains may add to the more frequently emphasized gains from technology transfer that accompany foreign direct investment (Razin, Sadka, and Yuen 2001, Hallward-Driemeier, Iarossi, and Sokoloff 2002).

The stability of the supply of foreign direct investment in emerging markets around crisis episodes is encouraging, all the more so as foreign direct investment grows more important as a means for channeling capital from developed countries to emerging markets. The data tell a dramatic story. According to the World Bank, net foreign direct investment flows to developing countries grew to a peak of $185 billion in 1999 from $24 billion in 1990, an eight-fold increase in only a decade. In 2000 and 2001, foreign direct investment net inflows to developing countries declined, but still remained at $168 billion in 2001. Clearly, the trend toward the globalization of investment via foreign direct investment has not been reversed by the high frequency of crises in emerging markets during the 1990s.

Similarly, foreign bank entry into emerging markets (itself a form of foreign direct investment) tends to be a stabilizing form of capital transfer. These banks could refuse to roll over debt during a crisis, repatriate profits, or even exit. But, in recent practice, foreign banks that establish local branches or affiliates in emerging markets (a class of investors that grew substantially in the 1990s) have been patient investors. Not only have they chosen to remain in-country during financial crises; they often use financial crises as opportunities to acquire weak banks and expand their local networks of operation. That was particularly true in the 1994–1995 Mexican crisis, where foreign banks eagerly acquired failed domestic banks' networks after laws restricting such acquisitions were changed in 1997.

Like foreign direct investment in manufacturing, bank foreign direct investment offers more than just new capital; it should bring advanced financial technology and skilled personnel to underdeveloped capital markets. Perhaps more important, it provides arms-length financing opportunities for productive firms that are denied access to funds because of widespread patronage and protectionist practices of domestic banks. Banks in poor countries often serve to distribute patronage rather than to make growth-promoting loans. Kane (1999) argues that another favorable consequence of bank foreign direct investment is that it changes the behavior of bank regulators. It encourages them to stop protecting nonviable banks, once their inefficiencies are revealed by competition. Indeed, Kane argues that "the banking crises that have roiled world markets in recent years [should be seen as] information-producing events that identify and discredit inefficient strategies of regulating banking markets." Research supports this favorable view.[6]

In summary, the literature on the role of capital flows in producing or exacerbating financial risk has produced five fairly robust findings:

- Debt magnifies the costs of macroeconomic shocks because currency depreciation raises the real burden of debt denominated in hard currencies.
- Unsustainable debt burdens produced by currency depreciation often create financial collapse of borrowers and domestic banks.
- Short-term debt denominated in dollars adds to the risk of financial collapse by adding to the risk of a sudden stop in capital flows.
- Manufacturing foreign direct investment and foreign bank entry into emerging markets offers a desirable combination of technology transfer, stability of capital flows, and competitive pressures that help to improve long-run productivity, capital allocation, and corporate governance.
- Unfortunately, access to the "right kinds" of capital flows is not universal; the riskiest emerging markets are constrained to rely more on risk-creating forms of capital flows.

This last conclusion has an important implication: It is not enough merely to point to the desirability of avoiding heavy reliance on short-term debt finance. High-risk emerging markets often do not have a choice. For many emerging markets, the choice appears to be between risky capital inflows and none at all. The policy challenge: how can emerging markets reduce the risk of their policy environments so that they can qualify for access to safer, better capital inflows? And if they are unable to do so, should emerging markets try to limit their reliance on global capital markets?

I will turn to these questions later, but first I will consider the evidence concerning the long-term growth gains that globalization of capital has produced for emerging markets.

Gains to Emerging Markets from Participating in Global Capital Markets

As we've seen, reliance on foreign capital by emerging markets is not without risk. Yet most countries have decided that the additional risks from relying on foreign capital are worthwhile, even when foreign capital takes the form of short-term foreign-denominated debt.

Positive effects of foreign capital on growth can be important, especially in a world where many liberalizing emerging markets face a beat-the-clock political problem. Liberalization is an act of political entrepreneurship. Costs are paid for political concessions, bargains are struck, and expectations are raised—often unrealistically high. If liberalization does not quickly deliver economic benefits, "reform fatigue" sets in and can lead to quick electoral reversals. In this context, foreign capital is more than a factor of production: *It is a political lifeline for economic reformers.*

Is there evidence that accessing global capital markets can substantially reduce the cost of financing investment and increase economic growth? Clearly, there are examples of both success and failure. Argentina was a success story in the early 1990s, as capital inflows financed purchases of capital goods, raising labor productivity and economic growth. But by 2000, over borrowing by the government had caused a reversal of capital flows. While there is no question that the Argentine crisis was the result of an unsustainable debt burden and a fundamental lack of fiscal discipline, the dependence on foreign capital made the economy more vulnerable.

Because the dependence on foreign capital can magnify the risk of shocks to the economy, some commentators argue that the potential increase in growth from accessing foreign capital comes at too high a price. A key question, however, is whether the reaction of foreign capital providers to financial trouble is more of a symptom than a cause of problems for emerging markets. If they could exercise more fiscal discipline, reduce corruption, improve contract enforcement, and strengthen discipline over bank risk taking, would markets be more patient in reacting to adverse shocks?

Let's consider what the history of international capital investment tells us about the impact of institutional preconditions on the growth and stability of capital flows, and their consequences for economic development.

Changing patterns of global trade and capital flows

Over the past five hundred years, international flows of capital have helped shape the world's political and economic landscape. Those flows (initially in the form of ships, guns, and other forms of imperialistic foreign direct investment) made possible the exploration and conquest of much of the world within the mercantilist system of empire building. That system was based on a partnership between merchant explorers and sovereigns, often codified in chartered companies, which oversaw the process of exploring new lands, conquering their inhabitants, populating those lands with Europeans, and monopolizing the trade of those new imperial outposts for the mother country.

By the late nineteenth century, globalization had taken on a different shape. Now relatively free global markets among many countries combined with a capital market in which investments (primarily involving bonds) connected business interests the world over. Capital was available to flow into newly developing areas because of the promise of growing trade between those areas and the home countries of the capital providers. Investors were willing to send capital abroad in expectation of a stream of future cash revenues back to the home country.

Those payments to foreign capital would be realized only if the developing area generated the export revenues to finance payments to capital. Thus, a necessary ingredient for access to foreign capital has always been the expectation of sufficient export growth in the destination country. Trade was and remains the basis for capital flows.

The early wave of liberalization and economic linkages across countries was undone by World War I, its aftermath, and World War II—a tumultuous period of international conflict that Winston Churchill dubbed the "second thirty years' war." In the wake of that chaotic period, it was difficult to reestablish trade linkages like those that existed prior to World War I. It took decades to reestablish faith in international trade as a mechanism for prosperity, particularly among developing countries. Developing countries that had liberalized their trade and capital markets prior to World War I had suffered enormous costs as the result of their dependence on global trade and capital markets as engines of growth.

The world was slow to reestablish pre–World War I levels of international trade after World War II. Not surprisingly, large capital market flows, which are based upon preexisting international trade flows, did not reemerge until later. As noted at the outset of this chapter, it is only in the past decade that capital flows of the pre–World War I magnitude (relative to world GDP) have been reestablished.

It is also worth remembering that the Bretton Woods Institutions created after World War II, including the International Monetary Fund and the World Bank, were established in an environment of collapsed international capital markets, and that the most prominent economists of the time had little faith in the desirability of restoring private international capital flows in the 1940s. John Maynard Keynes, one of the primary architects of the postwar international financial order, initially proposed a plan that would have actually taxed investors that financed countries' balance of payments deficits, as well as the countries that ran such deficits, on the grounds that doing so would stabilize global finance.

Keynes's view reflected a common perspective at the time. Imbalances, it was believed, create economic and accompanying political risks. He feared that a recession produced by capital outflows could drive countries to expand their flagging economies by devaluing their currency to boost exports and limit imports—a policy response that came to be known as "beggar-thy-neighbor" policy. Consequently, limits on capital flows were a common feature of virtually every major reform plan considered for reestablishing global trade in the 1940s. At the same time, the jaundiced view of capital flows espoused by Keynes and others was opposed by some prominent economists like Dennis Robertson, who saw the taxation of capital inflows as an impediment to the financing of international trade and economic development (Horsefield 1969: 19). [See Dani Rodrik's chapter in this volume for a related discussion.]

As late as the 1970s, most capital flows to developing countries took the form of official bilateral or multilateral loans to governments, sovereign bond issues, or bank loans to sovereigns or to a few large, well-established private borrowers. The growth in international trade in the 1970s and 1980s made substantial growth of foreign investment in developing countries feasible. At the same time, technological progress in the collection and distribution of information about enterprises has permitted the unprecedented growth of a global market in the equity and debt instruments of private corporations based in both developing and developed countries (Bordo, Eichengreen, and Kim 1998, Bordo, Eichengreen, and Irwin 1999, Calomiris 2002c), as shown in Table 3.9.

We now have a system of deep global capital markets. So we are once again faced with the question of whether reliance on private international capital markets is desirable. Was the costly collapse of global finance during World

TABLE 3.9   *Changes in the Composition of Capital Going to Developing Countries, As a Percentage of GDP, 1970–1997*

	1970	1975	1980	1985	1990	1995	1997
Stock of Debt							
Stock of Public Debt Issued	3.9	5.6	11.7	23.0	23.9	24.2	20.1
Stock of Private Debt Issued	1.6	1.9	2.9	3.4	1.7	4.2	5.7
Flows of Equity							
Net Inflows of Foreign							
Direct Investment	0.2	0.4	0.2	0.4	0.6	1.9	2.5
Net Portfolio Equity Inflows	0.0	0.0	0.0	0.0	0.1	0.6	0.5

Source: Calomiris (2002c), p. 311, based on World Bank, Global Development Finance, 2000.

War I and its aftermath proof that the international capital market is inevitably prone to collapse, or was World War I and its aftermath an aberration?

Benefits from International Capital Flows: The Historic Record

Most economic historians agree that, in the decades prior to World War I, the flow of factors of production (capital and labor) across borders was one of the most important contributors to economic growth and to the reduction of world poverty. Not only did those flows produce remarkable extensive growth (increased Gross Domestic Product) in the destination countries, they also were associated with intensive growth (higher labor productivity) and demonstrated that the most effective way to improve the lot of the poor was to move them from areas where their marginal productivity was low to areas of higher marginal product.[7] Angus Maddison (2001) reports that the population of Latin America doubled from 1870 to 1913, while the populations of the four major British offshoots, the U.S., Canada, Australia, and New Zealand, more than doubled. Gross Domestic Product per capita grew at an annual rate of 1.8 percent from 1870 to 1913, both in Latin America, and in the British offshoots. In contrast, in Latin America from 1820 to 1870, population had grown by roughly 10 percent and per capita GDP growth averaged 0.1 percent.

These facts are consistent with basic microeconomic theory, which suggests that the primary gain from factor mobility should be the long-run improvement in productivity that comes from equalizing the marginal productivity of factors across locations. An internationally integrated capital market will move capital to its most productive use to offset any local scarcity of funds.

That is not to say that capital flowed to poor countries, per se. Many poor countries of the pre–World War I era suffered from low productivity. Those countries did not experience capital inflows, since capital could be more productively employed in other destinations. For that reason, both labor and capital tended to flow to resource rich countries with institutional environments conducive to trade and growth. O'Rourke and Williamson (2000: 245) quantify and summarize that process and its consequences: "Late-nineteenth-century world capital flows were a force for divergence, not convergence, since much capital moved to some of the richest countries in the world. European capital tended to chase after European labor as both migrated to the land-abundant and labor-scarce new world."

When measuring capital market integration across countries, economists typically focus on yields on publicly traded debt instruments because these are the clearest indicators of funding costs within countries. Research of this kind has provided clear evidence for beneficial capital market integration resulting from removing barriers to capital flows (table 3.4, above). Interest rate levels in different countries became increasingly correlated in the pre–World War I era, as foreign sources of savings could be quickly mobilized to flow to high interest rate destinations (Obstfeld and Taylor 2003).[8]

From the standpoint of the business cycle, labor and capital mobility can have different effects on the welfare of laborers. Historically, immigration, when permitted, varied with the business cycle to mitigate the effects of economic downturns; bad times in the home country led to increased emigration, good times to less emigration or even migration back to the country of origin (Jerome 1926).

The effects of capital flows over the cycle were more complex. They either offset or aggravated cyclical shocks, depending on the nature of the shock. If the shock was perceived as having a permanent effect on the marginal product of capital in a country (say, a change in a country's long-run terms of trade), then capital outflows would hasten the painful adjustment to the new status (Bordo and Murshid 2002, Clemens and Williamson 2000). But if the shock was not of that kind—for example, if the shock were a short-run financial problem—then international capital flows often acted to insulate the economy from the effects of the shock.

Although observers of today's financial crises may be surprised to hear it, prior to World War I, when developing countries faced financial crises caused by temporary shortfalls of liquidity, foreign capital often came to the rescue. Eichengreen (1992) describes how this process was facilitated by cooperation among central banks. Under the classical gold standard, no single country was really in control of the supply of money, since the ultimate supply of money in any economy was determined by private decisions to import or export gold. If adverse shocks produced a scarcity of gold, balance was restored by gold inflows, and central banks coordinated actions to hasten that process. The extent to which countries experienced common financial market turbulence tended to reflect real global interdependence rather than volatility produced by financial markets (Neal and Weidenmeier 2002).

This historical portrait is very different from the portrayal common today, where foreign capital flows are often seen as the cause of financial crises rather than their solution, and where many see IMF aid as needed to offset capital flight by unwilling private market participants. What explains the relatively successful historical crisis resolution through the combined efforts of international bankers, governments, and central bankers? Why did private capital play a stabilizing role in the wake of historical crises?

Adherence to the classical gold standard is part of the explanation, for two reasons. First, countries depended on one another to manage the global supply of money because they were using the same ultimate definition of the value of money: gold. Shocks in one country that disrupted the world market for gold threatened all countries with exchange rate and price instability. Thus, both private and public sources of capital abroad had an interest in maintaining a stable world capital market.

Second, and even more important, the fundamental long-run credibility of policy was higher among developing countries. In particular, the fact that developing countries adhered to the gold standard as a long-run policy commitment meant that they were eligible for assistance when financial crises struck. Credible adherence to the gold standard allowed countries to maintain their eligibility for access to private markets because adherence to the gold standard ensured substantial fiscal and monetary policy discipline on the part of government. On the fiscal side, a country with a long-run commitment to fixed exchange parity with gold had to forego using the printing press to pay off its government debts, limiting fiscal profligacy. On the monetary side, adherence to gold parity circumscribed central banks' abilities to determine their domestic money supplies, even in the short run. After all, it is not possible to set the price of money (the gold exchange rate) and independently set its domestic supply since, in the presence of free capital markets, agents will be able to offset central bank manipulation of supply by borrowing gold from abroad.

Obstfeld and Taylor (2003) have termed the way that the combination of open capital markets and adherence to a fixed (e.g., gold) exchange rate constrains government policy the fixed exchange rate "trilemma."[9] A government may choose any two (but not all three) from the following list of policies: (1) a fixed exchange rate, (2) free capital flows, and (3) central bank control over the supply of money. For example, if a government maintains free capital flows and a fixed exchange rate, then it cannot determine the supply of money. If it tried to print lots of money, capital market speculators would see that the exchange rate was not sustainable and would flee.

During the pre–World War I era, central banks understood that they were constrained by the trilemma, and that markets would interpret any attempt to violate its logic as a sign of a potential lack of commitment to the gold standard. It became widely understood that the best way to react to a condition of "external imbalance" (e.g., an acceleration in gold outflows from any country) was to raise interest rates to attract gold into the country and hasten (rather than fight) the necessary long-run adjustment. Thus, the "rules of the game" demanded by the classical gold standard were simple and inflexible.

The Russian and Mexican examples

By pursuing these disciplined fiscal and monetary policies, countries gained the confidence of the capital market, as reflected in the lower average interest rates that they paid to borrow in international markets (Bordo and Rockoff 1996).

That confidence was also reflected in the ability to access markets during global financial crises. The cases of Russia in 1900 and Mexico in 1907 illustrate how long-term credibility was crucial for continuing access to international capital during a financial crisis.

A major recessionary shock in Europe in 1899 led to a contraction of credit in Western Europe, which produced a collapse of the Russian stock market, shut off trade credit for Russian exporters, and caused the insolvency or near insolvency of several Russian commercial banks. As severe as this imported crisis was for the Russian financial system, the swift actions of the Minister of Finance, Sergei Witte, allowed a rapid resolution of the crisis and avoided a systemic banking crisis. Witte personally examined commercial banks requesting assistance and helped only those he deemed close to solvency. This limited the amount of assistance offered to the private sector.

Russia remained on the gold standard during the crisis, and the Tsar's commitment to that discipline was never in question. Because of that credibility, and because the amount of loans offered by the government to domestic banks and firms was limited, the government was able to raise funds in the global capital market to support its local financial institutions and quickly restore confidence in the health of the banking system (Calomiris 2002a).

Mexico's Finance Minister, Jose Limantour, acted similarly in the fall of 1907 when the financial panic in New York City spread to Mexico. He offered loans to Mexican banks guaranteed by the Mexican government. As Russia had done, Mexico maintained its commitment to the gold standard and kept the amount of its exposure to loss limited. Consequently, Mexico was able to borrow from global capital markets for the purpose of restoring confidence in the domestic financial system. Limantour himself argued that adherence to the gold standard was crucial for Mexico's access to capital inflows during crises (Conant 1910, p. 88):

"[T]his influx of money, though very considerable, has occasioned no surprise to the authors of the new monetary regime. Indeed, the influx of foreign capital was precisely one of the objects sought to be obtained by the reform, not only because that capital fecundates all branches of the national wealth, but because it constitutes in itself one of the surest guarantees for the fixity of the gold value of our currency."

For Limantour, credible fixed exchange rates and access to capital flows during crises were complementary, mutually reinforcing phenomena. Credible long-term adherence to gold made access to capital markets during crises possible, and at the same time, access to capital markets during crises helped ensure credible long-term adherence to the gold standard.

Note how different the experiences during these two historical financial crises are from present-day crises in emerging markets. Today, governments of emerging markets seem powerless to defend their banking systems or their exchange rates from collapse. As their domestic financial systems teeter, their pegged exchange rates collapse, in a pattern now referred to as a "twin crisis." Governments of emerging markets appeal to the IMF for a bailout, which is then used to finance an across-the-board rescue of the domestic financial system at enormous fiscal cost.

By contrast, early twentieth-century Russia and Mexico dealt with severe financial crises largely by themselves, and without depreciating their currencies. They did not offer blanket assistance to failing banks, but rather moderate assistance to help offset a temporary loss of confidence. They accomplished their objectives with trivial fiscal costs.

Mexico and Russia were not unusual success stories. In fact, from 1873–1913 Calomiris (2002a) finds evidence of only three twin crises worldwide, all of them occurring in the 1890s, in Argentina, Brazil, and Italy. The Argentine case was the most severe crisis of the three. A lack of available data makes it difficult to analyze the Brazilian case, but in the other two cases there was a clear chain of causality connecting ex ante government guarantees of bank liabilities (risk subsidization of banks by the government) with subsequent large banking losses, the costs of which undermined the governments' abilities to maintain their exchange rate pegs. In other countries, not only were twin crises absent, but also banking sector losses during recessions remained small. There are a maximum of seven cases (as many as three in Brazil and one each in Argentina, Italy, Australia and Norway) of total banking sector insolvency in excess of one percent of annual GDP.

The comparable figure for the last two decades of the twentieth century shows more than a hundred cases of banking system insolvency with resolution costs in excess of one percent of GDP (Caprio and Klingebiel 1996, updated by the authors for Beim and Calomiris 2001, Appendix to chapter 7). It is worth emphasizing that what once were the exceptions of emerging finance have become the rule. The pattern of risk subsidization, banking collapse, and exchange rate depreciation that explains both of the well-documented cases of twin crises in the pre–World War I period (Argentina and Italy) has been repeated scores of times in the past two decades, most notably in Chile in 1982, Mexico in 1994, and Thailand, Indonesia, and Korea in 1997.

Effects of "The Rules of the Game"

Under the classical gold standard, adherence to gold constrained the use of fiscal or monetary policy to respond to adverse macroeconomic shocks. Monetary contraction was seen as a desirable response to domestic recession, helping to preserve external balance. The ability of fiscal policy to respond to downturns was limited by the need to maintain long-run credibility of the fixed exchange rate. That meant, in response to fundamental adverse shocks (such as an unfavorable change in a country's terms of trade), that capital would flow out of an economy, not into it, thus exacerbating the initial shock by lowering income and wages. Labor outflows, however, mitigated the effects of these shocks. Thus, under the pre–World War I system, capital flows offset the effects of temporary liquidity problems, but reinforced fundamental shocks to the macro economy.

That does not imply that capital mobility, on balance, had adverse effects on citizens of emerging markets prior to World War I. It is true that capital mobility encouraged adherence to the rules of the game, which sometimes aggravated business declines by requiring contractionary monetary policies during recessions, but at other times adherence to the gold standard helped to stabilize the economy. In particular, the responses of capital inflows to rises in domestic interest rates produced by domestic financial shocks helped to stabilize the domestic economy. Furthermore, from the standpoint of long-run growth, capital mobility encouraged adherence to the rules of the game under the gold standard by rewarding adherence and by ensuring that deviation from the rules would be punished economically. Foreign capital served both as a carrot and as a stick to encourage stable long-run macroeconomic policies, which were beneficial to both capital and labor.

Finally, because borrowing countries successfully adhered to the gold standard, they were able to avoid the problem of ballooning foreign debt burdens in the wake of exchange rate depreciation. Developing countries today have proven to be notoriously unable to maintain exchange rate parities for more than very brief episodes (Obstfeld and Rogoff 1995). But pre–World War I gold standard adherents could be confident that, over relatively long periods of time, the value of their wages, salaries, and domestic investments would rise and fall along with that of their foreign debts. Not only did gold standard adherence avoid costly debt service burdens, but also the low risk of depreciation contributed to the low yields paid on foreign debt.

Of course, the pre–World War I period was far from macroeconomically idyllic. The financial and monetary stability achieved by emerging markets operating on the gold standard, and the enormous growth produced by globalization of trade, capital, and labor, occurred despite enormous volatility in commodity prices and very pronounced business cycles, especially in the 1890s. Surprisingly, banking and currency crises remained rare.

Historians also have found that open capital markets brought risk-management advantages to both emerging markets and developed economies, raising financial system performance and probably helping to account for the remarkable stability of the global financial system. Globalization afforded new diversification opportunities in financial markets. Global portfolios of bonds and foreign direct investments allowed investors to hold more diversified portfolios, which permitted them to absorb more of the country-specific risks from financing development around the world.

Classical economists and modern-day economic historians have also stressed another route through which capital mobility, and globalization more generally, improved economic performance and reduced risk during the pre–World War I era. Global market access, especially capital mobility, fostered international competition for productive resources across differing political and regulatory regimes. To the extent that underdeveloped legal environments and misguided government policies impede growth and poverty reduction (Jones 1988, Landes 1999, Maddison 2001, Calomiris 2002b), capital mobility created strong incentives for countries to adopt market-friendly policies that promote domestic growth and poverty reduction.

In summary, economic history casts quite a favorable light on the international capital mobility of pre–World War I globalization. The same themes stressed by economic historians—efficient resource allocation, extensive and intensive growth, poverty reduction, portfolio diversification, and intergovernmental competition—have been emphasized by advocates of capital mobility today.

Are the long-run advantages of capital as great today as they were in the pre–World War I period?

Capital Flows and Growth in Today's World

In theory, the same advantages that attended global capital flows in the pre–World War I era should be available today. In fact, they should be enhanced, since new technologies now permit much better access to information about distant risks, which is apparent in the unprecedented ability of foreign firms to place risky equity offerings abroad. But financial crises—those that are narrowly confined to systemic bank insolvency and those involving both bank insolvency and exchange rate collapse—are more frequent today. Consequently, many critics of global capital markets argue that capital flows have helped cause financial crises, and some have advocated limiting or eliminating global capital flows.

If capital flows have played a role in causing crises, why did their role change from a stabilizing force prior to World War I to a sometimes destabilizing force today? And are there policy options that might permit more stable access to capital markets?

There is a large and rapidly evolving literature on the long-run determinants and effects of capital flows in developing countries (see the chapters in Feldstein 1999, Edwards 2000, and Edwards and Frankel 2002). Those who have measured the consequences of liberalizing capital flows have argued that destination countries benefit from capital mobility today, as in the past, through two channels. First, new inflows of savings reduce the cost of funds and help the economy to invest and grow faster. Second, diversification from cross-border trading in securities reduces the cost of capital by reducing the risk premium paid by firms, promoting investment and growth.

Some studies have found evidence that this second channel may be quite important. Bekaert and Harvey (2000) find that moments of stock market liberalization are associated with large movements of capital, which produce reductions in risk premiums and higher correlations of equity returns with global markets. They also find, interestingly, that capital market liberalization is associated with a reduction in exchange rate volatility.

Similarly, Henry (2000a) finds that permitting foreigners to purchase shares in a country produces, on average, a 3.3 percent appreciation of stock in the domestic market. There is a much larger effect (10.4 percent) for the firms that become eligible for purchase by foreigners (Chari and Henry 2002). Chari and Henry (2001) find that firms experiencing reductions in their cost of capital (as the result of global portfolio diversification) are the ones that account for the overall price rise.

Do the gains from stock market liberalization matter for real investment and growth? Henry (2000b) shows that stock market liberalizations are also associated with investment booms. Nine of eleven developing countries that liberalized their stock markets experienced growth rates of private investment above their non-liberalization median in the first year after liberalizing, and the average growth rate of private investment in the three years after stock market liberalization for the sample was 22 percent above average. Henry (2003) shows that higher investment also translates into higher output per worker, which rises by an additional 2.3 percent per year after stock market liberalizations.

Bekaert, Harvey, and Lundblad (2001) reinforce that conclusion. They find a one percent increase in annual growth, after accounting for inflation, over a five-year period after stock market liberalization. That effect holds after controlling for the effects of other simultaneous reforms and for business cycle phases.

Other research has offered a more nuanced view of the growth effects from broader financial liberalization (defined as "capital account liberalization"). Edwards (2001) examines not only cases of fully liberalized capital accounts but also partially liberalized countries. He considers various alternative measures of capital openness; separates capital flows in the form of foreign direct investment, debt, and portfolio equity; distinguishes among countries of six types (Industrial, African, Asian, Non-industrial European, Middle East, and Latin America); and examines how the effects of capital openness on GDP growth and total factor productivity depend on other economic factors.

Edwards finds that, overall, capital openness improves growth in output and productivity, but that the context affects the size of that impact. Specifically, capital openness only significantly improves economic performance once a country has reached a certain degree of development. Edwards also points out that previous studies that had found no positive effect of capital openness (e.g., Rodrik 1998) used data that did not properly take account of actual, as opposed to legal, impediments on capital mobility (see also Eichengreen 2001 and Klein and Olivei 1999).

Overall, Edwards' research suggests that for countries with a moderately developed economic and financial system (such as Mexico, Venezuela, Singapore, Israel, and Hong Kong) capital openness provides a significant boost, but for countries with very low initial conditions, capital mobility may not help, and in fact may even hurt—for example, through the negative consequences of volatility.

Other studies, however, challenge Edwards' definition of capital openness. Edison et al. (2002) consider new measures of capital openness (such as the stock of foreign claims relative to GDP, rather than flow measures), which they argue are less prone to measurement error. They also consider an extensive range of interactive terms to gauge the conditions under which capital flows contribute more or less to growth, and adopt new econometric methods that are designed to eliminate spurious correlations. They find that, after controlling for other effects, there is no significant effect of capital mobility *per se* on economic growth, regardless of the level of economic development or other institutional factors. They attribute earlier findings (like those of Edwards) mainly to the problem of reverse causality (growth causing capital inflows rather than vice versa).

Kaminsky and Schmukler (2002) have a different take on the question of financial liberalization (broadly defined) and growth. For them, the short-term pain (that is, the disruption caused by reform) is often a necessary condition for the long-run gains from liberalization. From this perspective, it may be very difficult to find growth effects when one looks at periods immediately following liberalization, even if, in the longer run, growth effects are large.

In summary, the literature on the effects of capital account liberalization on growth in recent times is still evolving. Studies that narrowly focus on the effects of foreign direct investment, foreign bank entry, and equity market liberalization tend to find clear evidence of long-run growth and efficiency improvements from liberalization. Studies that analyze broader trends in capital account policy are much more mixed in their results, partly due to controversies over how to measure openness, and partly due to differences in the time horizon over which growth effects are measured.

On balance, the evidence suggests that specific policies that liberalize the capital account in an emerging market economy both add to the short-term risk of financial collapse and to the potential long-term gains from economic growth.

CAPITAL FLOWS AND FINANCIAL CRISES

The question of whether and how capital flows contribute to the risk or severity of financial crises in emerging markets is a complex one. Teasing out causality during financial crises is complicated because, in a crisis, things happen very fast, many important aspects of the economy change simultaneously, and the observable economic variables are all potentially influenced by a wide variety of shocks.

Some proponents of the view that capital markets either breed or magnify shocks that produce financial crises tend to begin with jaundiced prior views about market efficiency (for example, along the lines of the theoretical framework of Minsky 1975). They argue that markets tend to overreact to news, and that capital markets are the main instrument of that overreaction.

Others argue for the crisis-producing role of capital by positing a multiple-equilibrium model—that is, an economic model that can deliver either a good or bad outcome, depending on which equilibrium is selected by the capital market. For example, if foreign debt is largely short-term, debt holders may be driven to demand immediate repayment only because they fear that other short-term creditors will demand repayment, and no one wants to be last in line to be repaid. The rush for the exits can produce a "bad equilibrium" even when, from a fundamental standpoint, such a bad equilibrium may not have been necessary. If creditors' actions could be coordinated (for example, through IMF intervention), then unnecessary crises could be avoided. This point of view became popular in the aftermath of the Mexican and Asian crises because of the large amount of short-term dollar-denominated debt that fled those countries during the crises.

Some capital market critics note that contagion across countries can exacerbate market reactions. That contagion can be either rational (driven by the need for securities holders to reduce risk exposure to country X in response to losses in country Y) or irrational (where asset liquidation is seen as an unnecessary, emotional reaction to loss).

It is hard to prove or disprove these arguments in regard to any particular crisis. Proponents of market irrationality or multiple equilibriums are often reduced to arguing, unconvincingly, that they personally were unable to identify any sufficiently severe fundamental weaknesses prior to a crisis in an emerging market. Needless to say, their opponents can be relied upon to offer a long list of such weaknesses. For example, even if on-balance sheet government debts are small, contingent government liabilities (such as explicit or implicit guarantees associated with bailouts) are often anticipated by the market (see Burnside, Eichenbaum, and Rebelo 1999 for an explanation of the East Asian crises that revolves around anticipated banking sector collapse). Thus, even though exchange collapses may precede bailouts, it may be reasonable to argue that such collapses are caused by anticipated bailouts.

Narrow versions of one or more of these arguments can be tested using data. For example, we can sometimes investigate whether foreign participants in capital markets are more likely to sell before domestic participants. Such studies of the Korean crisis found that foreigners did *not* drive selling pressure in the markets (Brown, Goetzmann and Park 1998, Choe, Kho and Stulz 1998).

Another type of study uses statistical analysis to identify predictors of financial crises using a sample of crisis countries. Authors of such studies construct measures that they claim capture particular influences, including financial market influences (such as the pre-crisis maturity structure of debt and the fundamental health of the domestic banking system), and then investigate which of the predicting variables included in the statistical model is helpful in predicting crises.

These studies are generally unconvincing. Sample sizes are small, and the potential for data mining is great. The interpretations attached to predicting variables are often suspect, and variable measurements are fraught with error (especially measures of the health of the domestic financial system, given the inaccuracy of banks' accounting for nonperforming loans). Furthermore, because future expectations have so much impact on current economic behavior, prediction and causality are hard to disentangle.

Perhaps most important, the predicting variables are often themselves affected by financial crises, which complicates any interpretation of their economic roles in causing the crises. It can be extremely hard to disentangle cause from effect when interpreting these correlations. For example, the fact that a high reliance on short-term capital flows tends to predict financial crises can be interpreted in a variety of ways. One interpretation is that short-term dollar-denominated debt causes crises to occur (as in a multiple-equilibrium model). Another interpretation is that, when fundamentals are weak and crises are likely, the only financing that is available is short-term debt (in part, because holders of short-term debt receive government and IMF protection). According to the first interpretation, crises are unwarranted results of multiple equilibriums; according to the second, both crises and the structure of capital flows are driven by weak fundamentals.

LOOKING TO HISTORY FOR ANSWERS

The inherent weakness of the current empirical literature on the connections between capital flows and crises should give weight to historical perspectives. I find it significant that in the pre–World War I period—when information processing was inferior, when macroeconomic shocks were at least as prevalent as the past two decades, when exchange rates were fixed, and capital flowed freely—twin crises were rare. It is also significant that the only pre–World War I twin crisis countries for which we have information (Italy and Argentina) were also unique cases in which governments subsidized banking sector risk.

I conclude that the new prevalence of costly twin crises cannot be ascribed to capital mobility, fixed exchange rates, or macroeconomic volatility *per se*. None of these factors is present today more than it was historically.

The combined factors that seem capable of explaining the new wave of twin crises (as well as the isolated historical instances of twin crises) are the subsidization of financial risk by government and the inability of government to maintain a credible commitment to an exchange rate peg. The two factors are related. Only if a country is willing to forego long-run fiscal discipline will it be able to offer a *carte blanche* bailout to its domestic financial system. Similarly, part of the economic cost of a lack of market discipline in the financial sector is a lack of fiscal discipline.

Perhaps the most interesting question is why governments prior to World War I chose to impose market discipline on banks, and to impose both credible exchange rate parities and fiscal discipline on themselves, but are unable or unwilling to do the same today. Any policy response to today's financial crises must come to grips with this central question.

I have no definitive answer to offer. Historically, political behavior has varied widely over time and across countries. Perhaps future empirical research will identify factors that explain such variation, but at the moment the best we can do is to make some informed guesses.

THE POLITICAL ECONOMY OF FRAGILITY

Eichengreen (1996) offers one hyphothesis; he argues that the expansion of the democratic franchise has made it increasingly difficult politically for governments to adhere to long-run exchange rate rules, since doing so would require them to forego short-term macroeconomic stabilization policies. In essence, the electoral constraints of democracy may make some beneficial long-run policies unattainable.

Similar logic applies to the trend away from market discipline in banking. Banking sector bailouts misdirect capital resources away from value-creating investments in favor of value destroying ones and undermine efficient competition in the banking sector that otherwise would favor prudent, skilled management (see the literature review in Beim and Calomiris 2001, chapter 7). Although governments like to justify bailouts as cyclically stabilizing (that is, as a means of avoiding credit contractions), empirical research indicates that bailouts do not even succeed in expanding the supply of credit. After all, bailout policies reward *all* kinds of risk-taking, not just lending risk. Weak or insolvent banks with little or nothing to lose often undertake substantial currency risks as part of high-risk "resurrection strategies." When the more likely outcome of financial collapse occurs, it typically takes years to rebuild the financial system, which places a substantial damper on economic growth.

However, bailouts do succeed at one thing: They serve to postpone the day of reckoning, which is an irresistible lure to populist politicians fighting to win elections, or to corrupt politicians seeking to protect their cronies.[10]

In summary, models of financial crises that view them as the unavoidable result of global capital market inefficiency, multiple equilibriums, or international contagion have the same basic flaw: They do not explain why, prior to World War I, emerging markets were capable of fixing exchange rates, maintaining open capital markets and private domestic banking systems without many twin crises, and with both growth-producing and cyclically stabilizing effects from international capital flows. If markets are always tottering toward instability because of contagion, inefficiency, and multiple equilibriums, then why were historical emerging markets so different?

The fundamental strength of historical emerging markets and the relative weakness of current emerging markets explains the changed role of capital markets in relation to financial crises, and points toward changes in the political environment for explanations of market fragility.

The developed countries and the multilateral institutions they created have exacerbated the problem of weak political fundamentals. Rather than forcing emerging markets to bear the costs of economic isolation, they have been establishing subsidies to encourage capital to flow to emerging markets despite fundamental weaknesses in their economies. Those policies have encouraged sovereign debt to balloon to unsustainable levels (as in, for example, Mexico in 1994, Argentina after 1999, and Brazil in 2002). Those policies have also encouraged imprudent lending to the private sector, especially to weak or insolvent private banks.

Consequently, foreign creditors holding short-term dollar-denominated debts believe (correctly, for the most part) that domestic governments will stand behind those debts and finance their redemption if things start to go awry, and that foreign multilateral institutions (encouraged by Wall Street, the U.S. Treasury, and the rest of the G7 governments) will provide the foreign exchange bridge loans necessary to finance those transfers. Ultimately, however, as the IMF loans are repaid (as they almost always are), the costs of the crises are borne almost entirely by the citizens of emerging markets themselves.

In this sense, it is true that capital flows are a fundamental part of the problem of emerging market crises and poverty. But the reason is that capital inflows are encouraged by the political choices of emerging markets and the G7 which subsidize rather than penalize the bad policies of emerging markets.

Proposed Solutions

Although many of the arguments linking free capital flows to financial crises are flawed, it does not follow that free capital flows are currently beneficial to all or most emerging markets. When emerging market financial systems are collapsing, capital flight certainly seems to make the problem worse, forcing sovereigns into default when their debts cease to be rolled over, crippling banks with massive withdrawals, and starving domestic users of capital when they need it most. What can be done to alleviate these problems?

The most important lesson that history offers is that when fiscal policy and bank regulatory policy are well chosen and credible, crises are infrequent, and capital flows play a stabilizing role in mitigating the costs of adverse shocks. By contrast, if fiscal and regulatory policies are ill-chosen or lack credibility, then crises are likely, and capital flows will exacerbate the costs of those crises. When capital enters for the wrong reason (as when governments and the IMF subsidize the costs of bearing risk in emerging markets), capital is also liable to exit during crises in a disruptive and costly way.

The obvious implications are that emerging markets need to improve their fiscal and regulatory policies, and that the IMF needs to restore proper risk-management incentives to the global financial markets. Both sets of reforms are easy to define and hard to do. In most countries, including the vast majority of emerging markets, government is crippled by populism, cronyism, corruption, and the short-sighted policies these beget. International competition in a free-market environment might help to encourage some change in policies of emerging markets, but competition is undermined by G7 realpolitik. Meanwhile, there is little chance that the G7 governments will adopt policies that maximize the welfare of poor inhabitants in emerging markets or of their own taxpayers. Election cycles set the time horizons of the G7 leaders, too. Quick fixes that avoid current costs to the global economy at the expense of skewed long-run incentives and lower long-run growth are often popular.

IMF reforms that try to limit bailouts have been undertaken with little success over the past several years. The recent bailouts advocated by the Bush administration (particularly Argentina in 2003) seem to point away from reform. The United States has given up on reform, in part, in order to support the war against Islamic terrorism (which motivates assistance to Turkey, Pakistan, and other countries fighting terrorism in Asia). And the recent weakness of the global economy made it politically difficult to deny aid to Brazil (Latin America's largest economy).

What, then, should a well-meaning policymaker in an emerging market (there are some) do to deal with the problem of crises? It may be appropriate for such reformers to try to limit capital flows, at least of some types, until they are able to adopt the fundamental fiscal and banking system policies that will enable them to raise capital on more stable footings. How should this be done?

First, limits on capital inflows should be focused on the sources and users of capital that are most likely to create problems. If the problem is the potential abuse of short-term dollar-denominated debt to fund excessive risk-taking by domestic banks or protected cronies, then limits on short-term hard-currency debt funding for these entities—not capital controls in the broad sense—should be the policy focus.

Broader policies to limit debt inflows or outflows are undesirable and hard to enforce. In today's world of complex derivatives contracting, taxes on various kinds of short-term debt inflows (like the Chilean *encaje*) can be hard to enforce, especially since such flows are often hidden from the authorities. Furthermore, as Edwards (1999a) argues, limits on short-term debt flows tend to disproportionately disadvantage small and medium-sized firms, breed corruption, and protect domestic cronies. With all this, they usually don't work. For example, they failed to stabilize the Chilean currency or capital account from 1991–1998. Chile, which was praised by many for its taxation of short-term debt, reduced the tax rate (reserve requirement) on its *encaje* to zero in 1998 to improve its access to foreign capital (DeGregorio, Edwards, and Valdes 2000).

Similarly, the record of limits on capital outflows for promoting stability and growth (used widely in Latin America in the 1980s and most recently in Malaysia in the wake of the Asian crises) is not encouraging. The Latin American countries that did not impose controls in the 1980s actually fared better than those that did (Edwards 1999a, Edwards 1999b). These policies also promote corruption (Johnson and Mitton 2001 argue this in the case of Malaysia), and their effectiveness is far from clear (see the recent debate over the Malaysian experience: Kaplan and Rodrik 2002, Dornbusch 2002, Hartwell 2001).

Finally, even if reformers succeeded in restricting *private* market inflows or outflows, that would still not preclude *sovereign* borrowing or government guarantees of private risks. In other words, corrupt governments in emerging markets can and do "arbitrage" capital controls when they need to, by borrowing abroad and then lending to private parties or guaranteeing (implicitly or explicitly) domestic private debts.

When we examine the twin crises of Mexico, East Asia, and other countries, we find that in every case governments bore substantial fiscal risks and suffered substantial fiscal costs from bailing out private banks and corporations. They financed those costs largely by printing money, and the market's anticipation of that fact largely explains why banking crises became currency crises. It is very hard for governments to tie their own hands fiscally, but unless they are able to do so, risk subsidization, excessive borrowing, and financial crises will likely continue, although the precise structure of "crisis intermediation" by governments will vary.

To the extent that there is an argument for limiting capital inflows, then, it is largely an argument for a particular form of domestic financial sector regulation: namely, limits on the extent to which banks can borrow short-term hard-currency funds or engage in derivatives contracts that amount to doing the same thing (Garber 1998). Limits on banks' dealings are easier to police than broader limits on all borrowers. And the need to control banks' risk taking and to prevent costly banking collapses is crucial to preserving both financial system stability and government fiscal health. More generally, establishing effective domestic regulation of banks is the key to creating an atmosphere in which foreign capital flows can boost growth without exposing the economy to the risks of excessive exchange rate exposures and sudden stops. As Calomiris (1999), Calomiris and Powell (2001), and Barth, Caprio, and Levine (2002) argue, establishing *market* discipline over bank-risk taking is both feasible and crucial to creating effective prudential regulation and supervision. If regulation gives market participants the incentives to monitor bank risk-taking, and if market opinions are harnessed by regulatory rules in ways that penalize excessive bank risk-taking, then banks and their borrowers will face strong incentives not to take excessive risks and not to abuse foreign capital to do so.

One of the best means of establishing market discipline is to encourage foreign institutions to hold the debts of domestic banks (as proposed in Calomiris 1999). If domestic banks are required to issue a class of credibly unprotected debt in the hands of sophisticated foreign investors, and if continuing market opinions about banks' abilities to repay that debt affect banks' abilities to undertake new risks, then required unprotected debt issues can serve as an antidote to risk subsidization through government guarantees. Thus, ironically, a properly designed prudential system would *depend upon* foreign-held bank debt as part of a system to limit financial sector risk. Regulation of financial sectors in emerging markets should limit domestic banks' exchange rate exposure from short-term borrowing or from derivative contracts, but should not discourage borrowing from abroad, per se. In fact, it should *require it*.

Note that changes in exchange rate policy, by themselves, will not put an end to costly financial crises. I agree with those who argue that a movement from pegged to floating exchange rates will reduce the costs of financial crises. If a country has no peg to defend, there will be no predictable, sudden exchange rate movement in the offing, reducing the potential for capital to suddenly flee. Floating rates should take some of the drama out of twin crises, and should also succeed in removing some of the subsidies that non-trade sector producers receive from overvalued pegged exchange rates. However, the adoption of flexible exchange rates will do little *per se* to solve the fundamental incentive problems that plague capital flows in emerging markets.

If fiscal and regulatory policy are weak, credit collapses will still occur and exchange rates will still depreciate, albeit more gradually. Capital misallocations ex ante, and outflows, ex post, will also still characterize the boom and bust cycle of liberalization and decline. The debt burdens produced by the combination of dollar-denominated debt and exchange rate depreciation will be similar.

The fact is that market economies function only as well as governments and their agents allow. Markets are never perfect, but their unusually poor performance in emerging markets over the past two decades owes much less to inherent capital market failings than to the inability of emerging markets and G7 governments to adhere to desirable long-term economic policies. Mechanical solutions to this problem cannot solve the core problem, which fundamentally revolves around the inability or unwillingness of governments to act in their own citizens' best interests.

NOTES

1. While some of today's developed economies, including the United States, relied on capital inflows to help finance a portion of their early growth, particularly in the construction of the transportation infrastructure (Davis and Cull 1994, Wilkins 1989, Davis and Gallman 2001), emerging market countries of the past financed most of their industrialization domestically, as they were able to rely on strong

domestic legal institutions and stable and efficient local financial intermediaries to channel savings to value-creating uses.

2. This combined foreign exchange rate, financial system, and economic collapse can be particularly acute and sudden when countries are pursuing so-called "exchange rate pegs." These take various forms, ranging from rigidly fixed exchange rates to target bands for exchange rate variation and "crawling pegs" that adjust gradually over time to accommodate inflation. Even many countries that claim to operate flexible exchange rate regimes, in fact, intervene to maintain targeted exchange rate values (Calvo and Reinhart 2001).

    The problem with pegs is that, when they become unsustainable, the adjustment that finally occurs after a long period of resistance can be enormous. Exchange rates can depreciate suddenly by very large amounts, often by 50 percent or more.

3. Montiel and Reinhart (1999) find that risky macroeconomic policies generate a greater reliance on short-term debt. Specifically, countries that pursue sterilized intervention in their monetary policy tend to attract increasing amounts of short-term debt finance. Essentially, sterilized intervention is a policy that fails to restrict monetary growth or to depreciate the currency in response to outflows of foreign reserves. Monetary contraction is necessary to protect central bank reserves against an attack on the currency.

4. Substantial amounts of long-term debt roll over annually. Claessens, Dooley, and Warner (1995) find little difference in the behavior of short- and long-term debt flows for their pre-1995 sample, although the subsequent experience of Mexico and East Asia have been widely regarded as providing evidence that short-term capital flows pose a unique threat by putting an EM economy at extreme risk (Radelet and Sachs 1998, Chang and Velasco 1998).

5. During the East Asian crises, total private capital flows to Asia fell from $100.5 billion in 1996, to $3.2 billion in 1997 and continued to fall, reaching -$55.1 billion in 1998. But foreign direct investment to Asia was nearly constant over these three years: $55.1 billion in 1996, $62.6 billion in 1997, and $50.0 billion in 1998. Lipsey (2001) studies foreign direct investment by manufacturers during three financial crises (Latin America in1982, Mexico in 1994, and East Asia in 1997) and finds that foreign direct investment behaved differently from other forms of investment (see also Ito 2000). Foreign direct investment inflows were more stable than portfolio flows or bank loans from abroad during these crises. In large part, that stability reflected the reaction of multinationals to new export opportunities in emerging markets in the wake of exchange rate depreciation during EM crises.

6. Claessens, Demirguc-Kunt, and Huizinga (1998) find that foreign entrants in developing countries tend to have higher interest rate margins and profits than their domestic counterparts. Furthermore, they find that permitting foreign entry tends to result in reduced profits and overhead expenses in domestic banks. Demirguc-Kunt, Levine, and Min (1999) also find that foreign bank participation lowers domestic bank profitability and overhead costs, but they are able to show important macroeconomic consequences, as well. Increased financial sector efficiency also raises economic growth

and lowers the probability of a banking crisis. Goldberg, Dages, and Kinney (2000) study the relative performance of foreign banks in Argentina and Mexico and find that foreign banks saw higher loan growth and lower volatility of lending, which largely reflected foreign banks' ability to maintain lending during financial crises. Barajas, Steiner, and Salazar (2000) study the effect of foreign bank entry in Colombia and find that it lowered intermediation costs and improved loan quality.

7. Capital and labor tended to move together from the old world to the new world, helping to augment productivity, wages, and profits in both the old and the new world (O'Rourke and Williamson 2000, Davis and Gallman 2001). In the post–World War I environment, emigration from poorer countries has not been as common a solution to poverty, as many relatively wealthy countries have limited immigration. Now trade and capital flows are the primary means through which developed economies can spur development abroad.

8. That approach can overstate the extent of capital market integration. For most firms, in and outside the United States, historically and today, access to national, much less international, capital markets remains a distant goal. Even within the United States there are many small local firms who depend on entrepreneurial wealth or local bank finance as their exclusive means of funding their activities. If international capital is only available through public securities markets, it may have little effect on those users of capital. Foreign bank entry, and foreign direct investment by companies or venture capitalists, however, can provide access to funds for firms that do not access securities markets. For that reason, the recent growth of capital flows in these categories is highly significant.

9. The basic insight of the "trilemma" was developed by Mundell (1963).

10. It is possible to argue that the cycle of liberalization and collapse in EMs is an intentional means of financing some favored producers in the economy at the expense of everyone else. Rojas-Suarez (2003) argues that the combination of pegged exchange rates and undisciplined banking systems provides significant short-term benefits to the nontradable good sector. These producers benefit from postliberalization easy credit and the temporary overvaluation of the currency that occurs prior to the exchange rate collapse. The implied subsidies, even if temporary, can be large.

REFERENCES

Barajas, Adolfo, Roberto Steiner, and Natalia Salazar. 2000. "The Impact of Liberalization and Foreign Investment in Colombia's Financial Sector." *Journal of Development Economics* 63 (October): 157–96.

Barth, James R., Gerard Caprio, Jr., and Ross Levine. 2002. "Bank Regulation and Supervision: What Works Best?" NBER Working Paper No. 9323.

Beim, David O., and Charles W. Calomiris. 2001. *Emerging Financial Markets.* New York: McGraw-Hill.

Bekaert, Geert, and Campbell R. Harvey. 2000. "Capital Flows and the Behavior of Emerging Market Equity Returns." In Sebastian Edwards, ed., *Capital Flows and the Emerging Economies.* Chicago: University of Chicago Press: 159–94.

Bekaert, Geert, Campbell R. Harvey, and Christian Lundblad. 2001. "Does Financial Liberalization Spur Growth?" NBER Working Paper No. 8245, April.

Bordo, Michael D., Barry Eichengreen, and Douglas Irwin. 1999. "Is Globalization Today Really Different Than Globalization a Hundred Years Ago?" NBER Working Paper No. 7195, June.

Bordo, Michael D., Barry Eichengreen, and Jongwoo Kim. 1998. "Was There Really an Earlier Period of International Financial Integration Comparable to Today?" NBER Working Paper No. 6738, September.

Bordo, Michael D., and Antu Panini Murshid. 2002. "Globalization and Changing Patterns in the International Transmission of Shocks in Financial Markets."NBER Working Paper No. 9019.

Bordo, Michael D., and Hugh Rockoff. 1996. "The Gold Standard as a 'Good Housekeeping Seal of Approval.' ." *Journal of Economic History* (June).

Brown, Stephen J., William N. Goetzmann, and James Park. 1998. "Hedge Funds and the Asian Currency Crisis of 1997." NBER Working Paper No. 6427.

Burnside, Craig, Martin Eichenbaum, and Sergio Rebelo. 1999. "Prospective Deficits and the Asian Currency Crisis." NBER Working Paper No. 6758.

Calomiris, Charles W.. 1999. "Building an Incentive-Compatible Safety Net." *Journal of Banking and Finance* 23 (October): 1499–1519.

Calomiris, Charles W.. 2002a. *Victorian Perspectives on the Twin Crises of the 1990s.* Manuscript, Columbia Business School.

Calomiris, Charles W.. 2002b. *A Globalist Manifesto for Public Policy: The Tenth Annual IEA Hayek Memorial Lecture.* London: Institute for Economic Affairs.

Calomiris, Charles W.. 2002c. "Banking and Financial Intermediation." In Benn Steil, David G. Victor, and Richard R. Nelson, eds., *Technological Innovation and Economic Performance.* Princeton: Princeton University Press: 285–313.

Calomiris, Charles W., and Andrew Powell. 2001. "Can Emerging Market Bank Regulators Establish Credible Discipline? The Case of Argentina, 1992–99." In Frederic S. Mishkin, ed., *Prudential Supervision: What Works and What Doesn't.* Chicago: University of Chicago Press: 147–96.

Calvo, Guillermo, and Carmen Reinhart. 2000. "When Capital Inflows Suddenly Stop: Consequences and Policy Options." In Peter B. Kenen and Alexander K. Swoboda, *Reforming the International Monetary and Financial System.* Washington D.C.: International Monetary Fund: 175–201.

Calvo, Guillermo, and Carmen Reinhart. 2001. "Fear of Floating." Working Paper, University of Maryland.

Caprio, Gerard, Jr., and Daniela Klingebiel. 1996. "Bank Insolvencies: Cross-Country Experience." Working Paper No. 1620. The World Bank.

Chang, R., and Andres Velasco. 1998. "The Asian Liquidity Crisis." NBER Working Paper No. 6796, November.

Chari, Anusha, and Peter B. Henry. 2001. "Stock Market Liberalizations and the Repricing of Systematic Risk." NBER Working Paper No. 8265.

Chari, Anusha, and Peter B. Henry. 2002. "Risk Sharing and Asset Prices: Evidence from a Natural Experiment." NBER Working Paper No. 8988.

Choe, Hyuk, Bong-Chan Kho, and Rene Stulz. 1998. "Do Foreign Investors Destabilize Stock Markets? The Korean Experience in 1997. NBER Working Paper No. 6661.

Claessens, Stijn, Michael P. Dooley, and Andrew Warner. 1995. "Portfolio Capital Flows: Hot or Cold?" *World Bank Economic Review* 9 (1): 153–74.

Claessens, Stijn, Asli Demirguc-Kunt, and Harry Huizinga. 1998. "How Does Foreign Entry Affect the Domestic Banking Market?" World Bank Policy Research Working-ing Paper 1918 (June).

Clemens, Michael A., and Jeffrey G. Williamson. 2000. "Where Did British Capital Go? Fundamentals, Failures and the Lucas Paradox: 1870–1913." NBER Working Paper No. 8028.

Conant, Charles A.. 1910. *The Banking System of Mexico.* Senate Document No. 493, 61st Congress, 2nd Session. Washington, D.C.: Government Printing Office.

Davis, Lance E., and Robert J. Cull. 1994. *International Capital Markets and American Economic Growth, 1820–1914.* Cambridge: Cambridge University Press.

Davis, Lance E., and Robert Gallman. 2001. *Evolving Financial Markets and International Capital Flows: Britain, The Americas, and Australia, 1865–1914.* Cambridge: Cambridge University Press.

Davis, Lance E., and Robert A. Huttenback. 1988. *Mammon and the Pursuit of Empire.* New York: Cambridge University Press.

DeGregorio, Jose, Sebastian Edwards, and Rodrigo Valdes. 2000. "Control on Capital Inflows: Do They Work?." *Journal of Development Economics* 63 (October): 59–83.

Demirguc-Kunt, Asli, Ross Levine, and Hong-Ghi Min. 1999. "Opening to Foreign Banks: Issues of Stability, Efficiency, and Growth." World Bank Working Paper.

Dornbusch, Rudiger. 2002. "Malaysia's Crisis: Was It Different?" In Sebastian Edwards and Jeffrey A. Frankel, eds., *Preventing Currency Crises in Emerging Markets.* Chicago: University of Chicago Press: 441–60.

Edison, Hali J., Ross Levine, Luca Ricci, and Torsten Slok. 2002. "International Financial Integration and Economic Growth." NBER Working Paper No. 9164.

Edwards, Sebastian. 1999a. "A Capital Idea? Reconsidering a Financial Quick Fix." *Foreign Affairs* (May/June): 18–22.

Edwards, Sebastian. 1999b. "Capital Flows to Latin America: A Stop-Go Story." In Martin Feldstein, ed., *International Capital Flows.* Chicago: University of Chicago Press: 5–42.

Edwards, Sebastian, ed. 2000. *Capital Flows and the Emerging Economies: Theory, Evidence, and Controversies.* Chicago: University of Chicago Press.

Edwards, Sebastian. 2001. "Capital Mobility and Economic Performance: Are Emerging Economies Different?" NBER Working Paper No. 8076.

Edwards, Sebastian and Jeffrey A. Frankel, eds. 2002. *Preventing Currency Crises in Emerging Markets.* Chicago: University of Chicago Press.

Eichengreen, Barry. 1992. *Golden Fetters: The Gold Standard and the Great Depression, 1919–1939.* New York: Oxford University Press.

Eichengreen, Barry. 1996. *Globalizing Capital: A History of the International Monetary System.* Princeton: Princeton University Press.

Eichengreen, Barry. 2001. "Capital Account Liberalization: What Do Cross-Country Studies Tell Us?" University of California, Berkeley, Working Paper.

Feldstein, Martin (Editor. 1999. *International Capital Flows*. Chicago: University of Chicago Press.

Garber, Peter. 1998. "Derivatives in International Capital Flows." NBER Working Paper No. 6623.

Goldberg, Linda, B. Gerard Dages, and Daniel Kinney. 2000. "Foreign and Domestic Bank Participation in Emerging Markets: Lessons from Mexico and Argentina." NBER Working Paper No. 7714.

Hallward-Driemeier, Mary, Giuseppe Iarossi, and Kenneth Sokoloff. 2002. "Exports and Manufacturing Productivity in East Asia: A Comparative Analysis of Firm-Level Data." NBER Working Paper No. 8894.

Hartwell, Christopher A.. 2001. "The Case Against Capital Controls." CATO Institute Policy Analysis No. 403, June 14.

Henry, Peter B.. 2000a. "Do Stock Market Liberalizations Cause Investment Booms?" *Journal of Financial Economics* 58: 301–34.

Henry, Peter B.. 2000b. "Stock Market Liberalization, Economic Reform, and Emerging Market Equity Prices." *Journal of Finance* 55 (April): 529–64.

Henry, Peter B.. 2003. "Capital Account Liberalization, the Cost of Capital, and Economic Growth." NBER Working Paper No. 9388.

Horsefield, J. Keith. 1969. *The International Monetary Fund, 1945–1965, Volume I: Chronicle*. Washington, D.C.: International Monetary Fund.

International Monetary Fund. 1998. *Capital Account Liberalization: Theoretical and Practical Aspects*. Occasional Paper 172. Washington, D.C.: IMF.

Ito, Takatoshi. 2000. "Capital Flows in Asia." In Sebastian Edwards, ed., *Capital Flows and the Emerging Economies*. Chicago: University of Chicago Press: 255–97.

Ito, Takatoshi, and Anne O. Krueger. 2001. *Regional and Global Capital Flows: Macroeconomic Causes and Consequences*. Chicago: University of Chicago Press.

Jerome, Harry. 1926. *Migration and Business Cycles*. New York: National Bureau of Economic Research.

Johnson, Simon, and Todd Mitton. 2001. "Who Gains from Capital Controls? Evidence from Malaysia." MIT Working Paper.

Jones, Eric L.. 1988. *The European Miracle*, Second Edition. Cambridge: Cambridge University Press.

Kaminsky, Graciela, and Sergio Schmukler. 2002. "Short-Run Pain, Long-Run Gain: The Effects of Financial Liberalizations." World Bank Working Paper, May.

Kane, Edward. 1999. "How Offshore Financial Competition Disciplines Exit Resistance by Incentive-Conflicted Bank Regulators." NBER Working Paper No. 7156.

Kaplan, Ethan, and Dani Rodrik. 2002. "Did the Malaysian Capital Controls Work?" In Sebastian Edwards and Jeffrey A. Frankel, eds., *Preventing Currency Crises in Emerging Markets*. Chicago: University of Chicago Press: 393–440.

Klein, M., and G. Olivei. 1999. "Capital Account Liberalization, Financial Depth and Economic Growth." NBER Working Paper No. 7384.

Krugman, Paul. 2000. "Fire-Sale Foreign Direct Investment." In Sebastian Edwards, ed., *Capital Flows and the Emerging Economies*. Chicago: University of Chicago Press: 43–59.

Landes, David. 1999. *The Wealth and Poverty of Nations.* New York: W.W. Norton.

Lipsey, Robert E.. 2001. "Foreign Direct Investors in Three Financial Crises." NBER Working Paper No. 8084.

Maddison, Angus. 2001. *The World Economy: A Millennial Perspective.* Paris: OECD Press.

Minsky, Hyman P.. 1975. *John Maynard Keynes.* New York: Columbia University Press.

Montiel, Peter, and Carmen Reinhart. 1999. "Do Capital Controls and Macroeconomic Policies Influence the Volume and Composition of Capital Flows? Evidence from the 1990s." *Journal of International Money and Finance* 18 (August): 619–35.

Mundell, Robert. 1963. "Capital Mobility and Stabilization Policy Under Fixed and Flexible Exchange Rates." *Canadian Journal of Economics and Political Science* (November), 475–85.

Neal, Larry, and Marc Weidenmeier. 2002. "Crises in the Global Economy from Tulips to Today: Contagion and Consequences." NBER Working Paper No. 9147.

Obstfeld, Maurice, and Kenneth Rogoff. 1995. "The Mirage of Fixed Exchange Rates." *Journal of Economic Perspectives* 9, 73–96.

Obstfeld, Maurice, and Alan M. Taylor. 2003. *Global Capital Markets: Integration, Crisis, and Growth.* Cambridge: Cambridge University Press, forthcoming.

O'Rourke, Kevin H., and Jeffrey G. Williamson. 2000. *Globalization and History: The Evolution of a Nineteenth-Century Atlantic Economy.* Cambridge: MIT Press.

Radelet, Steven, and Jeffrey D. Sachs. 1998. "The East Asian Financial Crisis: Diagnosis, Remedies, Prospects." *Brookings Papers on Economic Activity* (I): 1–90.

Razin, Assaf, Efraim Sadka, and Chi-Wa Yuen. 2001. "Social Benefits and Losses from Foreign Direct Investment: Two Nontraditional Views." In Takatoshi Ito and Anne O. Krueger. 2001. *Regional and Global Capital Flows: Macroeconomic Causes and Consequences.* Chicago: University of Chicago Press: 311–26.

Rodrik, Dani. 1998. "Who Needs Capital-Account Convertibility?" Harvard University Working Paper.

Rojas-Suarez, Liliana. 2003. "Monetary Policy and Exchange Rates: Guiding Principles for a Sustainable Regime." In Pedro P. Kuczynski and John Williamson, eds., *After the Washington Consensus: Restarting Growth and Reform in Latin America.* Institute for International Economics, forthcoming.

Wei, Shang-Jin. 2000. "Local Corruption and Global Capital Flows." *Brookings Papers on Economic Activity* (2): 303–46.

Wei, Shang-Jin, and Yi Wu. 2002. "Corruption, Composition of Capital Flows, and Currency Crises." In Sebastian Edward and Jeffrey A. Frankel, eds., *Preventing Currency Crises in Emerging Markets.* Chicago: University of Chicago Press: 461–501.

Wilkins, Mira. 1989. *The History of Foreign Investment in the United States to 1914.* Cambridge: Harvard University Press.

4

Globalization and Immigration

GEORGE J. BORJAS

T RADE AND IMMIGRATION are two aspects of the globalization of the world economy that are frequently linked. There are many obvious similarities between the two. Like international trade, immigration transports resources across national boundaries, with many economic effects. Like trade, immigration has increased significantly in recent decades. In the United States, the share of immigrants in the population has risen dramatically over the past three decades, with an increasing proportion of immigrants coming from the less-developed countries. At the same time, the ratio of exports and imports to Gross Domestic Product (GDP) has risen just as rapidly, with an increasing share of the imports again originating in less-developed countries.

Because of similarities such as these, many economists treat trade and immigration as virtually interchangeable aspects of globalization. Most theory supports this view. Standard economic models suggest that both trade and immigration alter national output and income distribution of income through the same mechanism—by increasing the nation's supply of relatively scarce factors of production. Thus, every time a Japanese-made car is unloaded at a Southern California dock, the country is importing (say) 350 man-hours of engineering know-how, 250 man-hours of low-skill labor, and so on. In effect, the importation of this automobile into the United States is equivalent to the immigration of workers with particular skills.

On this basis, many economists contend that the widespread acceptance of free trade ought to apply to immigration as well. If open borders for goods ultimately enhance the well-being of all nations, shouldn't open borders for people do the same? Economists who espouse this position in the ongoing debate over immigration policy often support it by appealing to the analogy with free trade.

But a deeper analysis suggests that the differences between immigration and trade are every bit as important as the similarities. Importing workers to harvest tomatoes is simply not the same thing as importing tomatoes. Immigration introduces cultural, political, and economic considerations that are absent when discussing the impact of foreign trade. The key difference is neatly captured by novelist Max Frisch's observation on the guest worker program that Germany used to import tens of thousands of Turks: "We asked for workers, and we got people." In this essay, I'll argue that the similarities and differences between immigration and trade need to be explicitly considered when trying to understand the impact of these two types of globalization. I'll review what is currently known about this impact with reference to the U.S. experience, which is better documented and more thoroughly analyzed than any other. And on the basis of this review, I would conclude that there does not have to be a contradiction if policymakers adopt differing positions with regards to trade and immigration: the United States could well benefit both from freer flows of goods across national boundaries and from restricting the number and types of immigrants admitted.

Trends in Immigration

The major impetus for the recent explosion of immigration to the United States, particularly from less-developed countries, came from the 1965 Amendments to the Immigration and Nationality Act. Before 1965, immigration to the United States was guided by the national-origins quota system. This scheme greatly restricted the annual number of immigrants, and allocated visas across countries based on the ethnic composition of the U.S. population in 1890. As a result, 60 percent of all available visas were awarded to applicants from only two countries, Germany and the United Kingdom.

The 1965 Amendments repealed the national-origins quota system. Along with subsequent minor legislation, the Amendments also set a higher worldwide numerical limit for immigration and enshrined a new objective for allocating entry visas among the many applicants: the reunification of families. Today, most legal immigrants (73.5 percent in 1999) get visas through family sponsorship.

The 1965 policy shift had an enormous impact. During the 1950s, only 250,000 legal immigrants entered the country annually; by the 1990s, the number was almost one million. In 1970, 4.8 percent of the population was foreign-born; by 2000, 11.1 percent was foreign-born. Immigration now accounts for more than half of the nation's population growth.

The 1965 Amendments also changed the national origin mix of the immigrant population. More than two-thirds of the legal immigrants admitted during the 1950s originated in Europe or Canada, 25 percent in Latin America, and

6 percent in Asia. By the 1990s, only 16 percent originated in Europe or Canada, 49 percent in Latin America, and 32 percent in Asia.

Remarkably, few of these effects were foreseen at the time of the 1965 Amendments. When asked about the prospect of increased Asian immigration, Attorney General Robert Kennedy responded that "five thousand immigrants could come in the first year, but we do not expect that there would be any great influx after that." Policymakers were apparently oblivious to the possibility that Asians and others who had previously been prevented from entering the United States would use available visas to establish a beachhead, then sponsor the entry of many close (and not-so-close) relatives under the family reunification provisions. They also failed to take into account that immigration decisions are largely motivated by economic factors, and that the sizable income differentials between the United States and many of the new potential source countries would generate huge demand for visas.

The evidence of a substantial increase in illegal immigration is plentiful. The latest wave apparently began in the late 1960s after the end of the *bracero* program, an agricultural guest worker program for Mexicans discontinued because of its perceived harm to the economic opportunities of competing native workers. Fueled by charges that illegal aliens were overrunning the country, Congress enacted the 1986 Immigration Reform and Control Act. This legislation gave amnesty to 3 million illegal aliens and introduced a system of employer sanctions designed to stem the flow of additional illegal workers. The legislation was a failure. In its most recent published estimate (in January 2003), the Immigration and Naturalization Service (INS) reported that 7 million illegal aliens resided in the United States in 2000, more than half from Mexico, and that this population was growing at the rate of 350,000 annually.

Historically, immigrants have clustered in a few places. In 2000, 70 percent of immigrants lived in six states (California, New York, Texas, Florida, Illinois, and New Jersey), with 30 percent in California alone. Similarly, 43 percent of immigrants lived in just four metropolitan areas (Los Angeles, New York, Miami, and Chicago), where just 15 percent of natives lived. This geographic concentration reflects both the immigrants' propensity to enter the country through a few gateway cities or states, and their slow later dispersal to other areas. As a result of this geographic clustering, the foreign-born share of the population increased very rapidly in California, from 10 percent in 1970 to 33 percent in 1998, and increased from 8 to 18 percent in the five other major immigrant-receiving states. In contrast, the foreign-born share in the rest of the country rose only slightly, from 3 to 5 percent.

Moreover, different immigrant groups tend to cluster in different parts of the country, giving rise to the ethnic enclaves that are prominent in many American cities. In 2000, for example, 15.3 percent of the population of Los Angeles was born in Mexico, as compared to only 1.9 percent in New York. Similarly, 25.2 percent of Miami's population was born in Cuba, as compared to only 0.3 percent of the population in Los Angeles.

Finally, the relative educational attainment and economic performance of the immigrant population in the United States changed markedly—and for the worse—in the last half of the twentieth century (see table 4.1). In 1960, for instance, 66 percent of immigrant men were high school dropouts and 10 percent were college graduates. This educational mix was only slightly worse than that of native men, where 55 percent were high school dropouts and 11 percent were college graduates. By the late 1990s, both groups were still just as likely to have a college degree, but immigrants were far more likely to be high school dropouts: 34 percent of immigrants lacked a high school diploma, as compared to only 9 percent of natives.

Partly as a result of the widening gap in educational attainment, the earnings advantage enjoyed by immigrant workers in 1960 turned into a huge disadvantage, with immigrants earning about 23 percent less than natives by 1998. I will show below that much of this wage differential persists over time—even over generations.

The available evidence also suggests that immigrants are more concentrated in lower-skill occupations than natives and work in somewhat different industries.[1] For example, there are relatively more immigrants working in farming

TABLE 4. 1   *Changing Skills of Immigrants and Natives*

	YEAR		
	1960	*1980*	*1998*
Percent high school dropouts			
Native men	55.0	23.3	9.0
Immigrant men	66.0	37.5	33.6
Percent college graduates			
Native men	11.4	22.8	29.8
Immigrant men	10.1	25.3	28.3
Percentage wage gap between			
immigrant men and native men	4.2	−9.2	−23.0

Source: George J. Borjas, Heaven's Door: Immigration policy and the American Economy (Princeton University Press, 1999), p. 21.

occupations, in service jobs, and as operators and fabricators. There are also relatively more immigrants in the agriculture sector, in manufacturing, and in wholesale and retail trade.

IMMIGRATION AND LABOR

Given the trends summarized above, how has the increased immigration since 1965 affected Americans? Let's begin by considering the effects of immigration on labor. Do immigrants harm the employment opportunities of native workers? If so, how large is the economic loss suffered by natives? And are all groups of native workers equally affected by immigration?

These questions have always been at the core of the immigration debate. The traditional approach to answering them typically takes a myopic, short-run perspective. According to this view, the entry of immigrants into a labor market should lower the wages of competing workers (that is, those with the same types of skills as the immigrants), and perhaps increase the wages of complementary workers (those whose skills become more valuable because of immigration). For example, an influx of foreign-born laborers should reduce the economic opportunities for local laborers, who now face stiffer competition in the job market. At the same time, high-skill natives may gain substantially. They'll pay less for the services that laborers provide, such as painting the house and mowing the lawn, while they themselves are freed up to specialize in work that demands their higher-level skills.

So states the conventional wisdom. But does the evidence support this picture?

Most of the research examining this question has tried to take advantage of the tendency of immigrants to cluster in a few states and cities by studying how wages of skilled and unskilled workers in a particular locality vary with the number of immigrants present. The data tend to suggest that the correlation between wages and immigration is indeed negative, but tiny. Thus, if City A has 10 percent more immigrants than City B, native wages in City A are likely to be only about 0.2 percent lower. The adverse impact of immigration on native workers is apparently minimal.

Moreover, case studies of specific labor markets show that immigration seems to have little local impact even when the market receives very large immigrant flows.[2] The classic real-life economic "experiment" of the Mariel boatlift is a notable example.

On April 20, 1980, Fidel Castro declared that Cuban nationals wishing to move to the United States could leave freely from the port of Mariel. By September, about 125,000 Cubans, mostly unskilled workers, had undertaken the journey. Almost overnight, Miami's labor force had grown by 7 percent. Yet the impact was minimal. Between 1980 and 1985, the trend in the unemployment rate of Miami's workers was similar to that in such cities as Los Angeles, Houston, and Atlanta, where the Mariel flow was not a factor. No wonder a National Academy of Sciences Panel concluded that "the weight of the empirical evidence suggests that the impact of immigration on the wages of competing native workers is small."[3]

In recent years, however, some economists have begun to question this conclusion. These revisionist studies stress that the cross-city correlations are difficult to interpret because, over time, natives will likely respond to the entry of immigrants in ways that compensate for and mask the original effects.

To illustrate, suppose that many low-skill immigrants settle in specific cities in California, substantially reducing the wages of low-skill workers in those cities. In time, employers who hire laborers will set up shop in those cities. The resulting capital flows will help dampen the adverse effects of immigration on the immigrant cities, while worsening economic conditions elsewhere. This equalizing effect ensures that cross-city comparisons will not be very revealing. Yet in the end, all laborers, regardless of where they live, are worse off because there are now many more of them.

Native workers may also respond to immigration, which reinforces the equalizing effects. Suppose that laborers living in Michigan or Mississippi are thinking

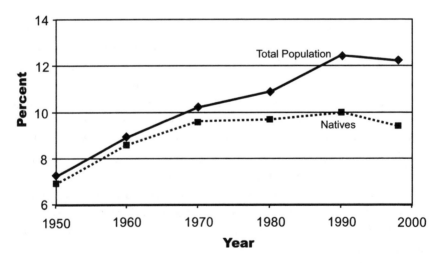

FIGURE 4.1   *Share of U.S. population living in California*
Source: George J. Borjas, Heaven's Door: Immigration Policy and the American Economy
(Princeton University Press, 1999), p. 74

about moving to California. If they do, their moves will reduce wages there, so that laborers from other states may decide to remain where they are or move elsewhere—and some Californians might actually leave the state in search of better opportunities. The migration of native workers within the United States, in effect, accomplishes what the immigrant flow, with its tendency to cluster in a small number of gateway cities, could not—a "spreading out" of the additional workers over the entire nation, rather than in just a limited number of localities. And again, a comparison of the employment opportunities of native workers in California and other states might show little or no difference because, in the end, immigration affected *every* locality, not just the ones that actually received immigrants.

Does the evidence suggest that natives actually respond to immigration in these ways? It's hard to say. Because there are few historical studies of the link between immigration and the internal mobility of labor and capital, the question must be examined indirectly. The resurgence of immigration in the United States began around 1968, when the policy changes in the 1965 Amendments became effective. It seems natural, therefore, to measure the impact of immigration by contrasting pre-1970 changes in the residential location of the native population with post-1970 changes.

In the years before 1970, the share of natives who lived in California, the major immigrant-receiving state, was rising rapidly (table 4.1). In 1950, 7 percent of all native-born persons lived in California; by 1970, this share had risen to 10 percent. Surprisingly, however, the share of natives living in California barely budged between 1970 and 1990; it was still around 10 percent in 1990. Nevertheless, California's share of the *total* population kept rising during this period, from 7 percent in 1950, to 10 percent in 1970, to 12 percent in 1990. Thus, while natives pouring into the state fueled California's population growth before 1970, immigrants alone fueled the post-1970 growth.

What do these facts tell us about the impact of immigration on the movements of native Americans? A possible interpretation is that, around 1970, native Americans simply lost their taste for California's sun and surf, and stopped moving there. According to this interpretation, if not for immigration, California's rapid population growth would have stalled after 1970. An alternative—and more provocative—interpretation is that immigration into California "displaced" the population growth that *would have occurred* in the immigrants' absence, and this displacement effectively diffused the economic impact of immigration from California to the rest of the country.

Neither of these hypotheses can be proved, but your own sense of plausibility may incline you to accept one or the other.

Because it's so hard to measure the impact of immigration through purely local studies, new approaches have been developed to measure the impact at the national level.[4] One popular approach compares the nation's actual supplies of workers in particular skill groups to those it would have had in the absence of immigration, and then uses outside information on how relative wages respond to changes in relative supplies to calculate the wage consequences of immigration.

To give a very simple example, suppose that in the absence of immigration there would have been one unskilled worker for every skilled worker in the national economy. Immigration changes this "skill ratio" so that there are now two unskilled workers for each skilled worker. Such a change in skill ratios will surely increase the wage gap between skilled and unskilled workers. If existing research provides a measure of the responsiveness of relative wages to changes in skill ratios, one could estimate to measure the impact of immigration on the wage gap between skilled and unskilled workers in the national economy.

Here is how this concept has played out in the real world. Between 1979 and 1995, the skill shift ratio shifted dramatically: immigration increased the supply of workers who are high school dropouts by nearly 21 percent, while increasing the supply of workers with at least a high school diploma by only 4 percent, which suggests that the impact of immigration is likely to be most adverse at the bottom end of the skill distribution. Specifically, it has been estimated that the earnings of the typical high school dropout (around $20,000 in 2000) may have been reduced by 5 percent ($1,000) as a result of immigration.[5]

Before we conclude our look at the labor market effects of immigration, remember that the same economic incentives that drive global trade flows motivate workers to move across international borders. Thus, trade and immigration, while not completely equivalent, will have overlapping effects. If there were no immigration of low-skill workers, the United States would probably import the low-priced goods produced by such workers. As a result, some of the wage losses suffered by native workers that we now attribute to immigration would have been observed in any case, only caused by trade rather than immigration.

Economic Benefits of Immigration

While advocates for labor and some economists focus on the potential impact of immigrants on wages, others emphasize the economic benefits that immigration generates for many Americans.

There's no doubt that some of these benefits are real. For example, immigrant consumers increase the demand for goods and services produced by native workers and firms, creating jobs for the workers and profits for the firms. And immigration can lower the price of many goods and services, benefiting American consumers. For instance, the availability of illegal alien labor in

Southern California surely improves the economic well-being of the many native households who hire them to tend the garden, do household chores, and care for the children.

However, measuring these economic gains accurately isn't easy. One needs to list all the possible channels through which immigration transforms the economy, then use this exhaustive list to estimate what the GDP of the United States would have been if the country had not admitted any immigrants. Comparing this counterfactual GDP with the actual GDP yields the increase in national income directly attributable to immigration. The same calculation can also show how much of the increase in national income accrues to natives as opposed to being paid directly to immigrants in return for their services.

This computation is obviously very difficult. It demands a model of the U.S. economy detailing how the various sectors of the economy operate and are linked together. One could then simulate how the economy changes when the labor market is flooded by millions of new workers, as well as the ripple effects of immigration on other sectors of the economy.

In recent years, economists have begun to apply their models of a free-market economy to estimate the benefits from immigration.[6] In the simplest "supply and-demand" framework, immigration introduces additional competition in the labor market and lowers the wage of native workers with similar skills. At the same time, however, native-owned firms gain by hiring workers at lower wages, and many native consumers gain because the lower labor costs eventually lead to cheaper goods and services.

According to these models, the gains accruing to the persons who use or consume immigrant services exceed the losses suffered by native workers. Hence, society as a whole is better off. Of course, this does *not* mean that every native-born person in the United States is better off. It simply means that the dollar value of the gains exceeds the dollar value of the losses.

It turns out, however, that the net benefits are relatively small. A review of the available evidence by the National Academy of Sciences concluded that the net gain accruing to the native population from the *entire* post-1965 resurgence of large-scale immigration is probably less than $10 billion a year, or somewhat less than $40 per native American.[7] On the other hand, this small net impact implies a substantial redistribution of wealth from workers who compete with immigrant labor to those who use immigrant services, amounting to some $140 billion annually. In other words, although immigration increases the size of the economic pie only slightly, it has a significant impact on the way the pie is divided.

This perspective clarifies the conflict at the core of the immigration debate. The question is not whether the United States as a whole is better off; the net gain seems to be undeniable, but so small as to be insignificant. The real conflict arises from the fact that some people gain substantially, while others lose. In short, the immigration debate reflects a tug-of-war between the winners and the losers.

Finally, don't forget that any estimate of the economic benefits from immigration must rely on a complex theoretical framework about the feedback effects which inevitably arise as the impact of immigration works its way through the economy. Inevitably, different models of the economy will lead to different estimates. Nonetheless, most plausible models make the economic benefits of immigration very small. In fact, recent theoretical work by trade economists suggests that, if one takes the perspective that the United States provides superior economic opportunities for all factors of production—so that capital as well as skilled and unskilled labor get higher returns by migrating to the United States—immigration might actually *lower* the GDP accruing to natives substantially (about $72 billion a year).[8] The loss arises because immigration forces us to share our superior opportunities with persons from abroad. In any case, there's certainly no current evidence to suggest that the economic benefits from immigration are enormous.

OTHER ECONOMIC EFFECTS OF IMMIGRATION

The most important change in immigration since 1965 has been a significant deterioration in the economic performance of immigrants. Compared to natives, the new immigrants are not so skilled or economically successful as those who came in earlier waves. The large-scale importation of low-skill labor into the United States raises significant social, cultural, and political issues. I'll discuss the economic aspects of two of these issues in detail: the problem of assimilation, and the link between immigration and the welfare state.

Assimilation

Concerns about assimilating new immigrants to the United States have been an important part of the immigration debate since colonial days. Benjamin Franklin, for example, worried that the German immigrants of his day were "the most stupid of their own nation." But Franklin also appreciated the benefits of assimilation and made specific policy recommendations designed to speed the process: "All that seems necessary is, to distribute them more equally, mix them with the English, [and] establish English schools where they are now too thick settled."

Although social, cultural, linguistic, and political assimilation are all significant issues for American policymakers, I'll focus on economic assimilation, which is often measured by calculating how the wage gap between natives and a specific wave of immigrants narrows over time (see figure 4.2). Consider, for example, male immigrants who arrived in the late 1960s and were 25 to 34 years old in 1970. This grouped earned 13 percent less than native workers of the same age. By 1998, when both immigrants and natives were between 53 and 62 years old, this wage gap had narrowed to about three percentage points. Overall, the process of economic assimilation reduced the initial wage disadvantage of these immigrants by ten percentage points over a thirty-year period, allowing them to almost catch up with native workers.

However, the young immigrants who arrived after 1970 face a much bleaker future, largely because they start out with a much greater disadvantage. Consider those who arrived in the late 1970s. By the late 1990s, twenty years after arrival, those immigrants were still earning 12 percent less than natives. The situation is even gloomier for those who arrived in the late 1980s. They started out with a 23 percent wage disadvantage, and this wage gap actually grew, rather than narrowed, during the 1990s.

How should policymakers respond to the growing persistence of the wage gap between immigrants and natives? It's typically assumed that economic assimilation benefits not only the immigrants, whose economic situation improves, but also the native-born population. Therefore, the United States should pursue policies that encourage and nurture the assimilation process.

Yet from a purely economic perspective, it's far from clear that the native population is better off when the immigrants assimilate rapidly. On the one hand, by narrowing the economic gap between less skilled immigrants

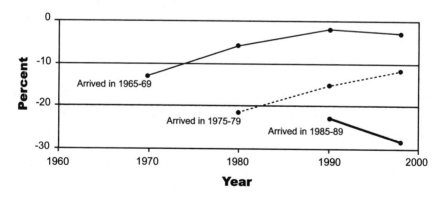

FIGURE 4.2 *Economic assimilation of immigrants. Relative wage of immigrants who arrived when they were 25–30 years old*

Source: George J. Borjas, Heaven's Door: Immigration Policy and the American Economy
(Princeton University Press, 1999), p. 30

and natives, assimilation reduces the drain on social services and lowers the chance that the immigrant population will become a new underclass, fomenting costly and troublesome social conflict. On the other hand, assimilation may actually wipe out the economic benefits from immigration discussed in the last section. These benefits arise because immigrants contribute scarce resources. It is often argued, for example, that the immigration of low-skill workers benefits the native population because the immigrants do jobs that natives reject. But as economic assimilation proceeds, and the skills of immigrants become more like those of natives, it becomes less and less likely that the immigrants will accept those jobs. Hence the presumed gains from immigration vanish, unless the low-skill immigrant population is replenished from outside.

Theory, then, is ambiguous as to whether the United States as a whole benefits from assimilation. Nonetheless, I suspect that the costs of addressing the social and economic problems created by a large underclass of immigrants would greatly exceed the (modest) economic benefits produced by immigration. On balance, the United States should encourage rapid economic assimilation, making it easier for immigrants to acquire the skills and human capital that will increase their marketability in their newly adopted country.

Ethnic Variations in Assimilation

It's well known that there is substantial dispersion in the relative wages of different ethnic groups among immigrants. In 1998, for instance, immigrants from the United Kingdom earned 20 percent more than the typical native worker in the United States, while immigrants from the Dominican Republic earned 40 percent less. The notion of the melting pot, which is the central myth through which many Americans view immigration, implies that these ethnic differences disappear quickly over time. But is this true?

To answer this crucial question, we can track the economic performance of the children and grandchildren of the immigrants who arrived in the United States a century ago. Nearly 24 million people entered the country between 1880 and 1924, in the vast human movement known as the Great Migration. Not surprisingly, there were sizable differences in economic achievement among the ethnic groups in this movement. In 1910, for instance, English immigrants earned 13 percent more than the typical worker, Portuguese immigrants earned 13 percent less, and Mexican immigrants earned 23 percent less.

Studies show that about half of the wage gap observed among ethnic groups in 1910 persisted into the second generation, and that about a quarter of the initial wage gap persisted into the third.[9] Roughly speaking, then, ethnic wage differences have a "half-life" of one generation.

The intergenerational "stickiness" of ethnic differences has important implications in assessing current immigration. In 1998, for instance, Canadian immigrants earned 120 percent more than Mexican immigrants and 90 percent more than Haitian immigrants. If the historical pattern holds, by the year 2100, the third-generation descendants of today's Canadian immigrants will still earn about 25 percent more than the descendants of today's Mexican or Haitian immigrants. Such differences will surely play a central role in debates over social policy for decades to come.

Is Assimilation Slowing Down?

Furthermore, there's reason to believe that immigrant assimilation in this century may not be as rapid as in the last. The large immigrant wave of the early 1900s, composed mainly of low-skill workers, helped build North America's manufacturing sector; three-quarters of the workers at the Ford Motor Company in 1914 were foreign-born. These manufacturing jobs evolved and eventually provided stable, well-paying opportunities to many immigrants and their descendants.

Conditions today are very different. The historic rise in the wage gap between high-skill and low-skill workers in the 1980s and 1990s indicates a worsening of opportunities for low-skill workers. As a result, it's doubtful that the economic conditions now facing low-skill immigrants will provide the same assimilation opportunities their counterparts enjoyed a century ago.

Moreover, the specific political reaction to the social and economic dislocations associated with the Great Migration may have helped to support the assimilation process. By 1924, the United States had adopted strict limitations on the number and type of persons who could enter the country. This policy shift, combined with the poor economic conditions during the Great Depression, effectively imposed a moratorium on immigration. In the 1930s, for example, only half a million persons entered the country. The moratorium provided a "breathing period" that may have fueled assimilation by cutting off the supply of new workers to ethnic enclaves and reducing economic and social contacts between immigrants and their countries of origin.

Finally, the ideological climate that favored cultural assimilation throughout much of the twentieth century has all but disappeared. Because cultural assimilation and economic assimilation are linked, it seems likely that the diminished pressure on today's immigrants to learn English and adopt American values and habits will retard their entry into the economic mainstream.

Since the assimilation experience of the Great Migration was determined by a unique set of economic and political circumstances, we shouldn't be surprised if ethnic differences among the post-1965 immigrant groups persist far longer than in the past.

IMMIGRATION AND WELFARE

One focus of the immigration debate has always been the possibility that immigrants may become public charges. In fact, the first restrictions on immigration into the territory that would eventually become the United States addressed precisely these concerns. As early as 1645, the Massachusetts colony enacted legislation prohibiting the entry of poor or indigent persons, and in 1691, New York introduced a bonding system to discourage the entry of potential public charges. After the Supreme Court invalidated state laws that restricted the entry of poor immigrants, Congress responded in 1882 by banning the entry of "any persons unable to take care of himself or herself without becoming a public charge." And in 1903, Congress approved the deportation of immigrants who became public charges within two years after arrival.

The current restrictions on public charges have changed little since then. The Immigration and Nationality Act states that "any alien who . . . is likely to become a public charge is inadmissible," and that "any alien who, within five years after the date of entry, has become a public charge . . . is deportable."

Nonetheless, recent decades have seen a rapid increase in the number of immigrants who received cash benefits from government (see figure 4.3). In 1970, immigrants were less likely to receive cash benefits than natives. By 2000, 8.0 percent of immigrant households received cash benefits, as compared to fewer than 6 percent of native households. And if one included both cash and non-cash benefits (such as Medicaid and food stamps) in the definition of public assistance, 20 percent of immigrants received some type of assistance in 2000, as compared to only 13 percent of natives.

Meanwhile, despite the laws forbidding immigrants from receiving public assistance, the INS deported only 58 immigrants for this reason between 1961 and 1980. After that, the INS simply stopped reporting the statistic.

Some worry that the relatively generous welfare programs offered by the United States have become a magnet for immigrants, attracting some who otherwise would not have migrated to the United States or discouraging immigrants who "fail" in the United States from returning to their source countries. These potential magnet effects raise questions about the political and economic viability of the welfare state: Who is entitled to the safety net that American

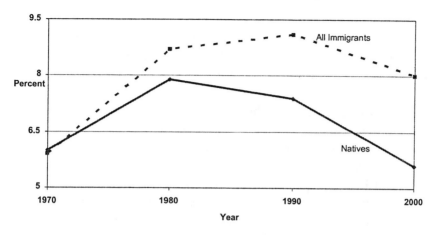

FIGURE 4.3   *Percent of households receiving cash benefits.*
Source: George J. Borjas, Heaven's Door: Immigration Policy and the American Economy
(Princeton University Press, 1999), p. 107

taxpayers pay for? And can the United States afford to extend that safety net to people from around the world? Yet surprisingly few studies have attempted to determine whether such magnet effects exist.

Much of the recent debate over the link between immigration and welfare has focused on the bottom line: Do immigrants pay their way in the welfare state? Many accounting exercises have purported to calculate the taxes paid by immigrants and balance these against the social expenditures they receive. Most of these studies are unconvincing, their conclusions determined by the accounting assumptions employed.

However, in 1996, the National Academy of Sciences attempted to settle the issue, and its report stands as the most careful investigation of this controversial subject.[10]

The National Academy considered the short-run impact of immigration on the ledger sheet of states and local governments in a particular fiscal year. For two major immigrant-receiving states (California and New Jersey), the National Academy conducted an item-by-item accounting of expenditures incurred and taxes collected, and calculated how immigration affected each of these entries.

California attracts a disproportionately large number of the welfare recipients in the immigrant population, and provides a wide array of expensive services, ranging from generous welfare assistance and world-class public universities to a sophisticated and well-maintained system of roads and freeways. According to the National Academy, immigration increased the state and local taxes paid by the typical native household in California in 1995 by $1,174 annually.

The cost-benefit calculation for New Jersey was less dramatic. Because New Jersey provides fewer state and local services, and because New Jersey attracts immigrants who are more skilled and less prone to using government services, immigration increased the annual tax bill of New Jersey's typical native household by only $229.

Extrapolating nationwide, the National Academy concluded that immigration increased the tax bill of the typical native-born household in 1995 by around $200 annually. With approximately 90 million such households in the United States, the national fiscal burden from immigration could be estimated at around $18 billion per year. Recall that the net economic gain from immigrants participating in the labor market is less than $10 billion annually.

In the short run, therefore, it seems unlikely that immigration is a great boon for the country. If anything, the evidence suggests that immigration produces a small net loss.

The Impact of PRWORA

Congress has reacted to these concerns by making it increasingly more difficult for immigrants to receive public benefits. The restrictions culminated in the inclusion of specific provisions in the welfare reform legislation of 1996 (the Personal Responsibility and Work Opportunity Reconciliation Act, or PRWORA) that denied most types of means-tested assistance to noncitizens who arrived after 1996 and limited the eligibility of many noncitizens already living in the United States.

However, another important, though little publicized, provision in PRWORA grants states the option to offer state-funded assistance to immigrants. And, in fact, five of the six states with the largest immigrant populations (California, New York, Florida, Illinois, and New Jersey) offered relatively generous state-funded assistance to immigrants in the aftermath of PRWORA (the only holdout was Texas).

There's evidence that the rate of welfare participation in immigrant households declined sharply (compared with the decline in native households) in the aftermath of PRWORA, but only in those states that chose not to make up for the cuts in federal assistance (see table 4.2). The percentage of noncitizens receiving assistance in the less-generous states (those that offered minimal levels of state-funded assistance) dropped by ten points, from 29 to 19 percent. By contrast, the percentage of non-citizens receiving assistance in the more generous states dropped by only four percentage points, from 27 to 23 percent. It seems clear, therefore, that the state-funded programs dissipated much of the impact that PRWORA might have had on immigrant welfare use.

TABLE 4.2 *Welfare Reform and Immigrant Participation in Welfare Programs*

	PERCENT OF HOUSEHOLDS RECEIVING ASSISTANCE	
	Natives	*Non-citizens*
Less generous states		
Pre-1996	16.4	28.8
Post-1996	14.3	19.1
Most generous states		
Pre-1996	14.3	27.0
Post-1996	13.1	22.8

Source: George J. Borjas, "Welfare Reform and Immigration," in The New World of Welfare: An Agenda for Reauthorization and Beyond, *edited by Rebecca Blank and Ron Haskins, Brookings Press, 2001, pp. 369-385. All data refer to non-refugee households; PRWORA did not restrict welfare use by refugees. The pre-1996 data refer to 1994-95, and the post-1996 data refer to 1997-98. The classification of states into "less" and "more" generous was made by the Urban Institute.*

There's a policy conundrum here. A few states that offer more generous safety nets than the one provided by the federal government could easily become magnets for immigration from other countries. But states are responsible for the cost of admitting immigrants only in the very short run. As soon as immigrants become naturalized citizens, many of the responsibilities shift to the federal government. The generosity of some states, therefore, could potentially harm the rest of the country.

In short, issues raised by the worrisome link between welfare and immigration were not solved by the welfare reform legislation of 1996, and they will surely remain part of the immigration debate for years to come.

LESSONS FROM THE AMERICAN EXPERIENCE

Although my discussion has focused on the American experience, there's little doubt that the resurgence of large-scale immigration will continue to transform countries around the world. Many European countries, for example, already have large immigrant populations. In the mid-1990s, the foreign-born share of the population was 10.4 percent in France, 6.4 percent in Germany, 8.9 percent in Sweden, and 6.5 percent in the United Kingdom.

European leaders today must wrestle with many of the same difficult cost / benefit analyses as American policymakers. Of course, the peculiar economic concerns of Europe put a particular spin on the debates. Some argue, for example, that immigration into Europe can help solve the fiscal problems created by the desire to provide generous levels of public services to native populations that are aging and shrinking. I suspect, however, that immigration may provide only a short-term fix for this problem. After all, the immigrants themselves will eventually get older and will need a young workforce to provide for *their* retirement. Unless the immigrants have very high fertility rates, they will need to import workers to solve their own fiscal problems a few decades from now.

Within the European Union, there is freedom of movement for capital, goods, services, and persons. In theory, this should create many additional economic opportunities for workers. Yet immigration policy continues to be a contentious issue in negotiations with countries trying to join the Union. Migration flows into the richer member states from the newly accepted nations could cause downward pressure on wages in the richer states and worsen their unemployment problems. And it's possible that the new member states could become transit stops for migration flows originating in countries further east or in Asia. Ironically, the expansion of the European Union may ultimately require the outer borders of the community to be *more* heavily monitored and guarded.

Let's conclude by returning to our first theme, the relationship between trade and immigration as aspects of globalization.

As economic theory holds, there are obvious similarities between immigration and trade. Most essentially, both transfer scarce resources into host economies across national boundaries. But there are equally important differences, which suggest that it is quite plausible that a particular country may benefit from both encouraging freer trade and restricting the number and type of immigrants admitted. The correct balance between trade and immigration as ways of capturing the benefits of globalization will continue to fuel debate for years to come.

ENDNOTES

1. Borjas, Freeman, and Katz (1997): 1–67.
2. Card (1990): 245–57.
3. Smith and Edmonston, eds. (1998): 220.
4. Borjas (2003): 1335–74.
5. Borjas, Freeman, and Katz (1997): 1–67.
6. Borjas (1995): 3–22; Johnson (1998): 17–50.
7. Smith and Edmonston, eds. (1998): 6.
8. Davis and Weinstein 2002.
9. Borjas (1994): 553–73.
10. Smith and Edmonston, eds. (1998): 254–96.

REFERENCES

Borjas, George J. 1994. "Long-Run Convergence of Ethnic Skill Differentials: The Children and Grandchildren of the Great Migration." *Industrial and Labor Relations Review* (July).

———. 1995. "The Economic Benefits from Immigration." *Journal of Economic Perspectives* (Spring).

———. 2004. "The Labor Demand Curve Is Downward Sloping: Reexamining the Impact of Immigration on the Labor Market." *Quarterly Journal of Ecnomics* (November).

———, Richard B. Freeman, and Lawrence F. Katz 1997. "How Much Do Immigration and Trade Affect Labor Market Outcomes?" *Brookings Papers on Economic Activity*.

Card, David. 1990. "The Impact of the Mariel Boatlift on the Miami Labor Market." *Industrial and Labor Relations Review* (January).

Davis, Donald R. and David E. Weinstein 2002. "Technological Superiority and the Losses from Migration," Department of Economics Working Paper 0102–60, Columbia University, May 2002.

Johnson, George E. 1998. "Estimation of the Impact of Immigration on the Distribution of Income among Minorities and Others." In Daniel S. Hamermesh and Frank D. Bean, eds. *Help or Hindrance? The Economic Implications of Immigration for African-Americans.* [Place:] Russell Sage Press.

Smith, James P. and Barry Edmonston, eds. 1998. *The New Americans: Economic, Demographic, and Fiscal Effects of Immigration.* Washington, DC: National Research Council.

5

Globalization, Poverty, and Inequality

DAVID DOLLAR

T HERE IS AN ODD disconnect between debates about globalization in the North and the South. Among intellectuals in the North, one often hears the claim that global economic integration is leading to rising global inequality—that it benefits the rich more than the poor:

> . . .globalization has dramatically increased inequality between and within nations. (Jay Mazur, *Foreign Affairs*)

> . . .inequality is soaring through the globalization period, within countries and across countries. And that's expected to continue. (Noam Chomsky)

Some even claim that the poor are actually worse off in absolute terms:

> . . .all the main parties support nonstop expansion in world trade and services although we all know it . . . makes rich people richer and poor people poorer. . . (Walter Schwarz, *The Guardian*)

In the South, on the other hand, intellectuals and policymakers often view globalization as providing good opportunities for their countries and their people:

> We are convinced that globalization is good and it's good when you do your homework . . . keep your fundamentals in line on the economy, build up high levels of education, respect rule of law. . . . when you do your part, we are convinced that you get the benefit. (President Vicente Fox of Mexico)

> There is no way you can sustain economic growth without accessing a big and sustained market. (President Yoweri Museveni of Uganda)

We take the challenge of international competition in a level playing field as an incentive to deepen the reform process for the overall sustained development of the economy. WTO membership works like a wrecking ball, smashing whatever is left in the old edifice of the former planned economy. (Jin Liqun, Vice Minister of Finance of China)

To be sure, the southern leaders aren't completely happy with the current state of globalization. President Museveni's comment above, for example, appears in the midst of a speech blasting the rich countries for their protectionist trade policies and demanding better market access for the poor. But the point of their critiques is generally that integration—through foreign trade, foreign investment, and immigration—is basically a good thing for poor countries, and that the rich countries could and should do more to facilitate this integration and make it freer.

Who is right—the anti-globalization intellectuals of the North, or the pro-globalization voices of the South? The goal of this essay is to help answer this question. It documents what we know about trends in global inequality and poverty, both over the long term and during the recent (post-1980) wave of globalization.

The heart of the essay is the second section, which presents evidence of five trends in inequality and poverty since 1980:

- Poor country growth rates have accelerated and are higher than rich country growth rates.
- The number of poor people in the world has declined significantly, the first such decline in history.
- Global inequality (among citizens of the world) has declined (modestly), reversing a 200-year-old trend toward higher inequality.
- There is no general trend toward higher inequality within countries.
- However, *wage* inequality is rising worldwide.

The essay then tries to draw a link between heightened global economic integration and accelerated growth and poverty reduction. Individual cases, cross-country statistical analysis, and micro evidence from firms all suggest that opening up to trade and direct investment has been a good strategy for such developing countries as China, Mexico, and Uganda.

My conclusions for policy are very much in the spirit of the comments from Presidents Fox and Museveni. Global integration can produce huge economic benefits for the developing world. But the world's poorer countries have a lot of homework to do to make effective use of integration as part of their development strategy. And rich countries could do much more to help. As Museveni indicates, globalization would work much better for the poor if developing countries and their people had freer access to those rich country markets.

THE GROWING INTEGRATION BETWEEN
NORTH AND SOUTH

Global economic integration has been going on for a long time. What is new in this most recent wave of globalization is the way in which developing countries are integrating with rich countries. This change is driven partly by technological advances in transport and communications, partly by deliberate policy changes.

The first great wave of modern globalization ran from about 1870 to 1914. It was spurred by the development of steam shipping and by an Anglo-French trade agreement. In this period, the world reached levels of economic integration comparable in many ways to those of today. The volume of trade, relative to world income, nearly doubled, from ten percent in 1870 to eighteen percent on the eve of World War I (table 5.1). There were also large capital flows to rapidly developing parts of the Americas, and the ownership of foreign assets (mostly Europeans owning assets in other countries) more than doubled, from 7 percent of world income to 18 percent.

Probably the most distinctive feature of this era of globalization was mass migration. Nearly 10 percent of the world's population relocated permanently in this era. Much of this was migration from poor parts of Europe to the Americas. But there was also considerable migration out of China and India (much of it forced migration in the case of India).

Of course, the 1870–1914 period was also the heyday of colonialism. Most of the world's people had scant opportunities to benefit from the expanding commerce. Colonies supplied raw materials to the metropolitan powers and had no freedom to develop modern economies. Thus, the economic integration of 1870–1914 was quite different from that of today.

Global integration took a big step backward during the period of the two world wars and the Great Depression—a powerful reminder that government policies can halt and reverse integration. The protectionist period undid half a century of integration; by the end of this dark era, both trade and foreign asset ownership had fallen back close to their levels of 1870. And the era of free migration was also at an end, as virtually all nations imposed restrictions on immigration.

In the period from the end of World War Two to about 1980, the industrial countries restored much of the integration that had existed earlier. They negotiated a series of mutual trade liberalizations under the auspices of the General Agreement on Tariffs and Trade (GATT). Liberalization of capital flows proceeded more slowly, and it was not until 1980 that the level of ownership of foreign assets returned to its 1914 level. Over this period, there was also modest liberalization of immigration in many of the industrial countries, especially the United States.

TABLE 5.1   *Measures of Global Integration*

	CAPITAL FLOWS	TRADE FLOWS	TRANSPORT AND COMMUNCATIONS COSTS (CONSTANT $)		
	Foreign assets/world GDP (%)	*Trade/GDP (%)*	*Sea Freight*	*Air Transport*	*Phonecall*
1820		2^d			
1870	6.9%	10	—	—	—
1890	—	12^e	—	—	—
1900	18.6	—	—	—	—
1914	17.5	18^{d,e}	—	—	—
1920	—	—	95	—	—
1930	8.4	18^d	60	0.68	245
1940	—	—	63	0.46	189
1945	4.9	—	—	—	—
1950	—	14^d	34	0.3	53
1960	6.4	16^e	27	0.24	46
1970	—	22.4/20^e	27	0.16	32
1980	17.7	—	24	0.1	5
1990	—	26	29	0.11	3
1995	56.8	—	—	—	—

a. *Average ocean freight and port chargers per ton*
b. *Average revenue per passenger mile*
c. *3 min. New York/London*
Sources: *Column 2, Crafts 2000; column 3, Maddison 1995(d) Crafts 2000(e); Columns 4–6, UNDP 1999*

In this second wave of modern globalization, many developing countries chose to sit on the sidelines. Most developing countries in Asia, Africa, and Latin America followed import-substituting industrialization strategies—that is, they kept their levels of import protection far higher than the industrial countries in order to encourage domestic production of manufactures. They also restricted direct foreign investment by multinational firms in order to encourage the growth of domestic firms (although quite a few developing countries turned to the expanding international bank borrowing in the 1970s and took on significant amounts of foreign debt).

The most recent wave of globalization starts, by my reckoning, in 1978 with the initiation of China's economic reform and the second oil shock, which contributed to external debt crises throughout Latin America and elsewhere in the developing world. In a growing number of countries, from Mexico and Brazil to India and Sub-Saharan Africa, political and intellectual leaders began to fundamentally rethink their development strategies. Thus, in this latest wave of globalization, the majority of the developing world (measured in terms of population) has shifted from an inward-focused strategy to a more outward-oriented one.

This altered strategy is reflected in the huge increase in trade integration among many developing countries over the past two decades. China's ratio of trade to national income has more than doubled, and countries such as Mexico, Bangladesh, Thailand, and India have seen large increases as well (figure 5.1).

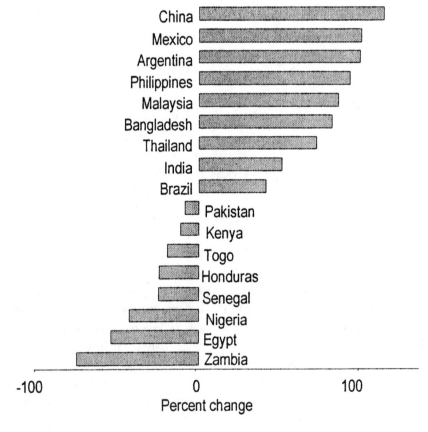

FIGURE 5.1   *Change in trade/GDP, 1977–97 (selected countries)*

However, quite a few developing countries trade *less* of their income than two decades ago, a point to which I will return.

The change has not just been in the amount, but in the nature of international trade. Twenty years ago, nearly 80 percent of developing country merchandise exports were primary products. The stereotype of poor countries exporting tin or bananas had a large element of truth. The big increase in merchandise exports in the past two decades has been of manufactured products. Today, 80 percent of merchandise exports from the South are manufactures (figure 5.2). Garments from Bangladesh, refrigerators from Mexico, computer peripherals from Thailand, CD players from China—this is the modern face of developing country exports. Service exports from the developing world have also increased enormously, including both traditional services, like tourism, and modern ones, like software.

Manufactured exports from the developing world are often part of multinational production networks. Nike contracts with firms in Vietnam to make shoes; General Motors buys auto parts from companies in many nations. Thus, part of the reason for the new globalization lies with technological advances that make integrated production feasible. (Refer back to table 5.1 to see the dramatic declines in the cost of air transport and international communications.)

But part of the answer clearly lies in the policy choices of developing countries as well. Before 1980, China and India had almost totally closed economies.

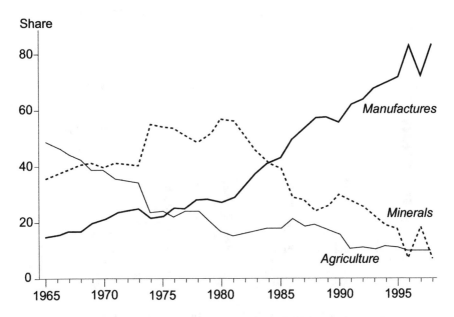

FIGURE 5.2 *Developing country exports have shifted toward manufactures*

Their increased integration would have been impossible without policy steps in these countries to gradually liberalize trade and direct foreign investment.

Some measure of this policy trend can be seen in average import tariff rates for the developing world. Average tariffs have declined sharply in South Asia, Latin America, and East Asia (though not in Africa and the Middle East) (figure 5.3). However, the most pernicious trade impediments are often non-tariff barriers, such as quotas, licensing schemes, and restrictions on purchasing foreign exchange for imports. Consider the example of China. In 1978, Chinese external trade was monopolized by a single government ministry. When China began allowing a growing number of firms, including private ones, to trade directly, and opened a foreign exchange market to facilitate this trade, a dramatic surge in trade resulted (figure 5.4).

Another major impediment to trade in many developing countries is inefficient ports and/or customs administration. For example, it is much more expensive to ship a container of textiles to the east coast of the U.S. from the port of Mombasa in Kenya than from Asian ports such as Bombay, Shanghai, Bangkok, or Kaohsiung, even though Mombasa is closer (figure 5.5). The extra cost, equivalent to an 8 percent export tax, traces back to inefficiencies and corruption in the port. Long customs delays often have a similar impact. Those developing countries that have become more integrated with the world economy have reasonably well-functioning ports and customs, often due to deliberate policy initiatives. Kenya is one of those countries that trade less of their income today than 20 years ago, and surely the country's inefficient ports and customs are part of the reason.

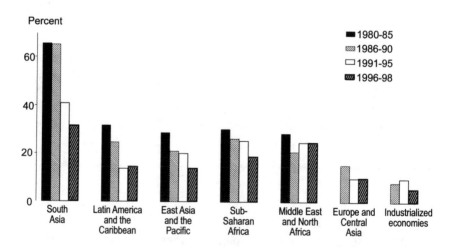

FIGURE 5.3 *Average unweighted tariff rates by region*
Source: Martin (2001)

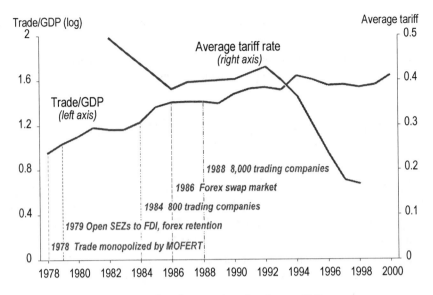

FIGURE 5.4 *Trade reforms and trade volumes, China 1978–2000*

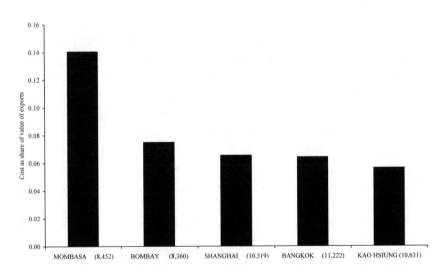

FIGURE 5.5 *Martime transport costs to the U.S. (East Coast: textiles)*

Thus, the way in which developing countries relate to the global economy has changed dramatically in the current wave of globalization. The developing world as a whole is now a major exporter of manufactures and services, many of which compete directly with goods from the industrial countries.

FIVE KEY IMPACTS OF THE NEW GLOBALIZATION

Some of the debate about globalization concerns its effects on poor countries and poor people. Earlier, I quoted a number of sweeping statements asserting that global economic integration is leading to growing poverty and inequality in the world. The reality is far more complex, and to some extent runs exactly counter to what is being claimed by anti-globalists.

Five key trends driven by the increase in world trade need to be understood. I'll consider each of the five in some detail in this section.

Poor Country Growth Rates Have Accelerated Since the Advent of the New Globalization

We have reasonably good data on economic growth going back to 1960 for about 125 countries, which make up the vast majority of the world's population. If you take the poorest one-fifth of countries in 1980 (about 25 countries), the *population-weighted* growth rate of this group was 4 percent per capita from 1980 to 1997, while the richest fifth of countries grew at just 1.7 percent (figure 5.6). This phenomenon of the fastest growth occurring in the poorest countries is historically new; the growth rates of these same countries for the prior two decades (1960–1980) were 1.8 percent for the poor group and 3.3 percent for the rich group. Data going back further in time are not as complete, but there is evidence that richer countries grew faster than poorer countries for a long time. No more.

Note that the adjective "population-weighted" is very important. If you ignore differences in population and just take an average of poor-country growth rates, you will find average growth of about zero for the world's poorest countries. Among the poorest quintile of countries in 1980 you have both China and India. You also have quite a few small countries, particularly in Africa. Ignoring population, the average growth rate of Chad and China is about zero, and the average growth of Togo and India is also about zero. However, taking account of differences in population, the average growth of poor countries over the past 20 years appears very strong.

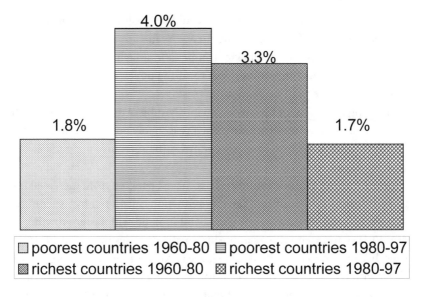

FIGURE 5.6   *Growth rates of the poorest and richest quintiles of countries*
(population weighted)

Fast-growing China obviously carries a large weight in any such calculation. But China is not the only poor country that has done well. India, Bangladesh, and Vietnam have also grown faster than rich countries in the recent period. So have a number of African economies, notably Uganda.

The Number of Poor People in the World Has Declined

Poverty reduction in low-income countries is very closely related to the growth rate in these countries. Hence, the accelerated growth of low-income countries has led to unprecedented poverty reduction. This trend is so important that it deserves somewhat detailed analysis.

In discussing poverty, it is important to be clear what poverty line one is talking about. Poverty is generally defined as subsistence below some absolute income threshold. Most poverty analysis is carried out using countries' own poverty lines, which are set in country context and naturally differ. (In global discussions, one often sees reference to international poverty lines of either $1 per day or $2 per day, and I will explain how these relate to national poverty lines.)

Most of the extreme poor in the world are peasants, and they subsist to a large extent on their own agricultural output. Since they have only limited involvement in the money economy, it would be misleading to consider only their money income. Thus, economic surveyors in China (for example) try to measure what households actually consume, and attach a value to this based on prices of different commodities. The resulting poverty line is meant to capture a certain real level of consumption.

Estimating the extent of poverty is obviously subject to error, but during the 1990s, more and more countries developed reasonably good household surveys and poverty analyses. Thus, in many countries the measures are good enough to pick up large trends.

Figure 5.7 shows five poor countries that have benefited from increased integration. In each case, significant poverty reduction, measured by the country's own poverty line and analysis, has gone hand in hand with faster growth.

It isn't easy to extend this relationship to all countries in the world or back in time, because good household surveys are lacking for many developing countries. However, discussions of global poverty during this most recent era of globalization are made easier by the fact that in 1980 a large majority of the world's poor lived in China and India, both of which have reasonably good national data on poverty.

Bourguignon and Morrisson estimate that there were 1.4 billion people in the world subsisting on less than $1 per day in 1980. This is a rough estimate, hedged with uncertainty. Still, it's clear that at least 60 percent of these poor were in

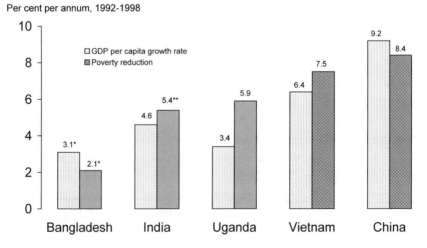

Per cent per annum, 1992-1998

* Bangladesh figures are for 1992-2000 ** India figures are for 1993-99

FIGURE 5.7 *Poverty reduction in Bangladesh, India, Uganda, Vietnam, and China closely related to growth*

China and India. So global poverty trends will depend to a very considerable extent on these two countries. The other areas with large numbers of extreme poor in 1980 were sub-Saharan Africa and several other large Asian countries (Bangladesh, Indonesia, Pakistan, Vietnam), and we will not lose sight of these as we proceed.

Taking China first, the national statistical bureau estimates that the number of people living below the country's poverty line declined from 250 million in 1978 to 34 million in 1999 (figure 5.8). Now, this Chinese poverty line is defined in constant Chinese *yuan*, and it is possible to translate it into U.S. dollars for purpose of comparison with other countries. This conversion is best done with a purchasing power parity (PPP) exchange rate, a rate that yields the same price in the U.S. and China for a representative basket of consumer goods. It is the normal basis for making international comparisons of living standards.

Evaluated at PPP in this way, the Chinese poverty line is about 70 cents per day—quite a low poverty line. Using information on the distribution of income in China, it is possible to make a rough estimate of the number of people living under a higher poverty line—for example, $1 per day at PPP. A rough estimate of $1 per day poverty in China in 1978 would be around 600 million. It may be surprising that the number is so much larger than the estimate of 250 million living on less than 70 cents per day. But in 1978, $1 per day at PPP was above the median in China, and a large mass of the population was in the range between 70 cents and $1.

India's official poverty data also show a marked drop in poverty over the past two decades. India's poverty line translates to about 85 U.S. cents at PPP.

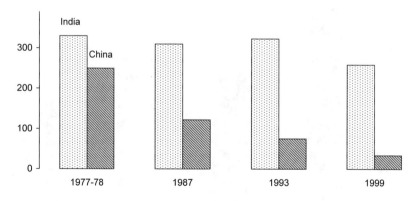

India's national poverty line: roughly $0.85 per day; China's national poverty line; roughly $0.70 per day

FIGURE 5.8 *Poverty has declined according to China's and India's national poverty lines*

By that line, the Indian statistical bureau estimates that there were 330 million poor people in India in 1977, declining to 259 million in 1999. Because India's population was growing rapidly over this period, the percent of the population living in poverty was halved over this period, from 51 percent to 26 percent. As with China, we can make a rough estimate of the number of poor living under a higher poverty line of $1 per day, using information on the distribution of income in Indian surveys.

In figure 5.9, I combine the rough estimates of $1 per day poverty in China and India. In 1977–78, there were roughly 1 billion people in these two giant countries who were subsisting on less than $1 per day at PPP; by 1997–98, the estimated number had fallen to about 650 million. This poverty reduction is all the more remarkable because the combined population of China and India increased by nearly 700 million people over this period. Thus, the percent of people living on less than $1 per day dropped sharply, from 62 percent in 1977–78 to 29 percent in 1997–98.

It is easy to quibble about specific numbers, but it's clear that there has been massive poverty reduction in China and India. And they are not the only countries in Asia that have had rapid poverty reduction. Bangladesh, Indonesia (despite its recent crisis), and Vietnam have also had significant declines in the share of the population living in poverty.

However, elsewhere in Asia, the economies of Burma and Pakistan have not done well in terms of growth and poverty reduction. It is also clear that poverty

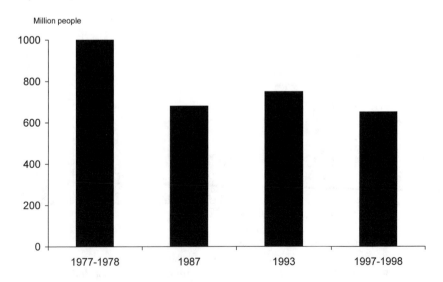

FIGURE 5.9 *Rough estimates of $1 per day poverty for China and India combined*

has been rising in Africa, where most economies have been growing slowly or not at all for the past twenty years. Chen and Ravallion (2001) estimate that the number of poor (subsisting on less than $1 per day) in Sub-Saharan Africa increased from 217 million in 1987 to 301 million in 1998. There is not comparably good data for 1980, but we know that the region was not doing well in the 1980–87 period. If the rate of increase of poverty was about the same in the 1980–87 period as in 1987–93, then the poor in Africa would have increased during the 1980–98 period by about 170 million people.

Nonetheless, there has been a large decline in the overall number of poor in the world because the decline in poverty in Asia has been significantly larger than the increase in poverty in Africa. This represents an important historical shift. Bourguignon and Morrisson (forthcoming) show that the number of poor people in the world ($1 per day line) increased through 1980 (figure 5.10). Between 1960 and 1980, for example, the number of poor grew by about 100 million. Between 1980 and 1992, however, the number of poor fell by about 100 million. Chen and Ravallion (2001) use a different methodology to estimate a further decline of about 100 million between 1993 and 1998. Chinese and Indian data for 1999–2000 show further declines that have not been incorporated in the global estimates for 1997–98.

On the basis of the well-documented poverty reduction in China and India, and their weight in world poverty, we can be confident that 200 million is a conservative estimate of the poverty reduction since 1980. In many ways, however,

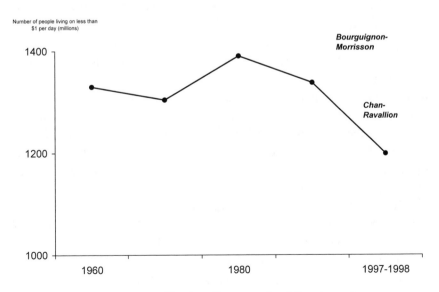

FIGURE 5.10   *Number of very poor has fallen since 1980*

adding up the good experiences and the bad experiences conceals more than it reveals. Certainly it is good news that large poor countries in Asia have done well. But that is no consolation to the growing number of poor in Africa, where most economies continue to languish.

Global Inequality Has Declined (Modestly)

People use the phrase "global inequality" casually to mean a number of different things. But the most sensible definition of inequality would be the same one generally used within a country: Line up all the people in the world from the poorest to the richest, and calculate a measure of inequality among their incomes.

There are a number of statistical measures of inequality, of which the Gini coefficient is the best known. Surjit Bhalla (2002) estimates that the world Gini coefficient declined from .67 in 1980 to .64 in 2000, after rising from .64 in 1960. Xavier Sala-I-Martin (2002) likewise finds that any of the standard measures of inequality shows a decline in global inequality since 1980.

Although this is a modest decline, it represents an important reversal of a long historical pattern of rising global inequality. Bourguignon and Morrisson (forthcoming) calculate the global Gini measure of inequality going back to 1820. Obviously we cannot have a lot of confidence in these early estimates, but the trend they outline is not seriously questioned: Global inequality has been on the rise throughout modern economic history. The B-M estimates of the global Gini have it rising from .50 in 1820 to about .65 around 1980 (figure 5.11). Xala-I-Martin estimates that the global Gini has since declined to .61.

The mean log deviation, another measure of inequality, shows a similar trend, rising up to about 1980 and then declining modestly since then (figure 5.12). (Roughly speaking, the mean log deviation is the percent difference between average income in the world and the income of a "typical person"—a randomly chosen individual.) Average income in the world today is around $5,000, but the typical person is living on $1,000, that is, 80 percent less. The mean log deviation has the advantage that it can be decomposed into inequality among countries (differences in per capita income across countries) and inequality within countries.

What this decomposition shows is that most of the inequality in the world can be attributed to inequality among countries. Global inequality rose from 1820 to 1980 primarily because countries already relatively rich in 1820 (Europe, North America) subsequently grew faster than poor locations. That pattern of growth was reversed starting around 1980, and the faster growth in poor locations such as China, India, Bangladesh, and Vietnam accounts for the modest

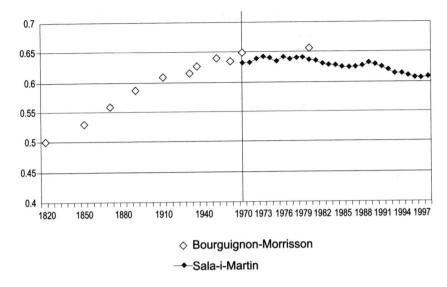

FIGURE 5.11 *Bourguignon-Morrisson and Sala-I-Martin: Global Gini Coefficent*

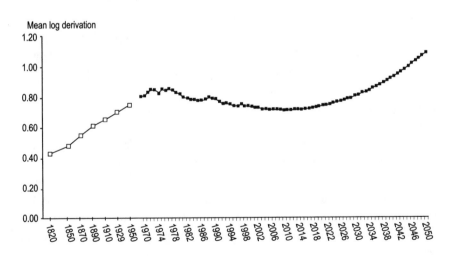

FIGURE 5.12 *Global household inequality has declined . . . but will rise again if same growth as 1980–98*

decline in global inequality since then. (Of course, slow growth in Africa tended to increase inequality, but the faster growth in low-income Asia had a greater impact overall.)[1]

Contrasting the experiences of Asia and Africa suggests what is likely to happen in the future. Rapid growth in Asia has been a force for greater global equality because that is where the majority of the world's poorest people lived in 1980. However, if the same growth trends persist, they will not continue to be a force for equality. According to Xala-I-Martin, if the growth rates of 1980–98 persist, global inequality will continue to decline until about 2015, after which it will rise sharply (see figure 5.12, above). With poverty increasingly concentrated in Africa, global inequality will eventually rise again unless Africa's slow growth can be remedied.

There Is No General Trend Toward Higher Inequality Within Countries

One of the common claims about globalization is that it is leading to greater inequality within countries and hence fostering social and political polarization. To assess this claim, Aart Kraay and I (forthcoming) collected income distribution data from over 100 countries, in some case going back decades.

We found that there is no general trend toward higher or lower inequality within countries. (Some countries in the 1990s, including China and the United States, had increases in inequality, while other countries had decreases.) One way to show this is to look at the growth rate of income of the poorest 20 percent of the population, relative to the growth rate of the whole economy. In general, growth rate of income of the poorest quintile is the same as the per capita growth rate (figure 5.13). This is equivalent to showing that the bottom quintile share (another common measure of inequality) does not vary with per capita income, and that this relationship has not changed over time.

Most important for the debate about globalization, we tried to use measures of integration to explain the changes in inequality that have occurred. We found no overall correlation between the two trends. That is, some countries in which trade integration has increased show rises in inequality, while others show declines (figure 5.14).

Figure 5.7 showed five good examples of poor countries that have integrated aggressively with the world economy. In two of these (Uganda and Vietnam) income distribution has shifted in favor of the poor during integration, which is why poverty reduction has been so strong in these cases. In low-income countries in particular, much of the former import protection served to benefit relatively rich and powerful groups, so that integration with the global market goes hand in hand with a decline in income inequality.

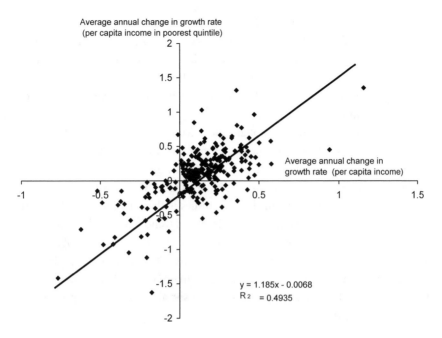

Average annual change in growth rate
(per capita income in poorest quintile)

Average annual change in
growth rate (per capita income)

$y = 1.185x - 0.0068$
$R^2 = 0.4935$

FIGURE 5.13   *Growth is good for the poor*

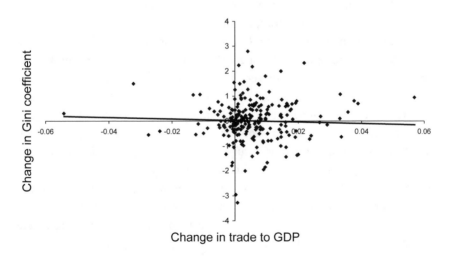

Change in Gini coefficient

Change in trade to GDP

FIGURE 5.14   *Increased trade has no correlation with changes in inequality*

A different picture of inequality trends emerges if one looks only at rich countries and only at the last decade. The Luxembourg Income Study (LIS) has produced high-quality income distribution data for most of the rich countries. This work finds no obvious trends in inequality up through the mid-to-late 1980s. But over the past decade, there have been increases in inequality in most of the rich countries.

Is this trend connected with globalization? Maybe. Because low-skilled workers in these countries are now competing more with workers in the developing world, it is certainly plausible that global economic integration creates pressures for higher inequality in rich countries, while having the opposite effect in poor countries. The good news from the LIS studies is that "Domestic policies and institutions still have large effects on the level and trend of inequality within rich and middle-income nations, even in a globalizing world . . . . [G]lobalization does not force any single outcome on any country" (Smeeding 2002). In other words, some rich countries have managed to maintain stable income distributions in this era of globalization through their social and economic policies (on taxes, education, welfare).

Wage Inequality Is Rising Worldwide

Much of the concern about globalization in rich countries relates to workers and labor issues. The most comprehensive examination of globalization and wages uses International Labour Organization data going back two decades (Freeman, Oostendrop, and Rama 2001). These data look across countries at what is happening to wages for very specific occupations (bricklayer, primary school teacher, nurse, auto worker). The study found that wages have generally been rising faster in globalizing developing countries than in rich ones, and faster in rich ones than in nonglobalizing developing countries (figure 5.15). Thus, the fastest wage growth is occurring in developing countries that are actively increasing their integration with the global economy.

While the general rise in wages is good news, however, the detailed findings from the Freeman, Oostendorp, and Rama study are more complex and indicate that certain types of workers benefit more than others. First, increased trade is related to a decline in the gender wage gap. More trade appears to lead to a more competitive labor market in which groups that have been traditionally discriminated against, such as women, fare especially well (Oostendorp 2002).

Second, the gains from increased trade appear to be larger for skilled workers. This finding is consistent with other work showing that there has been a worldwide trend toward greater wage inequality—that is, a larger pay gap—between educated workers and the less educated. Galbraith and Liu (2001), for

Wage Growth between 1980s and 1990s (percent)

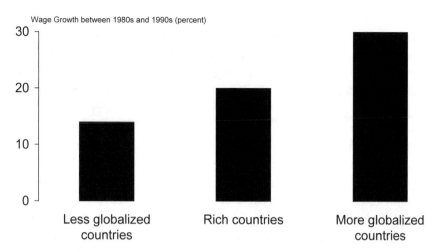

FIGURE 5.15 *Poor countries that globalize have seen the fastest growth in wages*

example, find a worldwide trend toward greater wage inequality among industries; that is, wages in skill-intensive industries (such as aircraft production) have been going up faster than wages in low-skill industries (such as garment manufacturing).

If wage inequality is going up worldwide, how is it possible that income inequality is not rising in most countries? Several factors explain this apparent inconsistency.

Most important, in the typical developing country, wage earners are a tiny fraction of the population. Even unskilled wage workers are a relatively elite group. Take Vietnam as an example—a low-income country where we have a survey of the same representative sample of households early in liberalization (1993) and five years later. The household data show that the price of the main agricultural output (rice) went up dramatically, while the price of the main purchased input (fertilizer) actually went down. These price movements are directly related to globalization, because over this period Vietnam became a major exporter of rice (supporting its price) and a major importer of fertilizer from cheaper producers (lowering its price). Thus the typical poor family—which in Vietnam is a peasant family—got a much bigger "wedge" between its input price and output price, and its real income went up dramatically (Benjamin and Brandt 2002). So one of the most important forces acting on income distribution in this low-income country has nothing to do with wages.

Quite a few rural households in Vietnam also sent a family member to a nearby city to work in a factory for the first time during this period. I worked on Vietnam for the World Bank from 1989 to 1995. When I first started visiting factories in the summer of 1989, the typical wage was the equivalent of $9 per month. Today, factory workers making contract shoes for U.S. brands often earn $50 per month or more. So the wage for a relatively unskilled worker has gone up something like five-fold. But wages for some of the skilled occupations—say, computer programmer or English interpreter—may have gone up ten times or even more.

Thus, a careful study of wage inequality in Vietnam is likely to show rising inequality. Yet the connection between wage inequality and household inequality is very complex. For a surplus worker from a large rural household who gets one of the newly created jobs in a shoe factory, earnings go from zero to $50 per month. Thus, if a large number of new wage jobs are created and if these typically pay a lot more than people earn in the rural or informal sector, then a country can have rising wage inequality but stable or even declining income inequality. (Sure enough, in Vietnam the Gini coefficient for household income inequality actually declined between 1993 and 1998.) In rich countries, on the other hand, where most people are wage earners, the higher wage inequality is likely to translate into higher household income inequality, which is what we have seen over the past decade.

A third point about inequality that is relevant for rich countries is that measures of wage inequality are often made pre-tax. If the country has a strongly progressive income tax, then inequality measures from household data (which are often post-tax) may not track wage inequality. In effect, tax policy may offset some of the trends in the labor market.

Finally, households can respond to increased wage inequality by investing more in the education of their children. A higher economic return to education is not a bad thing, provided that there is fair access to education for all. In Vietnam, there has been a tremendous increase in the secondary school enrollment rate in the 1990s (from 32 percent to 56 percent). This increase partly reflects the society's and the government's investment in schools (supported by aid donors), but it also reflects decisions by millions of individual households. Where there is little or no perceived return on education (that is, no jobs at the end of the road), it is much harder to get families in poor countries to send their children to school. Where the skill premium is high, it stimulates a shift of the labor force from low-skill to higher-skill occupations.

It should also be noted that there has been a large decline in child labor in Vietnam since the country started integrating with the global market. There is ample evidence that child labor is primarily driven by poverty and a lack of educational opportunity. Figure 5.16 shows the share of 6-to-15 year-olds working for different households ranked in terms of their 1993 level of income. It shows, unsurprisingly, that child labor is more prevalent in poor households. The fig-

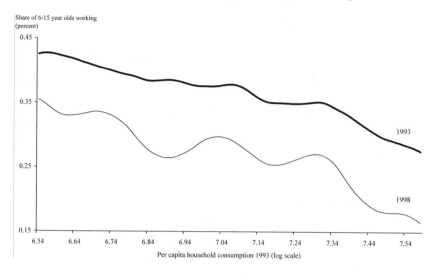

Share of 6-15 year olds working
(percent)

Per capita household consumption 1993 (log scale)

FIGURE 5.16   *Child labor and household consumption levels in Vietnam*

ure also shows that child labor has declined for all income groups. The change results from the fact that everyone is richer, and enjoys better educational opportunities, than five years earlier.

This discussion of wage trends makes it easy to see why some labor unions in rich countries are concerned about integration with the developing world. It is difficult to prove that the integration is leading to the greater wage inequality, but it's probably a factor. For example, imports of garments and footwear from countries such as Vietnam and Bangladesh create relatively high-paying jobs for workers in those countries, but they also put pressure on unskilled wages in the rich countries.

To summarize, the era of globalization has seen unprecedented poverty reduction and a modest decline in global inequality. However, it has put real pressure on less skilled workers in rich countries, and this competitive pressure is a key reason why the growing integration is controversial in the industrial countries.

IS THERE A LINK BETWEEN INTEGRATION AND POVERTY REDUCTION?

We've seen that developing countries have become more integrated with the global economy in the past two decades, and growth and poverty reduction have accelerated during the same period. Is there a link between the two? Could countries like Bangladesh, China, India, and Vietnam have grown as rapidly as they have without opening their borders to foreign trade and investment?

This kind of hypothetical question can never be answered with scientific certainty, but there are several types of evidence that we can bring to bear on it. First, let's consider what economic theory would predict. Consider the following from economist Paul Romer:

> To keep track of the wide range of explanations that are offered for persistent poverty in developing nations, it helps to keep two extreme views in mind. The first is based on an object gap: Nations are poor because they lack valuable objects like factories, roads, and raw materials. The second view invokes an idea gap: Nations are poor because their citizens do not have access to the ideas that are used in industrial nations to generate economic value. . . .
>
> Each gap imparts a distinctive thrust to the analysis of development policy. The notion of an object gap highlights saving and accumulation. The notion of an idea gap directs attention to the patterns of interaction and communication between a developing country and the rest of the world. (Romer 1993: 543–544)

As this suggests, traditional growth theory focuses on the "object gap" between poor countries and rich ones. If the important thing is just to increase the number of factories and workplaces, then it does not matter whether this is done in a closed environment or a state-dominated environment. This was the model followed by China and the Soviet Union, and to a lesser extent by most developing countries, who pursued import-substituting industrialization strategies throughout the 1960s and 1970s.

The disappointing results from this traditional approach led to new thinking both from policymakers in developing countries and from economists studying growth. Romer was one of the pioneers of the new growth theory that put more emphasis on how innovation occurs and is spread and the role of technological advances in improving the standard of living. According to this new model, several aspects of integration—sending students abroad to study, connecting to the Internet, allowing foreign firms to open plants, purchasing the latest equipment and components—can help overcome the "idea gap" that separates poor and rich nations.

Does the evidence support the idea that integration spurs growth? There are a large number of case studies that show how this process can work in particular countries. Among the countries that were very poor in 1980, China, India, Vietnam, and Uganda provide an interesting range of examples.

China. China's initial reforms in the late 1970s focused on the agricultural sector and emphasized strengthening property rights, liberalizing prices, and creating internal markets. As indicated in figure 5.4, liberalizing foreign trade and investment were also part of the initial reform program and played an increasingly important role in growth as the 1980s proceeded. The role of international linkages in China's growth is described in this excerpt from a case study by Richard Eckaus (1997: 415):

> The expansion of China's participation in international trade since the beginning of the reform movement in 1978, has been one of the most remarkable features of its remarkable [economic] transformation.
>
> While GNP was growing at 9 percent from 1978 to 1994, exports grew at about 14 percent and imports at an average of 13 percent per year.
>
> The successes contradict several customary generalizations about transition economies and large developing countries—for example, that the transition from central planning to market orientation cannot be made without passing through a difficult period of economic disorganization and, perhaps decline; and that the share of international trade in very large economies cannot grow quickly due to the difficulties of penetrating foreign markets on a larger scale.

India. It is well known that India pursued an inward-oriented growth strategy into the 1980s, and got disappointing results. Under this policy regime, India's growth in the 1960s (1.4 percent per annum) and 1970s (-0.3 percent) was disappointing. During the 1980s, India's economic performance improved. However, this surge was fueled by deficit spending and borrowing from abroad that was unsustainable. In fact, the spending spree led to a fiscal and balance of payments crisis that brought a new, reform government to power in 1991.

Srinivasan (1996) describes the key reform measures and their results as follows:

> In July 1991, the government announced a series of far reaching reforms. These included an initial devaluation of the rupee and subsequent market determination of its exchange rate, abolition of import licensing with the important exceptions that the restrictions on imports of manufactured consumer goods and on foreign trade in agriculture remained in place, convertibility (with some notable exceptions) of the rupee on the current account; reduction in the number of tariff lines as well as tariff rates; reduction in excise duties on a number of commodities; some limited reforms of direct taxes; abolition of industrial licensing except for investment in a few industries for locational reasons or for environmental considerations, relaxation of restrictions on large industrial houses under the Monopolies and Restrictive Trade Practices (MRTP) Act; easing of entry requirements (including equity participation)

for direct foreign investment; and allowing private investment in some industries hitherto reserved for public sector investment.

In general, India has gotten good results from its reform program, with per
capita income growth above 4 percent per annum in the 1990s. Growth and
poverty reduction have been particularly strong in states that have made the
most progress liberalizing the regulatory framework and providing a good environment for delivery of infrastructure services (Goswami et al. 2002).

Vietnam. The same collection that contains Eckaus's study of China also has
a case study of Vietnam:

> Vietnam has made a remarkable turnaround during the past decade. In
> the mid-1980s the country suffered from hyperinflation and economic stag-
> nation; it was not able to feed its population; and hundreds of thousands of
> people were signaling their dissatisfaction by fleeing in unsafe boats. A decade
> later, the government had restored macroeconomic stability; growth had ac-
> celerated to the 8–9 percent range; the country had become the second largest
> rice exporter in the world; and overseas Vietnamese were returning with their
> capital to take advantage of expanding investment opportunities. During this
> period there has also been a total transformation of Vietnam's foreign trade
> and investment, with the economy now far more open than ten years ago.
>
> That Vietnam was able to grow throughout its adjustment period can be
> attributed to the fact that the economy was being increasingly opened to the
> international market. As part of its overall effort to stabilize the economy,
> the government unified its various controlled exchange rates in 1989 and de-
> valued the unified rate to the level prevailing in the parallel market. This was
> tantamount to a 73 percent *real* devaluation; combined with relaxed adminis-
> trative procedures for imports and exports, this sharply increased the profit-
> ability of exporting.
>
> This . . . policy produced strong incentives for export throughout most
> of the 1989–94 period. During these years real export growth averaged more
> than 25 percent per annum, and exports were a leading sector spurring the
> expansion of the economy. Rice exports were a major part of this success in
> 1989; and in 1993–94 there was a wide range of exports on the rise, including
> processed primary products (e.g., rubber, cashews, and coffee), labor-inten-
> sive manufactures, and tourist services.
>
> The current account deficit declined from more than 10 percent of GDP
> in 1988 to zero in 1992. Normally, the collapse of financing in this way would
> require a sharp cutback in imports. However, Vietnam's export growth was
> sufficient to ensure that imports could grow throughout this adjustment pe-

riod. It is also remarkable that investment increased sharply between 1988 and 1992, while foreign aid [from the Soviet Union] was drying up. In response to stabilization, strengthened property rights, and greater openness to foreign trade, domestic savings increased by twenty percentage points of GDP, from negative levels in the mid-1980s to 16 percent of GDP in 1992. (Dollar and Ljunggren 1997: 439, 452–455)

Uganda. Uganda has been one of the most successful reformers in Africa during this recent wave of globalization, and its experience has interesting parallels with Vietnam's. It too was a country that was quite isolated economically and politically in the early 1980s. The role of trade reform in its larger reform is described in Collier and Reinikka (2001: 30–39):

> In 1986 the NRM government inherited a trade regime that included extensive nontariff barriers, biased government purchasing, and high export taxes, coupled with considerable smuggling. The nontariff barriers have gradually been removed since the introduction in 1991 of automatic licensing under an import certification scheme. Similarly, central government purchasing was reformed and is now subject to open tendering without a preference for domestic firms over imports.
>
> By the mid-1990s, the import tariff schedule had five *ad valorem* rates between 0 and 60 percent. For more than 95 percent of imported items the tariff was between 10 and 30 percent. During the latter half of the 1990s, the government implemented a major tariff reduction program. As a result, by 1999 the tariff system had been substantially rationalized and liberalized, which gave Uganda one of the lowest tariff structures in Africa. The maximum tariff is now 15 percent on consumer goods, and there are only two other tariff bands: zero for capital goods and 7 percent for intermediate imports.
>
> The average real GDP growth rate was 6.3 percent per year during the entire recovery period (1986–99) and 6.9 percent in the 1990s. The liberalization of trade has had a marked effect on export performance. In the 1990s export volumes grew (at constant prices) at an annualized rate of 15 percent, and import volumes grew at 13 percent. The value of noncoffee exports increased fivefold between 1992 and 1999.

These cases provide persuasive evidence that openness to foreign trade and investment—coupled with complementary reforms—can lead to faster growth in developing countries. But individual cases always raise the question: How typical are these results? Can every developing country that liberalizes foreign trade and investment expect good results?

Cross-country statistical analyses, which are useful in answering such questions, generally find a correlation between trade and growth. In general, countries that have had large increases in trade integration have also had accelerations in growth. This relationship persists after controlling for reverse causality from growth to trade and for changes in other institutions and policies (Dollar and Kraay 2001).

A final piece of evidence about integration and growth comes from firm-level studies. Developing countries often have large productivity dispersion across firms making similar things; high productivity and low productivity firms coexist, often with insufficient competition to spur innovation. Firm-level studies consistently show that openness leads to lower productivity dispersion as high-cost producers exit the market and are gradually replaced by more efficient, lower-cost entrants (Haddad 1993, Haddad and Harrison 1993, Harrison 1994).

Wacziarg (1998) uses eleven episodes of trade liberalization in the 1980s to look more closely at the issue of competition and market entry. Using data on the number of establishments in each sector, he calculates that entry rates were 20 percent higher among countries that liberalized compared to ones that did not. This estimate may reflect, in part, the effect of other policies that accompany trade liberalization such as privatization and deregulation, so this is likely to be an upper limit of the impact of trade liberalization. However, it is sizeable. The evidence also indicates that entry rates are usually of comparable to exit rates. Plant-level data from Morocco, Chile, and Columbia spanning several years in the 1980s when these countries initiated trade reforms indicate that exit rates range from 6 to 11 percent a year, while entry rates range from 6 to 13 percent. Over time, the cumulative turnover is quite impressive, with a quarter to a third of firms having turned over in four years (Roberts and Tybout 1996: 6).

The higher turnover rate of firms is an important source of the dynamic benefits of openness, since, in general, dying firms have falling productivity and new firms tend to increase their productivity over time (Liu and Tybout 1996, Roberts and Tybout 1996). In Taiwan, Aw, Chung and Roberts (2000) find that within a five-year period, the replacement of low productivity firms with new, higher productivity entrants accounts for half or more of the technological advance in many Taiwanese industries.

While these studies help explain why open economies are more innovative and dynamic, they also show why integration is controversial. An open, dynamic economy brings change and dislocation. If workers have good social protection and opportunities for developing new skills, then almost everyone may benefit. But without such policies, there may be some big losers.

Economic historians Peter Lindert and Jeffrey Williamson (2001) have neatly summarized the strength of the evidence linking integration to growth:

The doubts that one can retain about each individual study threaten to block our view of the overall forest of evidence. Even though no one study can establish that openness to trade has unambiguously helped the representative Third World economy, the preponderance of evidence supports this conclusion.

They go on to note that "countries that chose to be less open to trade and factor flows in the 1990s than in the 1960s and rose in the global living-standard ranks at the same time" constitute an "empty set." They conclude: "As far as we can tell, there are no anti-global victories to report for the postwar Third World. We infer that this is because freer trade stimulates growth in Third World economies today, regardless of its effects before 1940."

Making Globalization Work Better for the Poor

What are the implications of these findings—for developing countries, for rich countries, and for NGOs that focus on global poverty?

So far, the most recent wave of globalization starting around 1980 has been a powerful force for equality and poverty reduction. But it would be naïve to think that this will inevitably continue. Whether global economic integration continues to be an equalizing force will depend on the extent to which poor locations participate in this integration. That in turn will depend on both their own policies and the policies of the rich world.

True integration requires not just trade liberalization, but also wide-ranging reforms of institutions and policies. Many of the countries that are not participating very strongly in globalization have serious problems with the overall investment climate. Kenya, Pakistan, Burma, and Nigeria would all be examples. Some of these countries also have restrictive policies toward trade, but trade liberalization alone is unlikely to solve their economic problems.

It is not easy to predict the future of these countries. (Consider how surprising the reforms instituted by China, India, Uganda, and Vietnam were.) Building a coalition for reform in a developing country is not easy, and what outsiders can do to help is limited. But one thing that the rich countries can do is to make it easy for developing countries to join the club of free-trading nations. Unfortunately, in recent years the rich countries have been making it harder.

The GATT was originally built around agreements concerning trade practices. Now, however, a certain degree of institutional harmonization is required to join the WTO (for examples, on policies toward intellectual property rights). The current proposal to regulate labor standards and environmental standards through WTO sanctions would push this requirement for institutional harmonization much further, which developing countries see as inherently unfair and as a new protectionist tool that rich countries can wield against them.

To understand this perception, it's important to recognize that power in the WTO is inherently unbalanced. When it comes to dispute settlement, only larger countries can effectively threaten to retaliate against illegal measures. Thus, if the United States wins an unfair trade practices case against Bangladesh (for example), it is allowed to impose punitive duties on Bangladeshi products. Owing to the asymmetry in the size of these economies, the penalties are likely to impose a small cost on U.S. consumers and a large one on Bangladeshi producers. But suppose the situation is reversed and Bangladesh wins a judgment against the United States. For Bangladesh to impose punitive duties on U.S. products is likely to hurt its own economy much more than the United States.

Globalization will proceed more smoothly, and with broader benefits for humankind, if the rich countries make it easier for developing countries to benefit from trade and investment. Reciprocal trade liberalizations have worked well throughout the postwar period. There are still significant arenas of protectionism in OECD countries whose doors are shut to agricultural and labor-intensive imports like those produced by many developing nations. It would help substantially to reduce these protections. At the same time, developing countries would benefit from further opening of their own markets. They have a lot to gain from more trade in services.

On the other hand, 70 percent of the tariff barriers that developing countries face are imposed by other developing countries. So there is a lot of potential to expand trade among developing countries through further easing of trade restrictions. However, the trend to use trade agreements to try to impose an institutional model from the OECD countries on Third World countries makes it more difficult to reach trade agreements that benefit poor countries.

Another reason for pessimism concerns geography. There is no inherent reason why coastal China, or southern India, or Vietnam, or northern Mexico should be poor. These locations historically were held back by misguided policies, and with policy reform they can grow very rapidly and take their natural place in the world income distribution. But the same reforms will not have the same effect in Mali or Chad. Some countries are far from markets and have inherently high transport costs. Others face challenging health and agricultural problems. So it would be naïve to think that trade and investment can alleviate poverty in all countries.

For these geographically disadvantaged countries, more and better forms of foreign aid are essential. Aid targeted to developing medicines for malaria, AIDS, and other health problems of poor areas and to building infrastructure and institutions in these locations could produce enormous benefits. The promises of greater aid from the U.S. and Europe at the Monterrey Conference were encouraging, but it remains to be seen whether these promises will be fulfilled.

The importance of geography also raises the issue of migration—the missing flow in today's globalization. Migration from regions that are poor because of weak institutions and/or difficult geography could make a large contribution to reducing world poverty. Such migration raises the living standard of the migrant and benefits the sending country in three ways: Reducing the labor force raises wages for those who remain behind; migrants typically send money back home; and their presence in the OECD economy can support the development of trade and investment networks. These benefits are strongest if the migrant is relatively unskilled, since this is the part of the labor force that is in over-supply in much of the developing world.

Each year, 83 million people are added to the world population, 82 million of these in the developing world. Meanwhile, populations in Europe and Japan are aging, and without more migration, labor forces there will begin to shrink. So there are clear economic benefits to more migration of unskilled workers from the South to the North. Nonetheless, this flow remains highly restricted and very controversial because of its impact on society and culture. Because the economic pressures are so strong, however, growing volumes of illegal immigration are taking place—and some of the worst abuses of "globalization" occur because the world is not truly globalized when it comes to labor flows.

Realistically, none of the OECD countries is going to adopt open migration. But there is a good case for revisiting migration policies. Some of the OECD countries have a strong bias in their immigration policies toward highly skilled workers, spurring "brain drain" from the developing world. This policy pushes much of the unskilled flow into the illegal category. If OECD countries would accept more unskilled workers legally, it would help alleviate their own looming labor shortages, improve living standards in sending countries, and reduce the growing illegal human trade, with all its abuses.

We've seen, then, that integration of poor economies with richer ones has provided many opportunities for poor people to improve their lives. Beneficiaries of globalization may be found among Mexican migrants, Chinese factory workers, Vietnamese peasants, and Ugandan farmers. Yet much of the current debate about globalization ignores the unprecedented opportunities that it has provided to many poor people in the developing world.

After all of the rhetoric about globalization is stripped away, many of the practical policy issues come down to a single question: Are we going to make it easy or difficult for poor countries that want to integrate with the global economy to do so? The world's poor have a large stake in how the rich countries answer this question.

ENDNOTE

1. Milanovich (2001) estimates an increase in the global Gini coefficient for the short period between 1988 and 1993. How can this be reconciled with the Bhalla and Xala-I-Martin findings? Global inequality has declined over the past two decades primarily because poor people in China and India have seen increases in their incomes relative to incomes of rich people (that is, OECD populations). If you refer back to Figure 9, you will see that the period from 1988 to 1993 was the one period in the past 20 years that was not good for poor people in China and India. India had a serious crisis/recession in this period, and rural income growth in China was temporarily slowed in this period.

REFERENCES

Aw, B.Y., S. Chung, and M.J. Roberts. 2000. "Productivity and the Decision to Export: Micro Evidence from Taiwan and South Korea." *World Bank Economic Review* 14 (1): 65–90.

Benjamin, D., and L. Brandt. 2002. "Agriculture and Income Distribution in Rural Vietnam under Economic Reforms: A Tale of Two Regions." Policy Research Working Paper (forthcoming), World Bank, Washington, D.C.

Bhagwati, J. 1992. *India's Economy: The Shackled Giant*, Oxford: Clarendon Press.

Bhalla, Surjit. 2002. *Imagine There Is No Country: Poverty, Inequality, and Growth in the Era of Globalization.* Institute of International Economics.

Borjas, G. J., R. B. Freeman, and L. F. Katz. 1997. "How Much Do Immigration and Trade Affect Labor Market Outcomes." *Brookings Papers on Economic Activity* 1:1–90.

Bourguignon, F., and C. Morrisson (forthcoming). "Inequality among World Citizens: 1820–1992." *American Economic Review.*

Chen, S., and M. Ravallion. 2001. "How did the World's Poorest Fare in the 1990s?" *Review of Income and Wealth*, Series 47, no. 3, (September).

Collier, P., and R. Reinikka. 2001. "Reconstruction and Liberalization: An Overview." In P. Collier and R. Reinikka, eds., *Uganda's Recovery: The Role of Farms Firms, and Government*, Regional and Sectoral Studies, World Bank, Washington, D.C.

Crafts, N.. 2000. "Globalization and Growth in The Twentieth Century." International Monetary Fund Working Paper #00/44.

Dollar, David, and Aart Kraay. 2001. "Trade, Growth, and Poverty." Policy Research Working Paper No. 2199, World Bank, Washington, D.C.

——— and Aart Kraay (forthcoming). "Growth Is Good for the Poor." *Journal of Economic Growth.*

Dollar, David and Borje Ljunggren. 1997. "Going Global, Vietnam." In Padma Desai, ed., *Going Global: Transition from Plan to Market in the World Economy.* Cambridge: MIT Press, pp. 439–71.

Eckaus, R. 1997. "Going Global: China." in Padma Desai, ed. *Going Global: Transition from Plan to Market in the World Economy.* Cambridge: MIT Press, pp. 415–37.

Edmonds, E.. 2001. "Will Child Labor Decline with Improvements in Living Standards?" Dartmouth College Working Paper No. 01–09, July 1.

Freeman, R., R. Oostendorp, and M. Rama. 2001. "Globalization and Wages." World Bank, Washington, D.C. Processed.

Galbraith, James and Liaqing Liu. 2001. "Measuring the Evolution of Inequality in the Global Economy." In James Galbraith and Maureen Berner, eds. *Inequality and Industrial Change: A Global View,* New York: Cambridge University. Press.

Goswami, O., et. al. 2002. "Competitiveness of Indian Manufacturing: Results from a Firm-Level Survey." Research Report by Confederation of Indian Industry and The World Bank.

Haddad, M. 1993. "The Link Between Trade Liberalization and Multi-Factor Productivity: The Case of Morocco." World Bank Discussion Paper No. 4, Washington, D.C.

Haddad, M., and A. Harrison. 1993. "Are There Spillovers from Direct Foreign Investment? Evidence from Panel Data for Morocco." *Journal of Development Economics* 42 (1): 51–74.

Harrison, A. 1994. "Productivity, Imperfect Competition, and Trade Reform." *Journal of International Economics* 36(1–2): 53–73.

Lindert, P., and J. Williamson. 2001. "Does Globalization Make the World More Unequal?" National Bureau of Economic Research Working Paper No. 8228, National Bureau of Economic Research, Cambridge, MA.

Liu, L., and J. Tybout. 1996. "Productivity Growth in Chile and Columbia: The Role of Entry, Exit, and Learning." in M. Roberts and J. Tybout, eds., *Industrial Evolution in Developing Countries.* Oxford, UK: Oxford University Press.

Maddison, A. 1995. *Monitoring the World Economy 1820–1992.* Development Center Studies, Organization for Economic Co-operation and Development, Paris.

Mazur, J.. 2000. "Labor's New Internationalism." *Foreign Affairs.* New York.

Milanovic, B. 2002. "True World Income Distribution, 1988 and 1993: First Calculations Based on Household Surveys Alone." *The Economic Journal* 112 (January): 51–92. Royal Economic Society 2002. Published by Blackwell Publishers, Oxford, UK.

Oostendorp, R. 2002. "Does Globalization Reduce the Gender Wage Gap?" Economic and Social Institute, Free University, Amsterdam. Photocopy.

Roberts, M., and J. Tybout. 1996. *Industrial Evolution in Developing Countries: Micro Patterns of Turnover, Productivity and Market Structure.* New York: Oxford University Press.

Romer, P. 1986. "Increasing Returns and Long-Run Growth." *Journal of Political Economy* 94. No. 5.

_____. 1993. "Idea Gaps and Object Gaps in Economic Development." *Journal of Monetary Economics* (32).

Sala-I-Martin, X. 2002. "The Disturbing "Rise" of Global Income Inequality." Photocopy.

Smeeding, T. M. 2002. "Globalization, Inequality and the Rich Countries of the G-20: Updated Results from the Luxembourg Income Study (LIS) and other Places."

Prepared for the G-20 Meeting, Globalization, Living Standards and Inequality: Recent Progress and Continuing Challenges, Sydney, Australia, 26–28 May, 2002. Photocopy.

Srinivasan, T. N. 1996. "Indian Economic Reforms: Background, Rationale, Achievements, and Future Prospects." Photocopy.

Wacziarg, R. (1998. "Measuring Dynamic Gains from Trade." Policy Research Working Paper No. 2001, World Bank, Washington, D.C.

6

The Environment and Economic Globalization

JEFFREY A. FRANKEL

A T THE MINISTERIAL MEETING of the World Trade Organization in
Seattle in November 1999, when anti-globalization protestors launched
the first of their big demonstrations, some wore turtle costumes. These dem-
onstrators were concerned that international trade in shrimp was harming sea
turtles by ensnaring them in nets. They felt that a WTO panel had, in the name
of free trade, negated the ability of the United States to protect the turtles, simultaneously undermining the international environment and national sovereignty. Subsequently, anti-globalization protests became common at meetings
of multi-national organizations.

Perhaps no aspect of globalization worries the critics more than its implications for the environment. The concern is understandable. It is widely (if not
universally) accepted that the direct effects of globalization on the economy
are positive, as measured by Gross Domestic Product. Concerns rise more with
regard to "noneconomic" effects of globalization.[1] Of these, some, such as labor
rights, might be considered to be a subject properly of national sovereignty,
with each nation bearing the responsibility of deciding to what extent it wishes
to protect its own labor force, on the basis of its own values, capabilities, and
politics. When we turn to influences on the environment, however, the case
for countries sticking their noses into each other's business is stronger. We all
share a planet.

Pollution and other forms of environmental degradation are the classic instance of what economists call an externality: the condition under which individuals and firms, and sometimes even individual countries, lack the incentive to restrain their pollution, because under a market system the costs are
borne primarily by others. The phrase "tragedy of the commons" was originally
coined in the context of a village's shared pasture land, which would inevitably
be overgrazed if each farmer were allowed free and unrestricted use. It captures

the idea that we will foul our shared air and water supplies and deplete our natural resources unless somehow we are individually faced with the costs of our actions.

A central question for this chapter is whether globalization helps or hurts in achieving the best tradeoff between environmental and economic goals. Do international trade and investment allow countries to achieve more economic growth for any given level of environmental quality? Or do they undermine environmental quality for any given rate of economic growth? Globalization is a complex trend, encompassing many forces and many effects. It would be surprising if all of them were always unfavorable to the environment, or all of them favorable. The highest priority should be to determine ways in which globalization can be successfully harnessed to protect the environment rather than to degrade it.[2]

One point to be emphasized here is that it is an illusion to think that environmental issues could be effectively addressed if each country were insulated against incursions into its national sovereignty at the hands of international trade or the WTO. Increasingly, people living in one country want to protect the air, water, forests, and animals not just in their *own* countries, but also in *other* countries as well. To do so international cooperation is required. National sovereignty is the obstacle to such efforts, not the ally. Multilateral institutions are a potential ally, not the obstacle.

In the course of this chapter, we encounter three ways in which globalization can be a means of environmental improvement. So the author hopes to convince the reader, at any rate. Each has a component that is new.

First is the exercise of *consumer power*. There is the beginning of a worldwide trend toward labeling, codes of corporate conduct, and other ways that environmentally conscious consumers can use their purchasing power to give expression and weight to their wishes. These tools would not exist without international trade. American citizens would have few ways to dissuade Mexican fishermen from using dolphin-unfriendly nets if Americans did not import tuna to begin with. The attraction of labeling is that it suits a decentralized world, where we have both national sovereignty and consumer sovereignty. Nevertheless, labeling cannot be a completely laissez faire affair. For it to work, there need to be some rules or standards. Otherwise, any producer could inaccurately label its product as environmentally pure, and any country could unfairly put a pejorative label on imports from rival producers. This consideration leads to the second respect in which globalization can be a means of environmental improvement.

International environmental issues require international cooperation, a system in which countries interact under a set of *multilateral rules* determined in multilateral negotiations and monitored by multilateral institutions. This is just as true in the case of environmental objectives, which are increasingly cross-border, as of other objectives. It is true that, in the past, the economic objectives of international trade have been pursued more effectively by the GATT and other multilateral organizations than have environmental objectives. But multilateral institutions can be made a means of environmental protection. This will sound like pie-in-the-sky to the many who have been taken in by the mantra that recent WTO panel decisions have overruled legislative efforts to protect the environment. But the WTO has actually moved importantly in the environmentalists' direction in recent years.

The front lines of multilateral governance currently concern—not illusory alternatives of an all-powerful WTO versus none at all—but rather questions about how reasonably to balance both economic and environmental objectives. One question under debate is whether countries are to be allowed to adopt laws that may be trade-restricting, but that have as their objective influencing other countries' processes and production methods (PPMs), such as their fishermen's use of nets. While the issue is still controversial, the WTO has moved clearly in the direction of answering this question in the affirmative, that is, asserting in panel decisions countries' ability to adopt such laws. The only "catch" is that the measures cannot be unnecessarily unilateral or discriminatory. The environmentalist community has almost entirely failed to notice this major favorable development, because of confusion over the latter qualification. But not only is the qualification what a reasonable person would want, it is secondary to the primary issue of countries' rights under the trading system to implement such laws. By ignoring their victory on the main issue—the legitimacy of addressing PPMs— environmentalists risk losing the opportunity to consolidate it. Some players, particularly poor countries, would love to deny the precedent set in these panel decisions, and to return to a system where other countries cannot restrict trade in pursuit of others.

Third, countries can learn from others' experiences. There has recently accumulated *statistical evidence* on how globalization and growth tend to affect environmental objectives on average, even without multilateral institutions. Looking for patterns in the data across countries in recent decades can help us answer some important questions. Increased international trade turns out to have been beneficial for some environmental measures, such as SO_2 pollution. There is little evidence to support the contrary fear that international competition in practice works to lower environmental standards overall. Rather, globalization can aid the process whereby economic growth enables people to demand higher environmental quality. To be sure, effective government regulation is probably required if this demand is ever be translated into actual improvement; the environment cannot take care of itself. But the statistical evidence says that high-income countries do indeed eventually tend to use some of their wealth to clean up the environment, on average, for measures such as SO_2 pollution. For the increasingly important category of global environmental externalities, however, such as emission of greenhouse gases, regulation at the national level is not enough. An international agreement is necessary.

These three new reasons to think that globalization can be beneficial for the environment—consumer power, multilateralism, and cross-country statistical evidence—are very different in nature. But in each case what is striking is how little the facts correspond to the suspicions of critics that turning back the clock on globalization would somehow allow them to achieve environmental goals. The rise in globalization, with the attempts at international environmental accord and quasi-judicial oversight, is less a threat to the environment than an ally. It is unfettered national sovereignty that poses the larger threat.

This chapter will try to lay out the key conceptual points concerning the relationship of economic globalization and the environment, and to summarize the available empirical evidence, with an emphasis on what is new. We begin by clarifying some basic issues, such as defining objectives, before going on to consider the impact of globalization.

OBJECTIVES

It is important to begin a consideration of these issues by making clear that both economic income and environmental quality are worthy objectives. Individuals may disagree on the weight that should be placed on one objective or another. But we should not let such disagreements lead to deadlocked political outcomes in which the economy and the environment are both worse off than necessary. Can globalization be made to improve the environment that comes with a given level of income in market-measured terms? Many seem to believe that globalization necessarily makes things worse. If Mexico grows rapidly, is an increase in pollution inevitable? Is it likely, on average? If that growth arises from globalization, rather than from domestic sources, does that make environmental damage more likely? Less likely? Are there policies that can simultaneously promote *both* economic growth and an improved environment? These are the questions of interest.

Two Objectives: GDP and the Environment

An extreme version of environmental activism would argue that we should turn back the clock on industrialization—that it is worth deliberately impoverishing ourselves—if that is what it takes to save the environment. If the human species still consisted of a few million hunter-gatherers, man-made pollution would be close to zero. Thomas Malthus, writing in the early nineteenth century, predicted that geometric growth in population and in the economy would eventually and inevitably run into the natural resource limits of the carrying capacity of the planet.[3] In the 1960s, the Club of Rome picked up where Malthus had left off, warning that environmental disaster was coming soon. Some adherents to this school might favor the deliberate reversal of industrialization—reducing market-measured income below current levels in order to save the environment.[4]

But environmental concerns have become more mainstream since the 1960s. We have all had time to think about it. Most people believe that both a clean environment and economic growth are desirable, that we can have a combination of both, and it is a matter of finding the best tradeoff. Indeed, that is one possible interpretation of the popular phrase "sustainable development."

To evaluate the costs and benefits of globalization with regard to the environment, it is important to be precise conceptually, for example to make the distinction between effects on the environment that come *via* rapid economic growth and those that come *for a given level* of economic output.

We have a single concept, GDP, that attempts to measure the aggregate value of goods and services that are sold in the marketplace, and that does a relatively good job of it. Measurement of environmental quality is much less well advanced. There are many different aspects of the environment that we care about, and it is hard to know how to combine them into a single overall measure. It would be harder still to agree on how to combine such a measure with GDP to get a measure of overall welfare. Proponents of so-called *green GDP accounting* have tried to do exactly that, but so far the enterprise is very incomplete. For the time being, the best we can do is look at a variety of separate measures capturing various aspects of the environment.

A Classification of Environmental Objectives

For the purpose of this chapter, it is useful to array different aspects of the environment according to the extent to which damage is localized around specific sources, as opposed to spilling out over a geographically more extensive area.

The first category of environmental damage is pollution that is *internal* to the household or firm. Perhaps 80 percent (by population) of world exposure to particulates is indoor pollution in poor countries—smoke from indoor cooking fires—which need not involve any externality.[5] There may be a role for dissemination of information regarding long-term health impacts that are not immediately evident. Nevertheless, what households in such countries primarily lack are the economic resources to afford stoves that run on cleaner fuels.[6] In the case of internal pollution, higher incomes directly allow the solution of the problem.

Some other categories of environmental damage pose potential externalities, but could be internalized by assigning property rights. If a company has clear title to a depletable natural resource such as an oil well, it has some incentive to keep some of the oil for the future, rather than pumping it all today.[7] The biggest problems arise when the legal system fails to enforce clear divisions of property rights. Tropical forest land that anyone can enter to chop down trees will be rapidly over-logged. Many poor countries lack the institutional and economic resources to enforce laws protecting such resources. Often corrupt arms of the government themselves collude in the plundering. Another example is the dumping of waste. If someone agreed to be paid to let his land be used as a waste disposal site, voluntarily and without hidden adverse effects, economics says that there would not necessarily be anything wrong with the arrangement. Waste has to go somewhere. But the situation would be different if the government of a poor undemocratic country were to agree to be paid to accept waste that then hurt the environment and health of residents who lacked the information or political clout to participate in the policy decision or to share in the benefits.

A second category, *national externalities*, includes most kinds of air pollution and water pollution, the latter a particularly great health hazard in the third world. The pollution is external to the individual firm or household, and often external to the state or province as well, but most of the damage is felt within the country in question. Intervention by the government is necessary to control such pollution. There is no reason why each national government cannot undertake the necessary regulation on its own, though the adequacy of economic resources to pay the costs of the regulation is again an issue.

A third category is *international externalities*. Increasingly, as we will see, environmental problems cross national boundaries. Acid rain is an example. In these cases, some cooperation among countries is necessary. The strongest examples are purely *global externalities*: chemicals that deplete the stratospheric ozone layer, greenhouse gases that lead to global climate change, and habitat destruction that impairs biological diversity. Individual countries should not expect to be able to do much about global externalities on their own. The distinctions among internal pollution, national externalities, and global externalities will turn out to be important.

The Relationship Between Economic Production and the Environment

Scholars often catalog three intermediating variables or channels of influence that can determine the aggregate economic impacts of trade or growth on the environment.

1. The *scale* of economic activity: for physical reasons, more output means more pollution, other things equal. But other things are usually not equal.
2. The *composition* of economic activity: Trade and growth can shift the composition of output, for example, among the agricultural, manufacturing, and service sectors. Because environmental damage per unit of output varies across these sectors, the aggregate can shift.
3. The *techniques* of economic activity: Often the same commodity can be produced through a variety of different techniques, some cleaner than others. Electric power, for example, can be generated by a very wide range of fuels and techniques.[8] To the extent trade or growth involve the adoption of cleaner techniques, pollution per unit of GDP will fall.

The positive effects of international trade and investment on GDP are already moderately well established, both theoretically and empirically. The relationship between GDP and the environment is not quite as well understood, and is certainly less of a constant relationship. The relationship is rarely monotonic: sometimes a country's growth is first bad for the environment and later good. The reason is the three conflicting forces that were just noted. On the one hand, when GDP increases, the greater scale of production leads directly to more pollution and other environmental degradation. On the other hand, there tend to be favorable shifts in the composition of output and in the techniques of production. The question is whether the latter two effects can outweigh the first.

The Environmental Kuznets Curve

A look at data across countries or across time allows some rough generalization as to the usual outcome of these conflicting effects. For some important environmental measures, a U-shaped relationship appears: at relatively low levels of income per capita, growth leads to greater environmental damage, until it levels off at an intermediate level of income, after which further growth leads to improvements in the environment. This empirical relationship is known as the Environmental Kuznets Curve. The label is by analogy with the original Kuznets Curve, which was a U-shaped relationship between average income and inequality. The World Bank (1992) and Grossman and Krueger (1993, 1995) brought to public attention this statistical finding for a cross section of countries.[9] Grossman and Krueger (1995) estimated that SO_2 pollution peaked when a country's income was about $5,000–$6,000 per capita (in 1985 dollars). Most developing countries have not yet reached this threshold.

For countries where a long enough time series of data is available, there is also some evidence that the same U-shaped relationship can hold across time.

The air in London was far more polluted in the 1950s than it is today. (The infamous "pea soup" fogs were from pollution.) The same pattern has held in Tokyo, Los Angeles, and other cities. A similar pattern holds typically with respect to deforestation in rich countries: the percentage of U.S. land that was forested fell in the eighteenth century and first half of the nineteenth century, but rose in the twentieth century.[10]

The idea behind the Environmental Kuznets Curve is that growth is bad for air and water pollution at the initial stages of industrialization, but later on reduces pollution, as countries become rich enough to pay to clean up their environments. The dominant theoretical explanation is that production technology makes some pollution inevitable, but that demand for environmental quality rises with income. The standard rationale is thus that, at higher levels of income per capita, growth raises the public's demand for environmental quality, which can translate into environmental regulation. Environmental regulation, if effective, then translates into a cleaner environment. It operates largely through the techniques channel, encouraging or requiring the use of cleaner production techniques for given products, although regulation might also have a composition effect: raising the price of polluting goods and services relative to clean ones and thus encouraging consumers to buy more of the latter. [11]

It would be inaccurate to portray the Environmental Kuznets Curve as demonstrating—or even claiming—that if countries promote growth, the environment will eventually take care of itself. Only if pollution is largely confined within the home or within the firm does that Panglossian view necessarily apply.[12] Most pollution, such as SO_2, NO_x, etc., is external to the home or firm. For such externalities, higher income and a popular desire to clean up the environment are not enough. There must also be effective government regulation, which usually requires a democratic system to translate the popular will into action (something that was missing in the Soviet Union, for example), as well as the rule of law and reasonably intelligent mechanisms of regulation. The empirical evidence confirms that the participation of well-functioning democratic governments is an important part of the process. That is at the national level. The requirements for dealing with cross-border externalities are greater still.

Another possible explanation for the pattern of the Environmental Kuznets Curve is that it works naturally via the composition of output. In theory, the pattern could result from the usual stages of economic development: the transition from an agrarian economy to manufacturing, and then from manufacturing to services. Services tend to generate less pollution than heavy manufacturing.[13] This explanation is less likely than the conventional view to require the mechanism of effective government regulation. If the Kuznets Curve in practice resulted solely from this composition effect, however, then high incomes should lead to a better environment even when externalities arise at the international level, which is not the case. No Kuznets Curve has yet appeared for carbon dioxide, for example. Even though emissions per unit of GDP do tend to fall, this is not enough to reduce overall emissions, in the absence of a multilateral effort.

Regulation

It will help if we clarify one more fundamental set of issues before we turn to the main subject, the role of globalization per se.

It is logical to expect environmental regulation to cost something, to have a negative effect on measured productivity and income per capita. "There is no free lunch," Milton Friedman famously said. Most tangible good things in life cost something, and for many kinds of regulation, if effective, people will readily agree that the cost is worth paying. Cost-benefit tests and cost-minimization strategies are economists' tools for trying to make sure that policies deliver the best environment for a given economic cost, or the lowest economic cost for a given environmental goal. Taxes on energy, for example, particularly on hydrocarbon fuels, are quite an efficient mode of environmental regulation (if the revenue is "recycled" efficiently). Fuel efficiency standards are somewhat less efficient. (Differentiated CAFE standards for vehicles, for example, probably encouraged the birth of the SUV craze.) And crude "command and control" methods are less efficient still. (Government mandates regarding what specific technologies firms must use, for example, deny firms the flexibility to find better ways to achieve a given goal.) Some environmental regulations, when legislated or implemented poorly, can impose very large and unnecessary economic costs on firms, as well as on workers and consumers.

Occasionally there are policy measures that have both environmental and economic benefits. Usually these "win-win" ideas constitute the elimination of some previously existing distortion in public policy. Many countries have historically subsidized the use of coal. The United States subsidizes mining and cattle grazing on federal land, and sometimes logging and oil drilling as well, not to mention water use. Other countries have substantial subsidies for ocean fishing. Elimination of such subsidies would improve the environment and save money at the same time—not just for the federal budget, but for people's real income in the aggregate as well. Admittedly the economists' approach—taxing gasoline or making ranchers pay for grazing rights—is often extremely unpopular politically.

Another idea that would have economic and environmental benefits simultaneously would be to remove all barriers against international trade in environmental equipment and services, such as those involved in renewable energy generation, smokestack scrubbing, or waste treatment facilities. There would again be a double payoff: the growth-enhancing effect of elimination of barriers to exports (in a sector where the United States is likely to be able to develop a comparative advantage), together with the environment-enhancing effect of facilitating imports of the inputs that go into environmental protection. A precedent is the removal of barriers to the imports of fuel-efficient cars from Japan, which was a clear case of simultaneously promoting free trade and clean air.

A different school of thought claims that opportunities for saving money while simultaneously saving the environment are common rather than rare. The *Porter Hypothesis* holds that a tightening of environmental regulation stimulates technological innovation and thereby has positive effects on both the economy and the environment—for example, saving money by saving energy.[14] The analytical rationale for this view is not always made clear. (Is the claim that a change in regulation, regardless in what direction, stimulates innovation, or is there something special about environmental regulation? Is there something special about the energy sector?) Its proponents cite a number of real-world examples where a new environmental initiative turned out to be profitable for a given firm or industry. Such cases surely exist, but there is little reason to think that a link between regulation and productivity growth holds as a matter of generality. The hypothesis is perhaps better understood as making a point regarding "first mover advantage." That is, if the world is in the future to be moving in a particular direction, such as toward more environmentally friendly energy sources, then a country that innovates new products and new technologies of this sort before others do will be in a position to sell the fruits to the latecomers.

EFFECTS OF OPENNESS TO TRADE

The central topic of this chapter is the implications of trade for the environment. Some effects come via economic growth, and some come even for a given level of income. In both cases, the effects can be either beneficial or detrimental. Probably the strongest effects of trade are the first sort, via income. Much like saving and investment, technological progress, and other sources of growth, trade tends to raise income. As we have seen, higher income in turn has an effect on some environmental measures that is initially adverse but, according to the Environmental Kuznets Curve, eventually turns favorable.

What about effects of trade that do not operate via economic growth? They can be classified in three categories: systemwide effects that are adverse, systemwide effects that are beneficial, and effects that vary across countries depending on local "comparative advantage." We consider each in turn.

Race to the Bottom

The "*race to the bottom*" hypothesis is perhaps the strongest basis for fearing that international trade and investment specifically (rather than industrialization generally) will put downward pressure on countries' environmental standards and thus damage the environment across the global system. Leaders of industry, and of the unions whose members are employed in industry, are always concerned about competition from abroad. When domestic regulation raises their costs, they fear that they will lose competitiveness against firms in other countries. They warn of a loss of sales, employment, and investment to foreign competitors.[15] Thus domestic producers often sound the competitiveness alarm as a way of applying political pressure on their governments to minimize the burden of regulation.[16]

To some, the phrase "race to the bottom" connotes that the equilibrium will be a world of little or no regulation. Others emphasize that, in practice, it is not necessarily a matter of globalization leading to environmental standards that literally decline over time, but rather retarding the gradual raising of environmental standards that would otherwise occur. Either way, the concern is that, to the extent that countries are open to international trade and investment, environmental standards will be lower than they would otherwise be. But how important is this in practice? Some economists' research suggests that environmental regulation is not one of the more important determinants of firms' ability to compete internationally. When deciding where to locate, multinational firms seem to pay more attention to such issues as labor costs and market access than to the stringency of local environmental regulation.[17]

Once again, it is important to distinguish (1) the fear that globalization will lead to a race to the bottom in regulatory standards, from (2) fears that the environment will be damaged by the very process of industrialization and economic growth itself. Opening of national economies to international trade and investment could play a role in both cases, but the two possible channels are very different. In the first case, the race to the bottom hypothesis, the claim is that openness undermines environmental standards even for a given path of economic growth. This would be a damning conclusion from the standpoint of globalization, because it would imply that by limiting trade and investment in some way, we might be able to attain a better environment for any given level of GDP. In the second case, the implication would be that openness only affects the environment in the way that investment, or education, or productivity growth, or any other source of growth affects the environment, by moving the economy along the Environmental Kuznets Curve. Trying to restrict trade and investment would be a less attractive strategy in this case, because it would amount to deliberate self-impoverishment.

Gains from Trade

While the possibility that exposure to international competition might have an adverse effect on environmental regulation is familiar, less widely recognized and more surprising is the possibility of effects in the beneficial direction, which we will call the *gains from trade hypothesis*. Trade allows countries to attain more of what they want, which includes environmental goods in addition to market-measured output.

How could openness have a positive effect on environmental quality, once we set aside the possibility of accelerating progress down the beneficial slope of the Environmental Kuznets Curve? A first possibility concerns technological and managerial innovation. Openness encourages ongoing innovation.[18] It then seems possible that openness could encourage innovation beneficial to environmental improvement as well as economic progress. A second possibility is an international ratcheting up of environmental standards.[19] The largest political jurisdiction can set the pace for others. Within the United States, it is called the "California effect." When the largest state sets high standards for auto pollution control equipment, for example, the end result may be similar standards in other states as well. The United States can play the same role globally.

Multinational corporations (MNCs) are often the vehicle for these effects. They tend to bring clean state-of-the-art production techniques from high-standard countries of origin, to host countries where they are not yet known, for several reasons:

> First, many companies find that the efficiency of having a single set of management practices, pollution control technologies, and training programmes geared to a common set of standards outweighs any cost advantage that might be obtained by scaling back on environmental investments at overseas facilities. Second, multinational enterprises often operate on a large scale, and recognise that their visibility makes them especially attractive targets for local enforcement officials ... Third, the prospect of liability for failing to meet standards often motivates better environmental performance (Esty and Gentry 1997: 161).

The claim is not that all multinational corporations apply the highest environmental standards when operating in other countries, but rather that the standards tend on average to be higher than if the host country were undertaking the same activity on its own.[20] Corporate codes of conduct, as under the U.N. Global Compact promoted by Kofi Annan, offer a new way that residents of some countries can pursue environmental goals in other countries.[21] Formal international cooperation among governments is another way that interdependence can lead to higher environmental standards rather than lower.[22]

Furthermore, because trade offers consumers the opportunity to consume goods of greater variety, it allows countries to attain higher levels of welfare (for any given level of domestically produced output), which, as before, will raise the demand for environmental quality. Again, if the appropriate institutions are in place, this demand for higher environmental quality will translate into effective regulation and the desired reduction in pollution.

Attempts to Evaluate the Overall Effects of Trade on the Environment

If a set of countries opens up to trade, is it on average likely to have a positive or negative effect on the environment (for a given level of income)? Which tend in practice to dominate, the unfavorable "race to the bottom" effects or the favorable "gains from trade" effects? Econometrics can help answer the question.

Statistically, some measures of environmental quality are positively correlated with the level of trade. Figure 6.1 shows a rough inverse correlation between countries' openness to trade and their levels of SO_2 pollution. But the

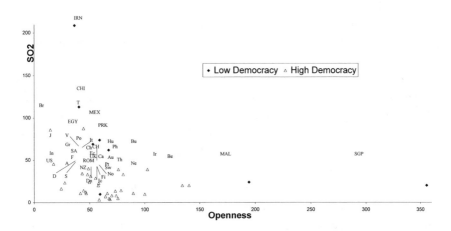

FIGURE 6.1 *Openness vs. SO_2 concentration in low- vs. high-democracy regimes, 1990*

causality is complex, running in many directions simultaneously. One would not want to claim that trade leads to a cleaner environment, if in reality they are both responding to some other third factor, such as economic growth or democracy.[23]

Eiras and Schaeffer (2001: 4) find: "In countries with an open economy, the average environmental sustainability score is more than 30 percent higher than the scores of countries with moderately open economies, and almost twice as high as those of countries with closed economies." Does this mean that trade is good for the environment? Not necessarily. It might be a result of the Porter hypothesis—environmental regulation stimulates productivity—together with the positive effect of income on trade. Or it might be because democracy leads to higher levels of environmental regulation, and democracy is causally intertwined with income and trade. As noted, democracy raises the demand for environmental regulation. Figure 6.1 suggests that the relationship between SO_2 concentrations and openness is even clear if one controls for the beneficial effect of democracy. But there remain other possible third factors.

A number of studies have sought to isolate the independent effect of openness. Lucas, et al. (1992), study the toxic intensity implied by the composition of manufacturing output in a sample of 80 countries, and find that a high degree of trade-distorting policies increased pollution in rapidly growing countries. The implication is that trade liberalization now is good for the environment. Harbaugh, Levinson, and Wilson (2000) report in passing a beneficial effect of trade on the environment, after controlling for income. Dean (2002) finds a detrimental direct of liberalization for a given level of income, via the terms of trade, though this is outweighed by a beneficial indirect effect via income.

Antweiler, Copeland and Taylor (2001) and Copeland and Taylor (2001, 2003a) represent an extensive body of empirical research explicitly focused on the effects of trade on the environment. They conclude that trade liberalization that raises the scale of economic activity by 1 percent works to raise SO_2 concentrations by .25 to .5 percent via the scale channel, but that the accompanying technique channel reduces concentrations by 1.25 to 1.5 percent, so that the overall effect is beneficial. But none of these studies makes allowance for the problem that trade may be the *result* of other factors rather than the cause. Antweiler et al. point out this potential weakness.[24]

Frankel and Rose (2003) attempt to disentangle the various causal relationships. The study focuses on exogenous variation in trade across countries, attributable to factors such as geographical location. It finds effects on several measures of air pollution (particularly SO_2 and NO_x concentrations), for a given level of income, that are more good than bad. This suggests that the "gains from trade" effects may be at least as powerful as the "race to the bottom" effect.

The findings are not so optimistic for other measures of environmental quality, however, particularly emissions of CO_2.

Differential Effects Arising from Comparative Advantage

So far we have only considered effects that could be expected to hold for the average country, to the extent that it is open to international trade and investment. What if the environment improves in some open countries and worsens in others? An oft-expressed concern is that, to the extent that countries are open to international trade and investment, some will specialize in producing dirty products, and export them to other countries. Such countries could be said to exploit a comparative advantage in pollution. The prediction is that the environment will be damaged more in this set of countries, as compared to what would happen without trade. The environment will be *cleaner* in the second set of countries, those that specialize in clean production and instead import the dirty products from the other countries. Leaving aside the possibility of a race to the bottom effect, the worldwide environment on average might even benefit somewhat, just as aggregate output should benefit, because of the gains from trade. But not everyone would approve of such a bargain.

What determines whether a given country is expected to be in the set of economies specializing in clean or dirty environmental production? There are several possible determinants of comparative advantage.

Endowments and Comparative Advantage
First, trade patterns could be determined by endowments of capital and labor, as in the standard neoclassical theory of trade, attributed to Heckscher, Ohlin, and Samuelson. Assume manufacturing is more polluting than alternative economic activities, such as services. (If the alternative sector, say agriculture, is instead just as polluting as manufacturing, then trade has no overall implications for the environment.) Since manufacturing is capital intensive, the country with the high capital/labor ratio—say Japan—will specialize in the dirty manufactured goods, while countries with low capital/labor ratios—say China—will specialize in cleaner goods.

For example, Grossman and Krueger predicted that NAFTA might reduce overall pollution in Mexico and raise it in the United States and Canada, because of the composition effect: Mexico has a comparative advantage in agriculture and labor-intensive manufacturing, which are relatively cleaner, versus the northern comparative advantage in more capital intensive sectors. This composition effect runs in the opposite direction from the usual worry, that trade would turn Mexico into a pollution haven as a result of high demand for environmental quality in the United States. That theory is discussed in the next section.

Second, comparative advantage could be determined by endowments of natural resources. A country with abundant hardwood forests will tend to export them if given the opportunity to do so. Here there cannot be much doubt that trade is indeed likely to damage the environment of such countries. True, in theory, if clear property rights can be allocated and enforced, someone will have the proper incentive to conserve these natural resources for the future. In practice, it seldom works this way. Poor miners and farmers cannot be kept out of large tracts of primitive forest. And even if there were clear property rights over the natural resources, private firms would not have the correct incentives to constrain external side effects of logging and mining, such as air and water pollution, soil erosion, loss of species, and so on. Government regulation is called for, but is often stymied by the problems of inadequate resources, at best, and corruption, at worst.

Pollution Havens   Third, comparative advantage could be deliberately created by differences in environmental regulation itself. This is the pollution haven hypothesis. The motivation for varying levels of regulation could be differences in demand for environmental quality, arising, for example, from differences in income per capita. Or the motivation could be differences in the supply of environmental quality, arising, for example, from differences in population density.

Many object to an "eco dumping" system according to which economic integration results in some countries exporting pollution to others, even if the overall global level of pollution does not rise.[25] They find distasteful the idea that the impersonal market system would deliberately allocate environmental damage to an "underdeveloped" country. A Chief Economist of the World Bank once signed his name to an internal memo with economists' language that read (in the summary sentence of its most inflammatory passage) "Just between you and me, shouldn't the World Bank be encouraging *more* migration of the dirty industries to the LDCs?" After the memo was leaked, public perceptions of the young Larry Summers were damaged for years.

There is a some empirical evidence, but not very much, to support the hypothesis that countries that have a particularly high demand for environmental quality—the rich countries—currently specialize in products that can be produced cleanly, and let the poor countries produce and sell the products that require pollution.[26] For the case of SO_2, the evidence appears to be, if anything, that trade leads to a reallocation of pollution from the poor country to the rich country, rather than the other way around.[27] This is consistent with the finding of Antweiler, Copeland and Taylor (2001) that trade has a significantly less favorable effect on SO_2 emissions in rich countries than in poor countries. Their explanation is that rich countries have higher capital/labor ratios, capital-intensive industries are more polluting, and this factor-based pollution-haven effect dominates the income-based pollution-haven effect.

Is the Majority of U.S. Trade and FDI with Low-Standard Countries?

To listen to some American discussion of globalization, one would think that the typical partner in U.S. trade and investment is a poor country with low environmental or labor standards. If so, it would help explain the fear that opening to international trade and investment in general puts downward pressure on U.S. standards. In fact, less than half of U.S. trade and investment takes place with partners who have lower wages and lower incomes than we do. Our most important partners have long been Canada, Japan, and the European Union (though Mexico has now become important as well). These trading partners often regard the United States as the low-standard country rather than the opposite

DOES ECONOMIC GLOBALIZATION CONFLICT WITH ENVIRONMENTAL REGULATION?

There is a popular sense that globalization is a powerful force undermining environmental regulation. This can be the case in some circumstances. The "race to the bottom" phenomenon can potentially put downward pressure on the regulatory standards of countries that compete internationally in trade and investment. But, as an argument against globalization, it leaves much out.

First is the point that, for most of us, environmental quality is one goal, but not the only goal. As already noted, we care also about income, and trade is one means of promoting economic growth. The goals often need to be balanced against each other.

Environmental concerns can be an excuse for protectionism. If policymakers give in to protectionist arguments and erect trade barriers, we will enjoy less growth in trade and income. We will not even necessarily end up with a better environment. Import-competing corporations (or their workers), in sectors that may themselves not be particularly friendly to the environment, sometimes seek to erect or retain barriers to imports in the name of environmental protection, when in reality it is their own pocketbooks they are trying to protect. In other words, environmentalism is an excuse for protectionism.

Often, the problem is less sinister, but more complex. To see how the political economy works, let us begin with the point that most policy debates are settled as the outcome of a complicated mix of multiple countervailing arguments and domestic interest groups on both sides. Most of the major viewpoints are in some way represented "at the table" in the federal government decisionmaking process. In the case of environmental measures, there are often representatives of adversely affected industry groups sitting across the table from the environmentalists, and they have an effect on the final political outcome. But when the commodity in question happens to be produced by firms in foreign countries, then that point of view largely disappears from the table around which the decision is made. If the issue is big enough, the State Department may weigh in to explain the potential costs facing foreign countries. But, understandably, the foreigners receive less weight in the policy process than would the identical firms if they were American. The result is that the environmental policies that are adopted on average can discriminate against foreign firms relative to domestic firms, without anyone ever deliberately having supported a measure out of protectionist intent.

One possible example is the strong opposition in Europe to Genetically Modified Organisms (GMOs). A Biosafety Agreement was negotiated in Montreal, January 29, 2000, in which the United States felt it had to agree to label grain shipments that might in part be bio-engineered, and to allow countries to block imports of GMOs.[28] In some ways, these negotiations might serve as a useful model for compromise in other areas.[29] But why have Europeans that they want to keep out genetically modified varieties of corn, despite the emergence of little or no scientific evidence against them as of yet, where American consumers are far less agitated? Is it because Europeans are predisposed to have higher standards for environmental issues? Perhaps.[30] An important part of the explanation, however, is that Monsanto and other U.S. technology companies, and U.S. farmers, are the ones who developed the technology and produce the stuff, not European companies or European farmers. Thus it is American producers, not Europeans, who stand to lose from the European squeamishness. European agriculture need not consciously launch a campaign against GMOs. All that the European movement needed was an absence around the table of producers who would be adversely affected by a ban. But the result is to reduce trade, hurt American producers, and benefit European farmers.

Whatever the source of different perceptions across countries, it is important to have a set of internationally agreed rules to govern trade, and if possible a mechanism for settling disputes that arise. That is the role of the WTO. The need for such an institution does not vanish when environmental issues are a part of the dispute. Certainly if one cares at all about trade and growth, then one cannot automatically sign on to each and every campaign seeking to block trade on environmental grounds. But even if one cares solely about the environment, claims need to be evaluated through some sort of neutral process. One can be easily misled; corporations make dubious claims to environmental motivations in, for example, seeking federal support of "Clean Coal" research or ethanol production. Most of the time, there is no substitute for investigating the details and merits of the case in question. One should not presume that an interest group's claims are right just because that group happens to be of one's own nationality.

The Impossible Trinity of Global Environmental Regulation

The concerns of anti-globalizers can be understood by means of a trilemma of regulation, called the principle of the Impossible Trinity of Global Governance. In designing a system of global governance, three kinds of goals are desirable. First, *globalization* is desirable, other things being equal, for its economic benefits if nothing else. Second, *regulation* is desirable when it comes to externalities like pollution, or other social goals not adequately addressed by the marketplace. Third, national *sovereignty* is desirable, because different

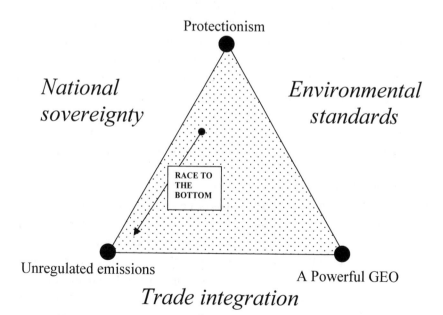

FIGURE 6.2 *The impossible trinity of global environmental regulation*

countries have different needs or preferences, and also because nations take pride in their political independence. The principle of the Impossible Trinity points out that it is feasible to design a system with any two of these attributes, but not with all three.

The three attributes are represented as the sides of the triangle in the accompanying figure. The lower left corner represents a system of complete laissez faire. The private market is given responsibility for everything. With no government regulation, there is nothing to coordinate internationally, and thus no loss in national sovereignty. If another country wants to make the mistake of heavy-handed intervention, that is its affair. One can imagine Friederich von Hayek, Ayn Rand, or Milton Friedman favoring the laissez faire corner.

The lower right corner represents a system of regulation at the global level. While there are not many "world federalists" around today, a proposal to establish a powerful World Environment Organization would be a step in this direction.

The top corner represents isolationism. Only if countries cut themselves off from trade, investment, and other international interactions can they preserve complete national sovereignty, while practicing whatever kind of regulation they wish. Two candidates in the 2000 U.S. presidential election, Ralph Nader and Pat Buchanan, seemed to want to move in this direction.

The environmental concerns created by globalization can be understood in terms of this diagram. The process of international economic integration is moving the United States and most other countries downward in the graph, toward the bottom side of the triangle. As a result, globalization is creating a growing conflict between the needs of environmental regulation and the demands of national sovereignty, or so goes the theory. National sovereignty has been winning, which means that the movement has been toward the lower left corner. The claim is that globalization has undermined the ability of sovereign governments to impose the level of environmental standards they would like.

Although the impossible trinity can be a useful way to think about the potential for globalization to undercut national environmental regulation, it can be very misleading in some contexts. There are two main reasons for this. First, even for environmental externalities that are largely confined within countries, such as local air pollution, there is little empirical evidence that the "race to the bottom" hypothesis in fact holds, i.e., that international trade and investment in fact put significant downward pressure on environmental regulation in the aggregate. Indeed, international trade and activities of multinational corporations may sometimes put upward pressure on environmental standards. Second, and more importantly, some environmental issues spill over across national borders even in the absence of international trade and investment, making it difficult for individual countries to address them through independent regulation.

Environmental Concerns Cross National Borders

Even those who do not care about trade at all should appreciate the need for some international agreements and institutions. The reason is the increasing importance of major sources of environmental damage that cross national borders, and that would do so even if there were no such thing as international trade. Some externalities have long spilled over from each country to its immediate neighbors—such as SO_2 pollution, which is responsible for acid rain, or water pollution, which flows downriver. They can be addressed by negotiations between the two countries involved (e.g., U.S. and Canada). An increasing number of environmental externalities are truly global, however. The best examples are greenhouse gases. A ton of carbon dioxide creates the same global warming potential regardless where in the world it is emitted. Other good examples of direct global externalities are stratospheric ozone depletion, depletion of ocean fish stocks, and threats to biodiversity.

Even localized environmental damage, such as deforestation, is increasingly seen as a valid object of international concern. A distinction is traditional between trade measures that target specific undesirable products, such as asbestos, and those that target *Processes and Production Methods* (PPMs), such as the use of prison labor in the manufacture of the commodity in question. It is clear that a country concerned about its own health or environment has the right to tax or ban products that it regards as harmful, so long as it does not discriminate against foreign producers. Indeed, such bans are less liable to become a vehicle for surreptitious protectionism than are attempts to pass judgment on other countries' production methods that are unrelated to the physical attributes of the product itself. But is it legitimate for importing countries also to discriminate according to how a given product was produced? Some ask what business is it of others whether the producing country wants to use its own prison labor, or cut down its own forests, or pollute its own environment?[31]

Often an international externality can be easily identified. Forests absorb carbon dioxide (a process called sequestration, or creating carbon sinks), so logging contributes to global climate change. An endangered species may contain a unique genetic element that someday could be useful to international scientists. Desertification can lead to social instability and political conflict, which can in turn produce problems for international security. Thus environmental damage in one country can have indirect effects on others.

But foreign residents increasingly care about localized environmental damage as well, even when they live far away and even when there is no evident link to their interests. The idea of "non-use value" is that many people place value on keeping, for example, a river canyon unspoiled, even if they know they will never see it. While the methodology of estimating the value according to what people say they would pay ("contingent valuation") is fraught with problems, the basic principle of non-use value is now widely accepted. This means that citizens in one country may have a stake in whether another country dams up a gorge, kills its wildlife, or pollutes its air and water.

Reversing Globalization Would Not End The Tension Of Regulation vs. Sovereignty

Thus, for an increasingly important set of environmental issues, the idea that individual countries could properly address the issues if left on their own is myth. If countries do not cooperate through multilateral institutions, each will be tempted to free ride on the efforts of others, and little will get done. Globalization and multilateral institutions are not the obstacle—and the appeal of national sovereignty is not an ally—in international efforts to protect the environment. Rather, environmentalists need global agreements and global agencies if they are going to get other countries to do the things they want them to do. It is the appeal of national sovereignty that is the obstacle.

The mistake of blaming all ills on globalization and multilateral institutions such as the WTO has yielded some very strange bedfellows. Environmentally concerned protestors have been treating labor unions and poor countries as comrades in arms, proud of the fact that a disparate set of groups have supposedly been brought together by a shared opposition to globalization. But in fact, some of these groups are on the other side of the environmental issue. U.S. labor unions are strong opponents of the Kyoto Protocol on Global Climate Change. Poor countries tend to be strong opponents of international environmental agreements in general. Both groups cite national sovereignty in support of their positions. It is particularly puzzling that some environmentalists see pro-sovereignty supporters as natural allies, when so many environmental problems in fact need to be addressed by means of multilateral institutions that in fact infringe on national sovereignty.

If labor unions and environmentalists can come together on an issue, that is fine. *But they have to agree on that issue.* They should share something more than an emotional antipathy to some particular multilateral institution: they should want the institution to move in the same direction, not opposite directions. They don't have to get into fine details, if they don't want to. But if, for example, one group thinks that the proper response to globalization is that the multilateral institutions should exercise less invasion of national sovereignty in the pursuit of environmental regulation and the other thinks the institutions should exercise more invasion of national sovereignty in that pursuit, then they are in truth hardly allies.

International Agreements And Institutions

Those who live in the world of international trade negotiations tell those who live in the environmentalist world along the lines that their concerns may be valid, but that they should address them by their own, separate, negotiations, and their own multilateral agencies.[32]

Multilateral Environmental Organizations

The one multilateral organization dedicated to environmental issues in general, the United Nations Environmental Program, is universally considered small and weak, even by the standards of UN agencies. Some may favor beefing it up. Many feel that it is not fixable, that—to begin with—it would have to be based somewhere like Geneva in order to be taken seriously, not in Nairobi as now. On these grounds, some have proposed a new, powerful, multilateral World Environment Organization.[33] Daniel Esty (1994) has proposed that it be called the Global Environmental Organization, providing the appropriate acronym GEO. But the source of the problem is not some accident of bureaucratic design history or geography. The problem, rather, is that there is very little support among the world's governments for a powerful multilateral agency in the area of the environment. They fear infringement on their sovereignty.

One can say that in concentrating their fire on the WTO, environmental activists are adopting a strategy of taking the multilateral trading system hostage. They envy the relative success of the WTO system. They are aware that international environmental treaties, even if successfully negotiated and ratified, may be toothless. The agreements made at Rio de Janeiro in 1992 are an example. The activists would ideally like to adopt trade sanctions as a means of enforcement, as does the WTO itself.

Such proposals do not explain attempts to take globalization hostage more broadly, for example by demonstrations at WTO ministerial meetings. There is nothing in the WTO to block multilateral environmental treaties from adopting penalties against relevant trade with nonmembers. Indeed, the Montreal Protocol on stratospheric ozone depletion has such trade controls, ran into no problems under international trade rules, and is generally considered to have been successful in achieving its goals. Admittedly there is strong resistance in other cases. Most governments do not favor international environmental agreements that are so aggressive as to include trade sanctions. Again, the failure does not mean that globalization and global institutions like the WTO are the problem. More likely it is the other way around: globalization is the ally, and national sovereignty is the obstacle.

Bilateral and Regional FTAs

Regional and bilateral agreements, such as the European Union or the Australia-New Zealand Closer Economic Relationship, have incorporated environmental components more often than have multilateral agreements. Whether because of cultural homogeneity or the small numbers involved, a group consisting of a few neighbors is usually readier to contemplate the sort of "deep integration" required for harmonization of environmental standards than are negotiators in groups with more than 100 diverse members, such as the WTO.

In the public debate over the North American Free Trade Agreement, one of the most prominent concerns of opponents was the pollution that had already accompanied industrialization in northern Mexico, particularly among the *maquilladoras* along the border, which in turn was a result of the ability to trade with the United States. The final agreement departed from previous U.S. trade agreements, or those in most other parts of the world, by taking into account environmental concerns, at least in a small way. The preamble includes environmentally friendly language, such as a stipulation that the NAFTA goals are to be pursued "in a manner consistent with environmental protection and conservation." Chapter 7B allows the member countries to continue adopting sanitary and phyto-sanitary standards. Chapter 9 allows countries to set whatever environmental standards they want, provided only that they do not discriminate or discourage trade unnecessarily.[34]

Nevertheless, environmental groups were unhappy with the subsequent outcome. Proposed side-agreements, for example, to establish a bank to finance environmental clean-up along the border, received a lot of attention during Bill Clinton's presidential campaign and during the subsequent NAFTA ratification campaign. Follow-up after the NAFTA went into effect in 1994, however, was disappointing.

Meanwhile, provisions under Chapter 11, which governs direct investment, have turned out to be important. On the one hand, the text reads "the Parties recognize that it is inappropriate to encourage investment by relaxing domestic health, safety or environmental measures." On the other hand, protection of the rights of investors has confirmed some environmentalists' fears, particularly a case brought by a Canadian company called Metalclad under the dispute settlement mechanism. Under a clause that forbids a signatory from taking measures "tantamount to nationalization or expropriation" of firms from other member countries, Metalclad in August 2000 won a judgment from a NAFTA tribunal against a local Mexican regulators' attempt to close its hazardous waste disposal plant without compensation. The finding that Mexican regulation had denied a foreign firm fair and equitable treatment was potentially an important precedent under the NAFTA.[35] But it would be strange, even from a pro-business viewpoint, if an American or Canadian firm were extensively protected against regulatory "takings" in Mexico when it would not be protected in its country of origin.

The NAFTA experience reinforced environmentalists' concerns with trade agreements. They urged the US government to bring environmental issues inside trade negotiations, for example, forbidding parties in trade agreements from relaxing environmental regulation in order to seek competitive advantage. A preferential trading arrangement negotiated by the United States at the end of the Clinton Administration, the Jordan-U.S. free trade agreement, incorporated such environmental provisions directly in the text, rather than as a side agreement, a precedent that was hoped to establish a "template" or precedent for future agreements. In addition, an Executive Order now requires that the government prepare an "environmental impact statement" whenever negotiating new trade agreements in the future, to guard against possible inadvertent side-effects adverse to the environment.[36]

The Failed Multilateral Agreement on Investment

The first time that NGOs using Internet-age methods successfully mobilized to block a major multilateral economic agreement was not in Seattle in 1999, but rather the preceding campaign against the Multilateral Agreement on Investment (MAI). Efforts to agree on rules governing cross-border investment tend to founder as soon as the circle of countries is broadened beyond a small regional grouping. The MAI was an attempt to negotiate such rules among the industrialized countries, at the OECD (Organization for Economic Cooperation and Development). Notwithstanding the weakness of the negotiated text and the seeming obscurity of the issue, environmentalist and other NGOs were energized by claims that the MAI would handcuff countries' regulatory efforts, and the MAI was not ratified.

The WTO and Some Panel Cases

In the postwar period, the vehicle for conducting the multilateral negotiations that succeeded in bringing down trade barriers in many countries was the General Agreement on Tariffs and Trade. An important outcome of the Uruguay Round of negotiations was the replacement of the GATT organization with a real agency, the World Trade Organization, which came into existence in 1995. One reason why the change was important is that the new institution featured a dispute settlement mechanism, whose findings were to be binding on the member countries. Previously, a party that did not like the ruling of a GATT panel could reject it.

Why do so many environmentalists apparently feel that the still-young WTO is a hostile power? Allegations concern lack of democratic accountability and negative effects on the environment. It is difficult to see how these allegations could apply to the process of setting WTO rules themselves. Regarding the alleged lack of democracy, the GATT and WTO are in principle one-country one-vote bodies that make decisions by consensus. Clearly in practice, some countries—particularly the United States—matter far more than others. But consider what it would mean to make this process more democratic. It would presumably mean giving less weight to U.S. views and more to the views, for example, of India, the world's most populous democracy. But, given India's preferences and its aversion to "eco-imperialism," this would clearly mean giving *less* attention in the WTO to environmental goals, not more.

The allegation that the GATT and WTO are hostile to environmental measures could conceivably arise from the core provisions of the GATT, which prohibit a member country from discriminating against the exports of another, in favor of "like products" made either by a third country (that is the Most Favored Nation provision of Article I) or by domestic producers (the national treatment provision of Article III). But Article XX allows for exceptions to the nondiscrimination principle for environmental reasons (among others), provided that the measures in question are not "a means of arbitrary or unjustifiable discrimination" or a "disguised restriction on international trade." Moreover, umbrella clauses allow countries to take actions to protect human, animal or plant life or health, and to conserve exhaustible natural resources.

Under the GATT, there was ambiguity of interpretation as to what was to happen when Article XX conflicted with the nondiscrimination articles. To clarify the matter, language was added to the preamble to the articles agreed to at Marrakech that established the WTO specifying that its objectives were not limited to promoting trade but included also optimal use of the world's resources, sustainable development, and environmental protection. Environmental objectives are also recognized specifically in the WTO agreements dealing with product standards, food safety, intellectual property protection, etc.

The protests are in a sense a puzzle. It would be easy to understand a political campaign in favor of the WTO taking a more aggressive pro-environment stance. But how does one explain the common view in the protest movement that the WTO currently is actively harmful to the environment?

When members of the protest movement identify specifics, they usually mention the rulings of WTO panels under the dispute settlement mechanism. The panels are quasi-judicial tribunals, whose job is to rule in disputes whether parties are abiding by the rules that they have already agreed to. Like most judicial proceedings, the panels themselves are not intended to be democratic. The rulings to date do not show a pattern of having been dominated by any particular country or interest group. There have been three or four fairly prominent WTO panel rulings that concern the environment in some way. Most within the environmentalist and NGO community have at some point acquired the belief that these rulings told the United States, or other defendant country, that their attempts to protect the environment must be repealed. The mystery is why this impression is so widespread, because it has little basis in fact.

The four WTO cases that will be briefly reviewed here are Canadian asbestos, Venezuelan reformulated gasoline, U.S. hormone-fed beef, and Asian shrimp and turtles. We will also touch on the Mexican tuna-dolphin case. Each of the cases involves an environmental measure that the producer plaintiff alleged to have trade-distorting effects. The complaints were not based, however, on the allegation that the goal of the measure was not valid, or that protectionism was the original motivation of the measure. In most of the cases, the allegation was that discrimination against foreigners was an incidental, and unnecessary, feature of the environmental measure.

Canadian asbestos   One case is considered a clear win for the environmentalists. The WTO Appellate Body in 2001 upheld a French ban on asbestos products, against a challenge by Canada, which had been exporting to France. This ruling made real the WTO claim that its charter gives priority to health, safety, and environmental requirements, in that for such purposes GATT Article XX explicitly allows exceptions to the Most Favored Nation and national treatment rules.[37]

Venezuelan reformulated gasoline.   In the reformulated gasoline case, Venezuela successfully claimed that U.S. law violated national treatment, i.e., discriminated in favor of domestic producers (with regard to whether refineries were allowed to use individual composition baselines when measuring pollution reduction). The case was unusual in that the intent to discriminate had at the time of passage been made explicit by U.S. administration officials seeking to please a domestic interest group. If the WTO had ruled in the U.S. favor, it would have been saying that it was fine for a country to discriminate needlessly and explicitly against foreign producers so long as the law came under an environmental label. Those who oppose this panel decision provide ready-made ammunition for the viewpoint that environmental activism is a false disguise worn by protectionist interests.

The United States was not blocked in implementing its targets, under the Clean Air Act, as commonly charged. Rather, the offending regulation was easily changed so as to be nondiscriminatory and thus to be permissible under the rules agreed to by members of the WTO. This case sent precisely the right message to the world's governments, that environmental measures should not and need not discriminate against foreign producers.

Hormone-fed beef   What happens if the commodity in question is produced entirely, or almost entirely, by foreign producers, so that it cannot be conclusively demonstrated whether a ban, or other penalty, is or is not discriminatory? The WTO has attempted to maintain the rule that such measures are fine so long as a scientific study has supported the claimed environmental or health benefits of the measure. In the hormone-fed beef case, the WTO ruled against an EU ban on beef raised with growth hormones because the EU conspicuously failed to produce a science-based risk assessment showing that it might be dangerous. It thus resembles the case of the EU moratorium on GMOs.

These are genuinely difficult cases. On the one hand, where popular beliefs regarding a scientific question vary widely, a useful role for a multilateral institution could be to rule on the scientific merits. Or at least a useful role could be, as under the current WTO procedures, to rule on whether the country seeking to impose the regulation has carried out internally a reasonable study of the scientific merits. This logic suggests overruling the EU bans. On the other hand, the world may not be ready for even this mild level of loss of national sovereignty. If a nation's intent is to protect its health or environment, even if the measure has little scientific basis and even if its primary burden would fall on foreign producers, perhaps ensuring that the ban does not unnecessarily discriminate among producing countries is the best that can be done.

Despite the WTO ruling on hormone-fed beef, the Europeans did not cancel the ban. Their strategy, which they justify with the name "precautionary principle," is to continue to study the matter before allowing the product in. The precautionary principle, as the Europeans apply it, says to prohibit new technologies that have not yet been proven safe, even if there is no evidence that they are dangerous.[38] At a minimum, it seems that they should be forced to allow imports of American beef subject to labeling requirements, as in the Montreal agreement on GMOs. Let the consumer decide.

Shrimp-turtle   Perceptions regarding the WTO panel ruling on a dispute about shrimp imports and the protection of sea turtles probably vary more widely than on any other case. The perception among many environmentalists is that the panel ruling struck down a U.S. law to protect sea turtles that are caught in the nets of shrimp fishermen in the Indian Ocean. (The provision was pursuant to the U.S. Endangered Species Act.) In reality, the dispute resembled the gasoline case in the respect that the ban on imports from countries without adequate regulatory regimes in place was unnecessarily selective and restrictive. The WTO panel and appellate body decided that the U.S. application of the law, in a complex variety of ways, was arbitrarily and unjustifiably discriminatory against the four plaintiff countries (Asian shrimp suppliers). The United States had unilaterally and inflexibly banned shrimp imports from countries that did not have in place for all production a specific turtle-protection regime of its own liking, one that mandated Turtle Excluder Devices.[39]

The case could in fact be considered a victory for the environmentalists, in that the WTO panel and the appeals body in 1998 explicitly stated that the United States could pursue the protection of endangered sea turtles against foreign fishermen. The United States subsequently allowed more flexibility in its regulation, and made good-faith efforts to negotiate an agreement with the Asian producers, which is what it should have done in the first place. The WTO panel and appellate body in 2001 found the new U.S. regime to be WTO-compliant.[40] The case set a precedent in clarifying support for the principle that the WTO rules allow countries to pass judgment on other countries' Processes and Production Methods, even if it means using trade controls to do so, provided only that the measures are not unnecessarily discriminatory.[41]

Tuna-dolphin.   In an earlier attempt to protect another large flippered sea animal, the United States (under the Marine Mammal Protection Act)] had banned imports of tuna from countries that allowed the fishermen to use nets that also caught dolphins. Mexico brought a case before the GATT, as this predated the WTO, and the GATT panel ruled against the U.S. law. Its report was never adopted. The parties instead in effect worked out their differences bilaterally, "out of court." The case could be considered a setback for trade-sensitive environmental measures, at least unilateral ones, but a setback that was to prove temporary. That the GATT ruling in the tuna case did not affirm the right of the United States to use trade bans to protect the dolphins shows how much the environmentalist cause has progressed under the WTO, in the subsequent gasoline, shrimp-turtle, and asbestos cases.

A system for labeling tuna in the US market as either "dolphin safe" or not was later found consistent with the GATT. The American consumer response turned out to be sufficiently great to accomplish the desired purpose. Since 1990, the major companies have sold only the dolphin-safe kind of tuna. The moral is not that the goal of protecting the dolphins was accomplished despite globalization in its GATT incarnation, but rather that *globalization was instrumental in the protection of the dolphins*. The goal could not have been accomplished without international trade, because American citizens would have had no effective way of putting pressure on Mexico. Leaving the U.S. government free to regulate its own fishermen would not have helped.[42]

Multilateral Environmental Agreements

When it comes to global externalities such as endangered species, stratospheric ozone depletion, and global climate change, it is particularly clear that the problem cannot be addressed by a system where each country pursues environmental measures on its own. Multilateral negotiations, agreements, and institutions are required. Furthermore, the point is not simply that global regulatory measures are needed to combat the effects of economic globalization. If countries had industrialized in isolation, without any international trade or investment among them, they would still be emitting greenhouse gases, and we would still need a globally coordinated response.

Multilateral environmental agreements (MEAs), even if they involve trade-restricting measures, are viewed more favorably under the international rules than unilateral environmental measures. Leaving aside the Law of the Sea, the Basel Convention on Hazardous Wastes, and a large number of relatively more minor agreements, three MEAs merit particular mention.

The Convention on International Trade in Endangered Species (CITES) was negotiated in 1973. Although it lacks the teeth that many would like, it was notable as a precedent establishing that MEAs are compatible with the GATT even if they restrict trade. An interesting issue relevant for species protection is whether a plan of using animals to support the economic livelihood of local residents can be a more sustainable form of protection than attempts to leave them untouched altogether.

The Montreal Protocol on Substances that Deplete the Ozone Layer is the most successful example of an MEA, as it has resulted in the phasing out of most use of CFCs (Chlorofluorocarbons) and other ozone-depleting chemicals. The success of this agreement is partly attributable to the enforcement role played by trade penalties: the protocol prohibits trade in controlled substances with countries that do not participate. This created the necessary incentive to push those developing countries that otherwise might have been reluctant into joining. If substantial numbers of countries had nevertheless remained outside the protocol, the trade controls would have also accomplished the second objective—minimizing *leakage*, that is, the migration of production of banned substances to nonparticipating countries.[43] One reason why the protocol succeeded was there were a relatively small number of producers. It also helped that there turned out to be good substitutes for the banned substances, though that was not known until the ban was tried.[44] One might say it also helped establish the principle that PPM-targeted measures were not necessarily incompatible with the GATT: the agreement threatened nonparticipants not only with a ban on trade in ozone-depleting chemicals themselves, but also a potential ban on trade in goods manufactured with such chemicals in the sense that governments were required to determine the feasibility of such a ban. But it never went further than that.

The Kyoto Protocol on Global Climate Change, negotiated in 1997, is the most ambitious attempt at a multilateral environment agreement to date. This is not the place to discuss the Kyoto Protocol at length. The task of addressing Climate Change while satisfying the political constraints of the various factions (particularly, the U.S., EU, and developing countries) was an inherently impossible task. Most economists emphasize that the agreement as it was written at Kyoto would impose large economic costs on the United States and other countries, while making only a minor dent in the problem. The Clinton Administration's interpretation of the protocol insisted on so-called flexibility mechanisms, such as international trading of emission permits, to bring the economic costs down to a modest range.[45] This interpretation was rejected by the Europeans at the Hague in November 2000. Without the flexibility mechanisms, the United States would be out of the protocol, even if the subsequent administration had been more environmentally friendly than it was. (Ironically, now that European and other countries are trying to go ahead without the United States, they are finding that they cannot manage without such trading mechanisms.)

Even most of those who for one reason or another do not believe that Kyoto was a useful step, however, should acknowledge that multilateral agreements will be necessary if the problem of Global Climate Change is to be tackled. The Bush administration has yet to face up to this. The point for present purposes is that a system in which each country insists, based on an appeal to national sovereignty, that it be left to formulate environmental policies on its own, would be a world in which global externalities like greenhouse gas emissions would not be effectively addressed.

SUMMARY OF CONCLUSIONS

The relationship between globalization and the environment is too complex to sum up in a single judgment—whether "good" or "bad." In many respects, global trade and investment operate like other sources of economic growth.

They tend to raise income as measured in the marketplace. On the one hand, the higher scale of output can mean more pollution, deforestation, and other kinds of environmental damage. On the other hand, changes in the composition and techniques of economic activity can lower the damage relative to income. Although it is not possible to generalize universally about the net effect of these channels, it is possible to put forward general answers to some major questions.

- A key question is whether openness to international trade undermines national attempts at environmental regulation, through a "race to the bottom" effect. This no doubt happens sometimes. But there is little statistical evidence, across countries, that the unfavorable effects on average outweigh favorable "gains from trade" effects on measures of pollution, such as SO_2 concentrations. If anything, the answer seems to be that favorable effects dominate.
- Perceptions that WTO panel rulings have interfered with the ability of individual countries to pursue environmental goals are poorly informed. In cases such as Canadian asbestos, Venezuelan gasoline, and Asian shrimp, the rulings have confirmed that countries can enact environmental measures, even if they affect trade and even if they concern others' Processes and Production Methods (PPMs), provided the measures do not unnecessarily discriminate among producer countries.
- People care both about the environment and the economy. As their real income rises, their demand for environmental quality rises. Under the right conditions, this can translate into environmental progress. The right conditions include democracy, effective regulation, and externalities that are largely confined within national borders and are therefore amenable to national regulation.
- Increasingly, however, environmental problems do in fact spill across national borders. The strongest examples are pure global externalities such as global climate change and ozone depletion. Economic growth alone will not address such problems, in a system where each country acts individually, due to the free rider problem. International institutions are required. This would be equally true in the absence of international trade. Indeed, trade offers a handle whereby citizens of one country can exercise a role in environmental problems of other countries that they would otherwise not have. Consumer labeling campaigns and corporate codes of conduct are examples.
- Many aspects of the environment that might have been considered purely domestic matters in the past, or that foreign residents might not even have

known about, are increasingly of concern to those living in other countries. This again means that multilateral institutions are needed to address the issues, and expressions of national sovereignty are the obstacle, not the other way around. Indeed, if one broadens the definition of globalization, beyond international trade and investment, to include the globalization of ideas and of NGO activities, then one can see the international environmental movement as itself an example of globalization.

ACKNOWLEDGMENT

The author would like to thank Steve Charnovitz, Dan Esty, Don Fullerton, Rob Stavins and Michael Weinstein for useful comments, Anne LeBrun for research assistance, and the Savitz Research Fund for support.

ENDNOTES

1. The quotation marks are necessary around "non-economic," because economists' conceptual framework fully incorporates such objectives as environmental quality, even though pollution is an externality that is not measured by GDP. For further reading on how economists think about the environment, see Hanley, Shogren, and White (1997) or Stavins (2000).
2. The literature on trade and the environment is surveyed in Dean (1992, 2001) and Copeland and Taylor (2003b).
3. Malthus was an economist. A contemporary commentator reacted by calling economics the dismal science. This description has stuck, long after ecology or environmental science broke off as independent fields of study, fields that in fact make economists look like sunny optimists by comparison.
4. Meadows, et al (1972), and Daly (1993). For a general survey of the issues, see Esty (2001).
5. Chaudhuri and Pfaff (2002) cite Smith (1993, p.551).
6. Some health risks in industrial production are analogous. Workers in every country voluntarily accept dangerous jobs, e.g., in mining, because they pay better than other jobs that are available to someone with the same set of skills. No externality is present.
7. Even when property rights are not in doubt and there is no externality, a common environmental concern is that the welfare of future generations does not receive enough weight, because they are not here to represent themselves. From the economists' viewpoint, the question is whether the interest rate that enters firms' decisions incorporates the correct *discount rate*. This topic is beyond the scope of this chapter, but Goulder and Stavins (2002) provide a concise survey.
8. The most important alternatives are: coal-fired plants (the dirtiest fuel, though there is a little scope for mitigating the damage, through low-sulfur coal, scrubbers,

and perhaps someday new carbon-sequestration technologies); petroleum products (not quite as dirty); solar (very clean, but much more expensive); and hydro and nuclear (clean with respect to pollution, but controversial on other environmental grounds).

9. Grossman and Krueger (1993, 1995) found the Kuznets Curve pattern for urban air pollution (SO_2 and smoke) and several measures of water pollution. Selden and Song (1994) found the pattern for SO_2, suspended particulate matter (PM), NO_x, and carbon monoxide. Shafik (1994) found evidence of the U shape for deforestation, suspended PM, and SO_2, but not for water pollution and some other measures. Among more recent studies, Hilton and Levinson (1998) find the U-shaped relationship for automotive lead emissions and Bradford, Schlieckert and Shore (2000) find some evidence of the environmental Kuznets Curve for arsenic, COD, dissolved oxygen, lead and SO_2, while obtaining more negative results in the cases of PM and some other measures of pollution. Bimonte (2001) finds the relationship for the percentage of land that is protected area, within national territory. Harbaugh, Levinson, and Wilson (2000) point out that the relationship is very sensitive with respect, for example, to functional form and updating of the data set. The evidence is generally against the proposition that the curve turns down in the case of CO_2 (e.g., Holtz-Eakin and Selden, 1995), as is discussed later.

10. Cropper and Griffiths (1994) find little evidence across countries of an EKC for forest growth. But Foster and Rosenzweig (2003) find supportive evidence in the time series for India.

11. Theoretical derivations of the environmental Kuznets Curve include Andreoni and Levinson (2001), Jaeger and Kolpin (2000), Selden and Song (1995) and Stokey (1998), among others.

12. Chaudhuri and Pfaff (2002) find a U-shaped relationship between income and the generation of indoor smoke, across households. In the poorest households, rising incomes mean more cooking and more indoor pollution. Still-higher incomes allow a switch to cleaner fuels. Individual families make the switch on their own, as they gain the wherewithal to do so. Government intervention is not required.

13. Arrow, et al, (1995); Panayotou (1993).

14. Porter and van der Linde (1995).

15. Levinson and Taylor (2001) find that those U.S. industries experiencing the largest rise in environmental control costs have indeed also experienced the largest increases in net imports.

16. What is competitiveness? Economists tend to argue that concerns regarding international competitiveness, if interpreted as fears of trade deficits, are misplaced, which would seem to imply they should not affect rational policymaking. (Or else, to the extent competitiveness concerns can be interpreted as downward pressure on regulation commensurate with cost considerations, economists figure that they may be appropriate and efficient.) But Esty and Gerardin (1998: 17–21) point out that competitiveness fears, under actual political economy conditions, may inhibit environmental regulation even if they are not fully rational. Ederington and Minier (2002) find econometrically that countries do indeed use environmental regula-

tion to reduce trade flows—that they tend to adopt less-stringent environmental regulations for their import-competing industries than for others.

17. Jaffe, et al. (1995), Grossman and Krueger (1993), Low and Yeats (1992), and Tobey (1990). Other empirical researchers, however, have found more of an effect of environmental regulation on direct investment decisions: Smarzynska and Wei (2001). Theoretical analyses include Copeland and Taylor (1994, 1995, 2001) and Liddle (2001).

18. Trade speeds the absorption of frontier technologies and best-practice management. This explains why countries that trade more appear to experience a sustained increase in growth rather than just the one-time increase in the level of real income predicted by classical trade theory.

19. E.g., Vogel (1995), Braithwaite and Drahos (2000), Porter (1990, 1991) and Porter and van der Linde (1995). This ratcheting up may be more effective for product standards than for standards regarding processes and production methods.

20. Esty and Gentry (1997: 157, 161, 163) and Schmidheiny (1992).

21. Ruggie (2002).

22. Neumayer (2002). Multilateral environmental agreeements (MEAs) are discussed in a subsequent section.

23. Barrett and Graddy (2000) is one of several studies to find that an increase in civil and political freedoms significantly reduces some measures of pollution.

24. A few authors have sought to address some aspects of the problem of endogeneity. Levinson (1999) shows that controlling for endogeneity of environmental regulation can change results, in his study of hazardous waste trade. Dean (2002) treats income as endogenous in her study of the effect of trade liberalization on water pollution across Chinese provinces. But the existing research does not directly address the problem that trade may be simultaneously determined with income and environmental outcomes.

25. The desire to "harmonize" environmental regulation across countries, and the arguments against it, are analyzed by Bhagwati and Srinivasan (1996).

26. E.g., Suri and Chapman (1998) find that middle-income countries' growth leads to lower domestic pollution only if they increase imports of manufactures. Muradian, O'Connor and Martinez-Alier (2001) find evidence that the imports of rich countries embody more air pollution than their exports. Ederington, Levinson and Minier (2003) find that pollution abatement costs are relevant for only a small subset of trade: imports from developing countries in sectors that are especially mobile geographically.

27. Frankel and Rose (2004). We do not find significant evidence of other pollution-haven effects, based on population density or factor endowments, or for other pollutants.

28. *The Economist*, Feb. 5, 2000. So far, the United States has been reluctant to bring the GMO case to the WTO, out of a fear of that the outcome might be a political failure even if a legal success. As Victor and Runge (2002: 112–13) argue, the Europeans were sufficiently traumatized in the 1990s by a series of scandals in the regulation of their food, such as the UK government's failure to stop "Mad

Cow" disease, that an attempt by the United States to use the WTO dispute settlement process to pry the European market open for GMOs would be counterproductive, regardless of the scientific evidence. But the United States may go ahead anyway.

29. Environmental NGOs were allowed inside the meeting hall, a new precedent. *FT*, Feb. 1, 2000.

30. But it is interesting that some health issues have gone the other way. The United States has in the past cared more about feared carcinogens than Europeans. The U.S. requires cheese to be pasteurized, and the EU does not. (David Vogel, 1995.)

31. See Charnovitz (2002a) on the history, law, and analysis of PPMs, and for other references. He argues that the public failure to understand environment-friendly developments in the late 1990s within GATT/WTO jurisprudence regarding PPMs is now an obstacle to further progress (e.g., in the WTO Committee on Trade and Environment, pp. 64, 103–4).

32. The most prominent and articulate spokesman of the viewpoint opposing linkage between trade and unrelated issues is probably Jagdish Bhagwati (2000).

33. Charnovitz (2002b) surveys the proposals. Juma (2000) argues in opposition, on the grounds that decentralized agreements can do the job better.

34. Hufbauer, et al. (2000).

35. Ibid. pp. 8–14.

36. The Executive Order was issued by President Clinton in 1999. But President George Bush announced he would continue to abide by it, e.g., in preparing free-trade agreements with Singapore, Chile, and the Americas. Martin Crutsinger, *AP* April 21, 2001 [e.g., *Boston Globe*].

37. *New York Times*, July 25, 2000.

38. Does the precautionary principle derive from risk aversion? Someone should point out that risk-aversion in the presence of uncertainty is not necessarily sufficient to justify it. For poor residents of developing countries, the risk may be higher from drought or pests or disease in their crops, or from existing pesticides, than from the new GMOs that are designed to combat them more safely. Does the precautionary principle say that society should persist with what is natural and traditional, even if the current state of scientific evidence suggests a better, artificial, substitute? Then Asian men concerned about maintaining virility should continue to buy powdered rhino horn rather than switching to Viagra. (Gollier, 2001, offers another economist's perspective on the precautionary principle.)

39. For example, the Asian suppliers had been given only four months' notice, thus discriminating against them and in favor of Caribbean suppliers. (The U.S. measure has also been pronounced unnecessarily restrictive in another sense: the majority of suppliers in India raise shrimp by aquaculture, where no sea turtles are endangered. Jagdish Bhagwati, *Financial Times*, December 21, 1999.)

40. Charnovitz (2002a, p. 98–99).

41. For a full explanation of the legal issues, see Charnovitz (2002a). Also Michael Weinstein, "Greens and Globalization: Declaring Defeat in the Face of Victory," *NY Times*, April 22, 2001. Charnovitz and Weinstein (2001) argue that the envi-

ronmentalists fail to realize the progress they have made in recent WTO panel cases, and may thereby miss an opportunity to consolidate those gains. It is not only environmentalists who are under the impression that the GATT rules do not allow PPMs. Some developing countries also claim that PPMs violate the GATT. The motive of the first group is to fight the GATT, while the motive of the second group is to fight PPMs.

42. Thomas Friedman, *New York Times*, p. A31, December 8, 1999. Presumably, iwithout the opportunity to export to the United States, Mexican fisherman would not have caught so many tuna, which would have limited the dolphin casualties somewhat. It is not known whether the much-reduced number of dolphins still killed under the current system is less than in the hypothetical no-trade case. But working through the channel of voting power represented by U.S. imports was surely a better way to have accomplished the goal. Telling Mexican fisherman they must remain poor, and telling American consumers that they couldn't eat tuna, would have been a less satisfactory solution to the problem.

43. Brack (1996).

44. Parson (2002).

45. The author was one of the few economists sympathetic to the Clinton Administration policy on the Kyoto Protocol. Two claims: (1) Quantitative targets à la Kyoto are the "least impossible" way politically to structure an international agreement (see Frankel, 2003, for my response to the arguments of Cooper, 1998, Nordhaus, 2001, and Schelling, 2002, against assignment of quantitative targets). And (2) Bill Clinton's approach—signing the treaty but announcing his intention not to submit for ratification unless the Europeans agreed to unrestricted international trading of emission permits and unless developing countries agreed to participate in the system—was the least impossible way, subject to the existing political constraints, of demonstrating U.S. willingness to address climate change. We hope that when the world is ready to make a more serious attempt, it will build on the good aspects of the Kyoto Protocol, particularly the role for international permit trading and other flexibility mechanisms.

REFERENCES

Andreoni, James, and Arik Levinson. 2001. "The Simple Analytics of the Environmental Kuznets Curve." *NBER Working Paper* no. 6739. *Journal of Public Economics* 80 (May): 269–86.

Antweiler, Werner, Brian Copeland and M. Scott Taylor. 2001. "Is Free Trade Good for the Environment?" *NBER Working Paper* No. 6707. *American Economic Review*, 91, no. 4 (September): 877–908.

Arrow, K., R. Bolin, P. Costanza, P. Dasgupta, C. Folke, C.S.Holling, B.O. Jansson, S.Levin, K.G. Maler, C.Perrings, and D.Pimentel. 1995. "Economic Growth, Carrying Capacity, and the Environment." *Science* (April 28) 268: 520–521.

Barrett, Scott, and Kathryn Graddy. 2000. "Freedom, Growth, and the Environment." *Environment and Development Economics* 5: 433–56.

Bhagwati, Jadgish. 2000. "On Thinking Clearly About the Linkage Between Trade and the Environment." In *The Wind of the Hundred Days: How Washington Mismanaged Globalization*. Cambridge: MIT Press.

———, and T. N. Srinivasan. 1996. "Trade and the Environment: Does Environmental Diversity Detract from the Case for Free Trade." In Jagdish Bhagwati and Robert Hudec, eds. *Fair Trade and Harmonization—Vol. 1: Economic Analysis,* Cambridge: MIT Press, pp. 159–223.

Bimonte, Salvatore. 2001. "Model of Growth and Environmental Quality: A New Evidence of the Environmental Kuznets Curve." *Universita degli studi di Siena, Quaderni*, no. 321 (April).

Brack, Duncan. 1996. *International Trade and the Montreal Protocol.* London: The Royal Institute of International Affairs and Earthscan Publications.

Bradford, David, Rebecca Schlieckert and Stephen Shore. 2000. "The Environmental Kuznets Curve: Exploring a Fresh Specification." *NBER Working Paper* no. 8001. Forthcoming, *Topics in Economic Analysis and Policy.*

Braithwaite, John, and Peter Drahos. 2000. *Global Business Regulation.* Cambridge: Cambridge University Press.

Charnovitz, Steve. 2002a, "The Law of Environmental 'PPMs' in the WTO: Debunking the Myth of Illegality." *The Yale Journal of International Law* 27, no. 1 (Winter): 59–110.

———. 2002b, "A World Environment Organization." *Columbia Journal of Environmental Law,* 27, no. 2, 323–362.

———, and Michael Weinstein. 2001. "The Greening of the WTO." *Foreign Affairs* 80, no. 6: 147–156.

Chaudhuri, Shubham, and Alexander Pfaff. 2002. "Economic Growth and the Environment: What Can We Learn from Household Data?" Columbia University, February.

Cooper, Richard. 1998. "Why Kyoto Won't Work." *Foreign Affairs*, March/April.

Copeland, Brian, and M. Scott Taylor. 1994. "North-South Trade and the Environment." *Quarterly Journal of Economics* 109: 755–87.

———. 1995. Trade and the Environment: A Partial Synthesis." *American Journal of Agricultural Economics* 77: 765–71.

———. 2001. "International Trade and the Environment: A Framework for Analysis." *NBER Working Paper* No. 8540, Oct.

———. 2003a, *Trade and the Environment: Theory and Evidence.* Princeton: Princeton University Press.

———. 2003b, "Trade, Growth and the Environment." NBER Working Paper No. 9823, July.

Cropper, Maureen, and Charles Griffiths. 1994. "The Interaction of Population Growth and Evironmental Quality." *American Economic Review* 84, no. 2 (May): 250–54.

Daly, Herman. 1993. "The Perils of Free Trade." *Scientific American* (November): 51–55.

Dean, Judy. 1992. "Trade and the Environment: A Survey of the Literature." In Patrick Low, ed., *International Trade and the Environment*, World Bank Discussion Paper No. 159.

————. 2001. "Overview." In Dean, ed., *International Trade and the Environment*. International Library of Environmental Economics and Policy Series. UK: Ashgate Publishing.

————. 2002. "Does Trade Liberalization Harm the Environment? A New Test." *Canadian Journal of Economics* 35, no. 4 (November): 819–42.

Dua, Andre, and Daniel Esty. 1997. *Sustaining the Asia Pacific Miracle: Environmental Protection and Economic Integration*. Washington, DC: Institute for International Economics.

Ederington, Josh, and Jenny Minier. 2002. "Is Environmental Policy a Secondary Trade Barrier? An Empirical Analysis." *Canadian Journal of Economics*, forthcoming.

————, Arik Levinson and Jenny Minier. 2003. "Footloose and Pollution-Free." NBER Working Paper No. 9718, May.

Eiras, Ana, and Brett Schaefer. 2001. "Trade: The Best Way to Protect the Environment." *Backgrounder*, The Heritage Foundation no. 1480, September 27.

Esty, Daniel. 1994. *Greening the GATT: Trade, Environment, and the Future*. Washington, DC: Institute for International Economics.

————. 2001. "Bridging the Trade-Environment Divide." *Journal of Economic Perspectives* 15, no. 3 (Summer): 113–30.

————, and Bradford Gentry. 1997. "Foreign Investment, Globalisation, and the Environment." In Tom Jones, ed. *Globalization and the Environment*. Paris: Organization for Economic Cooperation and Development.

————, and Damien Giradin. 1998. "Environmental Protection and International Competitiveness: A Conceptual Framework." *Journal of World Trade*, 32, no. 3, (June): 5–46.

————, and Michael Porter. 2001. "Measuring National Environmental Performance and Its Determinants." Yale Law School and Harvard Business School, April.

Foster, Andrew, and Mark Rosenzweig. 2003. "Economic Growth and the Rise of Forests." *Quarterly Journal of Economics* 118, no. 2 (May): 601–38.

Frankel, Jeffrey. 2003. "You're Getting Warmer: The Most Feasible Path for Addressing Global Climate Change Does Run Through Kyoto." Fondazione Eni Enrico Mattei, Milan, Italy. In John Maxwell, with Marialuisa Tamborra, eds. *Trade and the Environment in the Perspective of the EU Enlargement*. UK: Elgar Publishers, Ltd.

Frankel, Jeffrey, and Andrew Rose. 2003. "Is Trade Good or Bad for the Environment? Sorting Out the Causality." RWP03–038, Kennedy School of Government, Harvard University, September. Revised version of NBER Working Paper 9201. Forthcoming, *Review of Economics and Statistics*.

Gollier, Christian. 2001. "Should We Beware the Precautionary Principle?" *Economic Policy* 33 (October): 303–27.

Goulder, Lawrence, and Robert Stavins. 2002. "An Eye on the Future." *Nature*, 419, (October 17): 673–74.

Grossman, Gene, and Alan Krueger. 1993. "Environmental Impacts of a North American Free Trade Agreement." In Peter Garber, ed. *The U.S.-Mexico Free Trade Agreement*. Cambridge: MIT Press.

———. 1995. "Economic Growth and the Environment." *Quarterly Journal of Economics*, 110, no. 2 (May): 353–77.

Hanley, Nick, Jason Shogren, and Ben White. 1997. *Environmental Economics in Theory and Practice*, New York: Oxford University Press.

Harbaugh, William, Arik Levinson, and David Wilson. 2000. "Reexamining the Empirical Evidence for an Environmental Kuznets Curve." *NBER Working Paper* No. 7711, May.

Hilton, F.G. Hank, and Arik Levinson. 1998. "Factoring the Environmental Kuznets Curve: Evidence from Automotive Lead Emissions." *Journal of Environmental Economics and Management* 35: 126–41.

Holtz-Eakin and T. Selden. 1995. "Stoking the Fires? CO_2 Emissions and Economic Growth." *Journal of Public Economics* 57 (May): 85–101.

Hufbauer, Gary, Daniel Esty, Diana Orejas, Luis Rubio, and Jeffrey Schott. 2000. *NAFTA and the Environment: Seven Years Later, Policy Analyses in International Economics* no. 61 (October). Washington, DC: Institute for International Economics.

Jaeger, William and Van Kolpin 2000. "Economic Growth and Environmental Resource Allocation." Williams University and University of Oregon, August 22.

Jaffe, Adam, S. R. Peterson, Paul Portney and Robert Stavins. 1995. "Environmental Regulation and the Competitiveness of U.S. Manufacturing: What Does the Evidence Tell Us?" *Journal of Economic Literature* 33: 132–63.

Juma, Calestous. 2000. "The Perils of Centralizing Global Environmental Goverance." *Environment* 42, no. 9 (November): 44_45.

Levinson, Arik. 1999. "State Taxes and Interstate Hazardous Waste Shipments." *American Economic Review*, no. 3 (June).

Levinson, Arik, and M. Scott Taylor. 2001. "Trade and the Environment: Unmasking the Pollution Haven Effect." Georgetown University and University of Wisconsin.

Liddle, Brantley. 2001. "Free Trade and the Environment-Development System." *Ecological Economics* 39: 21–36.

Low, P., and A. Yeats. 1992. "Do 'Dirty' Industries Migrate?" in P. Low, ed., *International Trade and the Environment*. World Bank, pp. 89–104.

Lucas, Robert E.B., David Wheeler, and Hememala Hettige. 1992. "Economic Development, Environmental Regulation and the Internaitonal Migration of Toxic Industrial Pollution: 1960–1988." In Patrick Low, ed. *International Trade and the Environment*. World Bank Discussion Papers no. 159. Washington, DC: The World Bank.

Meadows, Donella, Dennis Meadows, Jorgen Randers, and William Behrens, 1972. *The Limits to Growth*. New York: Universe Books.

Muradian, Roldan, Martin O'Connor and Joan Martinez-Alier. 2001. "Embodied Pollution in Trade: Estimating the 'Environmental Load Displacement' of Industrialised Countries." *FEEM Working Paper* No. 57, July, Milan.

Neumayer, Eric. 2002. "Does Trade Openness Promote Multilateral Environmental Cooperation?" *The World Economy* 25, no. 6: 812–832.

Nordhaus, William. 2001. "After Kyoto: Alternative Mechanisms to Control Global Warming." American Economic Association, Atlanta, Jan. 4.

Panayotou, Theo. 1993. "Empirical Tests and Policy Analysis of Environmental Degradation at Different Stages of Development." Working Paper WP238, Technology and Employment Programme (International Labor Office: Geneva).

Parson, Edward. 2002. *Protecting the Ozone Layer: Science, Strategy, and Negotiation in the Shaping of a Global Environmental Regime* Oxford: Oxford University Press.

Porter, Michael. 1990. *The Competitive Advantage of Nations.* New York: MacMillan.

———. 1991. "America's Green Strategy." *Scientific American,* April.

———, and Claas van der Linde. 1995. "Toward a New Conception of the Environment-Competitiveness Relationship." *Journal of Economic Perspectives* 9, no. 4.

Ruggie, John. 2002. "Trade, Sustainability and Global Governance." *Columbia Journal of Environmental Law* 27: 297–307.

Schelling, Thomas. 2002. "What Makes Greenhouse Sense?" *Foreign Affairs,* 81, no. 3, May/June.

Selden, Thomas, and Daqing Song. 1994. "Environmental Quality and Development: Is There a Kuznets Curve for Air Pollution Emissions?" *Journal of Environmental Economics and Management* 27: 147–62.

Selden, Thomas, and Daqing Song. 1995. "Neoclassical Growth, the J Curve for Abatement, and the Inverted U Curve for Pollution." *Journal of Environmental Economics and Management* 29: 162–68.

Shafik, Nemat. 1994. "Economic Development and Environmental Quality: An Econometric Analysis." *Oxford Economic Papers* 46: 757–73.

Smarzynska, Beata, and Shang-Jin Wei. 2001. "Pollution Havens and Foreign Direct Investment: Dirty Secret or Popular Myth?" *NBER Working Paper* No. 8465, September.

Stavins, Robert. 2000. *Economics of the Environment: Selected Readings,* 4th ed. New York: Norton.

Stokey, Nancy. 1998. "Are There Limits to Growth?" *Intenational Economic Review* 39, no. 1 (February): 1–31.

Suri, Vivek, and Duane Chapman. 1998. "Economic Growth, Trade and Energy: Implications for the Environmental Kuznets Curve." *Ecological Economics* 25, no. 2 (May): 147–60.

Tobey, James A.. 1990. "The Effects of Domestic Environmental Policies on Patterns of World Trade: An Empirical Test." *Kyklos* 43: 191–209.

Victor, David, and C. Ford Runge. 2002. "Farming the Genetic Frontier." *Foreign Affairs,* 81, no. 3: 107–21.

Vogel, David. 1995. *Trading Up: Consumer and Environmental Regulation in a Global Economy.* Cambridge: Harvard University Press.

World Bank. 1992. *Development and the Environment,* World Development Report.

7

The Rich Have Markets, The Poor Have Bureaucrats

WILLIAM EASTERLY

T HE TRAGEDY OF FOREIGN AID is not that it doesn't work, but that it has never really been tried. It's not that funds haven't been provided to encourage development and reduce poverty. The problem is that the donor nations have tolerated—make that demanded—an aid system that does little to relieve human suffering. Afraid to compete, developed countries coordinate their aid efforts, in effect creating a cartel. The cartel acts to protect many small, inefficient aid programs for poor countries, and a bureaucratic nightmare for recipients.

Proof of the inefficiency of aid in reducing poverty emerges from the World Bank's own estimate that donor countries spend $1 billion in aid to lift 284,000 people a year out of extreme poverty. Thus, it takes about $3,500 a year to raise a poor person's income above $365 a year, the Bank's standard of poverty. By contrast, consider the efficiency of the globalized private markets. In less than five minutes, I can order a $450 Fabergé silver caviar server made in Italy from the Saks Fifth Avenue web site and have it shipped to my home. In another five minutes, I can order in a $382 tin of Russian Beluga caviar from a different website, also to be shipped overnight. By tomorrow, I could serve my guests Russian-produced caviar in a Italian-made server bought from companies based in New York and Seattle.

The world's one billion people who live in extreme poverty can't afford to buy caviar, or even enough corn meal, on global markets. No wonder so many people are justly outraged that the world economy does such a good job at producing caviar for the rich and such a bad job at producing food for starving children.

There is an ongoing debate about whether worldwide incomes are slowly converging or diverging (see figure 7.1). If each country is treated as an independent natural experiment, rich and poor countries are diverging. The median country has grown more slowly than the rich countries, and the bottom 5 percent of countries have not grown at all. But if countries are weighted by population, rich and poor countries are converging, because the massive populations of China and India, after starting from a very low base, have been catching up to the rich countries since 1980. Nonetheless, average incomes of China and India remain below one-eighth of average incomes in rich countries, and historical experience teaches that the rapid rates of growth in China and India are unlikely to continue.

In any case, whether there is slow convergence or divergence over time makes little difference to the typical malnourished child today over his formative years, so there is widespread demand for some additional action. The rich

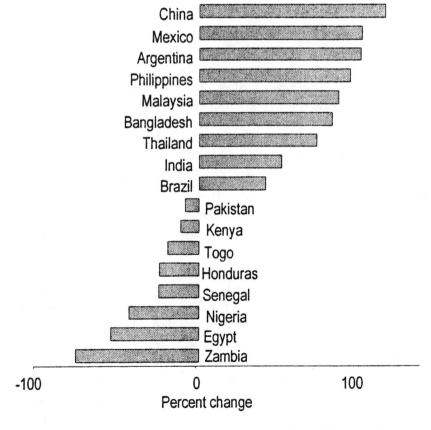

FIGURE 7.1 *Change in trade/GDP, 1977–1997 (selected countries)*

governments' response has been foreign aid. Unfortunately, foreign aid over the last decade has developed an increasingly byzantine bureaucracy that delivers help at an excruciatingly slow pace—if at all.

ONE FATHER IN ETHIOPIA

More than 50 percent of rural Ethiopian children are malnourished—the world's highest incidence of hunger. Consider a typical father in the Ethiopian countryside, with an income of around 74 cents a day in purchasing-power-adjusted dollars.[1]

Let's call him Malik. How would his needs fit into the foreign aid process?

Here's how the current system works. Let's imagine that Malik somehow communicates his desire for aid to "civil society representatives" and/orNGOs, who allegedly articulate his needs through the government of Ethiopia to international donors.

The Ethiopian government then looks to foreign aid for financing of improved nutrition and general economic development that would eventually reach Malik and his family. Suppose the national government solicits one of the World Bank's new "poverty reduction support credits" (PRSC) and one of the International Monetary Fund's (IMF) new Poverty Reduction and Growth Facilities (PRGF). To get these loans, the government must first complete a satisfactory poverty reduction strategy paper (PRSP) in consultation with civil society, NGOs, and other donors and creditors. The government prepares the PRSP in light of the 14-point Comprehensive Development Framework (CDF) of the World Bank, unveiled in 1999. The World Bank then follows a series of internal steps to approve a PRSC, including the preparation of a Country Assistance Strategy (CAS), a pre-appraisal mission, an appraisal mission, negotiations, and Board approval, all in accordance with OD 8.60, OP 4.01, and Interim PRSC Guidelines. So far, so good.

The government also seeks to qualify for the Enhanced Heavily Indebted Poor Countries (HIPC) Initiative, so that the new loan doesn't simply go to service old loans. The creditors and the government conduct a debt sustainability analysis (DSA). In response, HIPC, PRSC, and PRGF require numerous reform conditions, such as participation of the poor, the monitoring of poverty-reducing government expenditures through annual Public Expenditure Reviews (PERs), the setting of fiscal deficit and revenue mobilization targets, and recently prescribed reforms such as the implementation of a Financial Information Management System (FIMS) in government, financial sector reform in line with the Basel standards and the 11 areas of International Standards and Codes recommended by the IMF and World Bank, control of money laundering, and the lowering of trade barriers in ways governed by the World Trade Organization (WTO), perhaps by applying the "Integrated Framework for Trade-Related Technical Assistance to Least Developed Countries."

Hundreds of pages of documents are required to verify these reforms. They take months and years to prepare and a lifetime to implement. For example, the Ethiopian government completed an "interim" PRSP in November, 2000 that listed 152 recommended actions for the government to implement over the next three years. The full PRSP was completed in July 2002.[2] The PRSP may or may not include money that could finance hunger relief for Malik. The amount of money available for hunger relief will depend on the prioritization of various needs in the multi-year medium-term expenditure framework (MTEF). The recently released thousand-page *Poverty Reduction Strategy Paper Sourcebook* of the World Bank provides guidance like the following for prioritizing spending on different areas:

> The sector ministries prepare medium-term strategic plans that set out the sector's key objectives, together with their associated outcomes, outputs, and expenditure forecasts (within the limits agreed upon by the Cabinet). These plans should consider the costs of both ongoing and new programs. Ideally, spending should be presented by program and spending category with financing needs for salaries, operations and maintenance, and investment clearly distinguished.[3]

Meanwhile, if beleaguered Ethiopian government officials have any time left, the PRSP Sourcebook also suggests that they cost out the various ways the government is making progress toward the International Development Goals (IDGs), which include targets for hunger, poverty, infant and maternal mortality, primary education, clean water, contraceptive use, AIDS, gender equality, and the environment, and improved government institutions to participate in a "partnership for development."

Of course, the calendars of Ethiopian officials are getting increasingly crowded, as other international bodies would like to comment upon the Ethiopian PRSP. They include the United Nations Development Program (UNDP), the World Food Programme (WFP), the African Development Bank (ADB), the Consultative Group to Help the Poorest, the United Nations Conference on Trade and Development (UNCTAD), the Food and Agriculture Organization (FAO), the World Trade Organization (WTO), the World Health Organization (WHO), the International Labor Organization (ILO), the European Union (EU), the United Nations Children's Education Fund (UNICEF), the United Nations High Commissioner for Refugees (UNHCR), and the Development

Assistance Group (DAG), which includes representatives of national aid agencies such as those from Austria, Belgium, Canada, Finland, France, Germany, Ireland, Italy, Japan, Netherlands, Norway, Spain, Sweden, Switzerland, United Kingdom (DFID), and the United States (USAID).

If the international lenders and donors approve the PRSP and release new funds to Ethiopia, the government will allocate the money in accordance with the MTEF, CDF, PRGF, PRSC, and PRSP. If all goes well, some of these funds might reach Malik's hungry children. In the best-case scenario, if lots of shaky empirical relationships and assumptions hold, a continuing flow of aid might raise the country's economic growth by one percentage point a year. This means that ten years from now, the aid program will have increased Malik's income by a grand total of eight cents per day.

UNDERSTANDING THE GROWTH OF GRIDLOCK

How did the business of delivering foreign aid services to poor people in poor countries come to involve so much unproductive bureaucracy? It's not that aid bureaucrats are bad. In fact, many smart, hard-working, dedicated professionals toil in the world's top aid agencies. Their obtuse behavior is explained by the increasingly perverse incentives they face.

Bureaucracy works best where there is high feedback from beneficiaries, high incentives to respond to the feedback, easily observable outcomes, high probability that bureaucratic effort will translate into favorable outcomes, and competitive pressure from other bureaucracies and agencies.[4] In short, bureaucracy works best when it functions something like a free market.

For foreign aid, all of these conditions have become increasingly rare in recent years.

Foreign aid today is approved by the increasingly skeptical voters of rich country A, influenced by increasingly powerful and often hostile NGOs. The national government gives money through its own aid bureaucracy and international aid bureaucracies to the government of poor country B, which in turn is supposed to use the money to aid poor people. The poor people in country B have little voice in their own government, much less a voice in the distant national aid bureaucracies, the international aid bureaucracies, and the NGOs in rich country A. These aid bureaucracies, although well intentioned, have little incentive to pay attention to the wishes of poor people from country B who do not vote or lobby in country A.

Although a poor person in Ethiopia can easily observe whether his children are hungry, it is hard for a foreign aid agency to continuously monitor which and how many people are malnourished in country B. Moreover, it is very hard for aid bureaucracies to investigate and learn from past mistakes (such as the redirecting of funds intended for food into fighter jets), because any admission of past failure is a threat to getting aid in the future. In the absence of feedback, foreign aid over time drifts increasingly out of touch with reality.

Exacerbating the problem is the fact that the number of actors in foreign aid has exploded in the last decade thanks to the multiplication of NGOs and government agencies scrutinizing foreign aid outcomes. Social-science theories about the interaction of principals (NGOs and government agencies) and their agents (aid agencies) suggest that having multiple principals dramatically weakens the incentives for the agent. Each principal will try to get the agent (the aid agency) to pursue the principal's objectives. In the aggregate, the incentives for the agent to follow become weak. [5] That is exactly what is happening in foreign aid.

To make matters worse, the principals have pushed the aid agencies into areas where the agents' (aid agencies') performance is even harder to measure (empowering the poor, mainstreaming gender, etc.), reducing the aid agencies' incentives to exert effort towards the principals' goals..[6]The resulting lack of accountability has allowed foreign aid agencies to form a cartel. I call it The Cartel of Good Intentions. Cartels thrive when customers have little opportunity to complain or find alternative suppliers. The typical aid agency acts as a mini-monopoly, forcing governments to work exclusively with its own bureaucracy—its project appraisal and selection apparatus, its economic and social analysts, its procurement procedures, and its own interests and objectives. The collection of all these mini-monopolies forms a cartel.

Finally, the agencies handle the increasingly high risks in foreign aid by the time-honored bureaucratic strategy of sharing blame. Evaluators of foreign aid don't know whom to blame for bad outcomes. Is it mistakes by the international aid community or by the national recipient governments? Is it the bad economic design of aid programs, or the bad politics that undermines their implementation? Is it the excessive austerity imposed by International Monetary Fund or the failure of the World Bank to preserve high return areas from public expenditure cuts? Who knows? This sharing of blame produces a convenient equilibrium for the aid-agency cartel.

Critical evaluation of past aid efforts is suppressed by all agencies because it threatens the overall aid budget. Advocates of various aid objectives agree to support one another, in a process that a political economist might dub "log-rolling." Conversely, aid agencies refuse to criticize one another's interventions.[7] The feedback from experimentation and learning by doing that is essential to success in any activity is therefore mostly absent, robbing the aid community of its historical memory.

In sum, an increasingly baroque bureaucracy in foreign aid has evolved to face an increasingly hostile environment.[8] The resulting edifice of national and international bureaucracies provides services effectively to the world's poor. Rich country donors use this systemic failure as an excuse to decrease aid to the world's poor.

The heartbreaking reality of aid isn't so much that it doesn't work as that we in rich countries behave as if we don't really care whether it does.

THROWING MONEY AT THE PROBLEM

Even a brief glimpse of the history of foreign aid reveals the good intentions and hopeful expectations of those offering the aid. A convenient starting point for such an overview is the Point Four program of Harry S. Truman, which he announced in his inaugural address on January 20, 1949: "We must embark on a bold new program for . . . the improvement and growth of underdeveloped areas. More than half the people of the world are living in conditions approaching misery. . . . For the first time in history, humanity possesses the knowledge and the skill to relieve the suffering of these people." I believe this was the first call for peacetime aid from one state to another in history. At the moment of its birth, we have some characteristics of foreign aid that will last through the years: the call for a new program, the rationale in terms of poverty, and the optimism that foreign aid programs can make a big difference.

A statement two years later by a group of UN experts was more precise: "a 2 percent increase in the per capita national incomes cannot be brought about without . . . a sum of money . . .of about $3 billion a year" (UN Expert Group 1951). This started a fashion of setting precise targets, calculating aid "requirements" to achieve this target, and then calling for an aid increase. So Walt Rostow in his famous *Stages of Growth* declared that "an increase of $4 billion in external aid would be required to lift all of Asia, the Middle East, Africa, and Latin America into regular growth, at an increase of per capita income of say, 1.5% per annum" (Rostow 1960). This recommendation would have approximately doubled current aid spending. Rostow, like others at the time and for many years afterward, assumed that aid was temporary—that within ten to fifteen years, poor countries would attain "self-sustaining" growth for which aid would no longer be necessary.

Over the following decades, similar statements advocating increased aid continued. "Existing foreign aid programs and concepts are largely unsatisfactory . . .we intend during this coming decade of development to achieve a decisive turnaround in the fate of the less-developed world, looking toward the ultimate day . . .when foreign aid will no longer be needed" (John F. Kennedy 1961). "We recommend a substantial increase in official aid flows" (Pearson Commission 1969). "The current flow of ODA . . . is only half the modest target prescribed by the internationally accepted United Nations Strategy for the Second Development Decade" (World Bank President Robert McNamara, 1973). "Additional concessionary resources would be required to achieve both higher rates of growth in the poorest countries" (World Bank, IDA-6, 1980). "A cut of just 10 percent in military spending by the countries of the North Atlantic Treaty Organization would pay for a doubling of aid. . .real growth in aid of only 2 percent a year is an unacceptably weak response to the challenge of global poverty" (World Bank WDR 1990).

How did the wealthy nations respond to these calls for increased aid? In fact, the amounts given grew throughout this period (figure 7.2), doubling several times between 1949 and the present. The cumulative sums involved are impressive. In fact, if all foreign aid given since 1950 had been invested in US Treasury Bills, the assets of poor countries by 2001 would have amounted to $2.3 trillion.

Of course, the aid was not invested in any such fashion. Instead, much of it went to build a foreign aid bureaucracy. For example, the World Bank's administrative expenses grew from $81 million in 1959–60 to $1.5 billion in 1993–94 (in constant fy1993 dollars), while its staff grew from 657 to 7,106 (Kapur et al. 1997). Meanwhile, the typical poor country has stagnated. There have been individual success stories and progress on specific indicators, like infant mortality and school enrollment. But the goal of increased living standards and reduced poverty in the typical poor country was not attained.

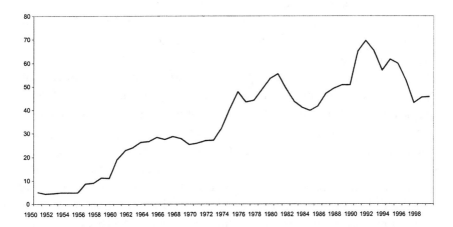

FIGURE 7.2 *Overseas development assistance in 1999 billions of dollars*

Thus by the second half of the 1990s, aid agencies faced a public relations crisis.[9] The doubling of aid monies stopped; in fact, aid flows actually declined in the second half of the 1990s.

Nonetheless, the calls for doubling of aid continue today, based perhaps on a mixture of historical amnesia and chutzpah: "If we are serious about ensuring a beneficial globalization and meeting multilateral development goals we have all signed on to, we must double ODA from its current level of about $50 billion a year" (World Bank President James Wolfensohn, 2001). A World Bank technical study on the cost of meeting the international goals concurred on doubling: "An increase in foreign aid of an amount equal to current foreign aid . . . is about the right order of magnitude for achieving the development goals" (World Bank 2002).[10]

In response, the increasingly resistant rich country politicians console themselves with the belief that they have done all they could for the world's poor. Rich countries and aid agencies find it convenient to blame the governments of poor countries for aid failures, as opposed to rich country politicking, inefficient donor bureaucracies, and the dysfunctional operations of the global aid cartel.

THE CARTEL IN ACTION: "COORDINATION" RATHER THAN COMPETITION

As indicated, the ineffectiveness of the aid cartel can be measured by the enormous gap between its functioning and that of the typical free market. Let's consider four specific symptoms of this gap: (1) the emphasis on "coordination" of aid efforts rather than competition among agencies; (2) the redefining of "outputs" so as to create the appearance of success even when poverty is unaffected; (3) the focus on spin control and public relations rather than genuine progress; and (4) the historical amnesia that prevents aid agencies from learning from the failures and successes of the past.

From the earliest days, the emphasis of all participants in the foreign aid process has been on coordination rather than competition. President Truman signaled in 1949 that "this should be a cooperative enterprise in which all nations work together through the United Nations and its specialized agencies wherever practicable." Two decades later, an aid commission repeated, "A serious effort is necessary to coordinate the efforts of multilateral and bilateral aid-givers and those of aid-receivers" (Pearson Commission 1969). The World Bank's 1981 Berg report on Africa agreed that "Aid coordination, both within recipient countries and among major financing agencies, has been recognized as increasingly important." (World Bank, 1981).

Yet despite the repeated calls for coordination, there is never enough. "Donors must act more in concert—with each other and with recipients. This report suggests six ways to improve coordination" (World Bank Africa report, 1986). "Better coordination among international financial institutions is needed." (World Bank, IDA-12, 1998). "Deputies encouraged Management . . . to maintain close collaboration with other multilateral development banks (MDBs), the OECD-DAC Task Force on Donor Practices, the Strategic Partnership with Africa (SPA), the United Nations and its specialized agencies, and bilateral development assistance agencies" (World Bank, IDA-13, 2001).

Thus, the hoped-for level of cooperation in foreign aid is always just a little out of reach. This phenomenon is consistent with the natural tensions inherent in a cartel, where agencies formally forswear competition but are forever tempted to encroach on one another's turf.

The emphasis on "coordination" in foreign aid protects a growing number of tiny players in the business, even when dealing with them drives the poor countries' governments to distraction. One wonders whether the transactions costs were worth the effort for the Senegalese government to receive 3,344 Euros from the Finnish Ministry for Foreign Affairs Department for International Development Cooperation in 2001,[11] or how well Yasser Arafat is monitoring tenders in November 2001, for Consultancy Services for the Palestinian–Finnish Education Programme, Phase I. As the World Bank said in 1998, "It is hard to explain this behavior, except that different donors like to "plant their flags."

The increasing awareness of the bad outcomes of "coordination" has recently impelled calls for recipient governments to organize what the aid community cannot:

> **Negotiating an external assistance strategy in the context of the PRSP process** that explicitly identifies the priority sectors and programs for donor financing. . . . More detailed external assistance strategies can then be developed for key areas through sectoral working groups in which representatives of major donors and line agencies participate . . .

> **Agreeing on financing priorities for individual donors within the framework of a global external assistance strategy**, rather than through bilateral agreements. . . (World Bank Poverty Reduction Strategy Sourcebook, 2001)

This asks recipient governments to do central planning, which even rich countries with far more administrative capacity than poor countries have a hard time doing. Not only must the understaffed government of Ethiopia decide where and whether a given hungry child gets help, but it must then "coordinate" which amongst a sea of donors and programs will do the job.

Make no mistake, there is a valid need for coordinating the actions of different agents. In a market economy, the need for coordination is met either by decentralized markets or by management within a firm. Unfortunately, the aid community uses neither method. Instead, it occupies a halfway house where monopoly substitutes for competition.

This produces a series of unfortunate results. First, the cartel enables agencies to escape pressure for cost reductions. Second, the agencies present a united front to the well-intentioned people in the rich countries who want to assist the poor, making it difficult for them to discriminate among agencies on the basis of efficiency. Third, the cartel imposes an unequal relationship on the recipient governments, who can only take or leave what the United Donors offer. Finally, The Cartel of Good Intentions embraces the local government bureaucracy.

In the end, it is the intended beneficiaries who suffer. There are many reports like the one in Ukraine of the "humiliation that one endures from government bureaucrats, infamous for their ferocious and insulting tone." In Esmeraldas, Ecuador, a group of villagers reported "The mayor even slapped a woman who asked for help" (World Bank, *Voices of the Poor* 2000b). Likewise, Filmer and Pritchett 2001 report "a client survey of women who had a birth in the past 2 years at rural health centers in the Mutasa district of Tanzania revealed the most frequently cited disadvantages of giving birth in an institution were: ridiculed by nurses for not having baby clothes (22 percent). . . and nurses hit mothers during delivery (13 percent)."

No one can say with certainty how representative such examples are. Still, one could probably improve a system where the bureaucrats beat the beneficiaries.[12]

The current emphasis on "coordination" also undermines the potential gains from specialization and division of labor among agencies. Aid organizations are notorious for trying to do it all. The IMF, World Bank, and regional banks all get involved in short-run financial crises, just as the IMF, World Bank, and regional banks all get involved in reducing long-run poverty. The aid agencies also discourage staff members from developing specialized skills. For example, they prevent them becoming country experts by rotating them frequently. Thus, knowledge of local history, politics, and languages is rare.

Redefining Output

In response to outside pressures and criticism, aid bureaucracies seek to produce observable "outputs." However, the primary output that foreign aid agencies advertise is the volume of money they disburse. In effect, this means the agencies redefine inputs to development as outputs.

For example, in its defense against recent critics, the World Bank's IDA defines itself in terms of volume in 2001: "IDA, as the largest source of concessional assistance to the world's poorest countries, plays a critical role in their efforts to achieve growth and poverty reduction." A World Bank publication in 2001 advertised ten accomplishments of the organization. All ten involved volumes of assistance for different purposes.[13]

This emphasis on moving money has a number of consequences for the aid business. Since the weak institutions of the recipient are often the critical bottleneck in disbursing funds, donors have increasingly substituted their own institutions for those of the recipient so as the keep the money flowing. The World Bank's 1998 aid report said, "Faced with low implementation capacity and pressure to 'move the money,' aid agencies have a long history of attempting to 'cocoon' their projects using free-standing technical assistance, independent project implementation units, and foreign experts—rather than trying to improve the institutional environment for service provision." In Tanzania in the early 1990s, donors were implementing 15 separate stand-alone projects in the health sector (Van de Walle 2001). An aid worker reported to me that Honduras has 57 different projects in the education sector as of this writing, and that the impoverished country was "floating in aid money."

Increased critical scrutiny leads to stress on other kinds of output as well, like international meetings of statesmen, glossy reports for the public, and the proliferation of framework and strategy papers. The standard response to any Third World tragedy has become to hold a meeting about it. In a recent report, UNDP discussed its success at arranging meetings:

> Trust Fund resources have been used to support the preparation and dissemination of social sector expenditure reviews in seven African countries. . . . Five of these reports have already been finalized and a workshop has been or will be held to discuss their findings and recommendations. Preliminary findings of these studies were shared in three regional meetings, co-sponsored by UNDP and UNICEF, which served to sensitize policy-makers about the 20/20 initiative and prepare them for the international meeting which took place in Hanoi in October 1998.[14]

A rich, complex, and voluminous flow of verbiage is another output that the aid agencies like to boast about. IDA's 2001 draft document discussed the interlocking strategies and frameworks produced by different aid organizations, with an output by one organization often serving as an input to another: "The UN Common Country Assessment, the Bank's Economic and Sector Work (ESW), and the IMF's analytical and technical assistance work would contribute to governments' analytical base for PRSPs [Poverty Reduction Strategy Papers]. [IDA Deputies] also welcomed the European Union's decision to base its Africa, Caribbean and Pacific (ACP) assistance programs on the PRSPs."

In response to criticism that they are not doing enough for the poor, aid agencies like to produce observable "frameworks" that avoid hard choices between a number of competing claims on their scarce implementation resources. Such frameworks typically include a Christmas tree of aims like "an increased focus on issues like good governance at national and international levels and the fight against corruption, respect for all internationally recognized human rights, gender issues, capacity and institutional building, social services supply and environmental concerns" (UN Conference on the Least Developed Countries 2001). Likewise World Bank President James Wolfensohn set out his "Comprehensive Development Framework" in 1999 with a checklist of 14 items, each with multiple sub-items.[15] Similarly, the UN in its preparatory documents for the 2002 Johannesburg Summit on Sustainable Development recommends 185 actions by rich and poor nations.

Since the outputs that really matter are what is observable to the electorate in rich countries, aid agencies often strive to produce side effects for rich countries. For example, aid agencies are attentive to the need to reward political allies of the rich countries with aid. Such indicators as the frequency with which a recipient country votes with the donor in the UN and whether the recipient is an ex-colony of the donor can explain recent aid flows (Alesina and Dollar 2000, World Bank 1998). After September 11, 2001 there was anecdotal evidence of new aid resources for allies in the war against terrorism, like Pakistan, Turkey, and Uzbekistan.

The inverse of donors' desire to produce observable positive outputs is their fear of producing observable negative outputs. Donors feel this more than ever in recent years with the increased success of NGOs in popularizing particular causes in the rich country media. For example, NGOs will blame donors for an aid project that produces visible environmental damage, with the degree of blame often out of proportion to real damage produced. As a result, the aid agencies choose increasingly elaborate control procedures to minimize the risk of visible negative outputs. The unfortunate officer on a World Bank country desk is required to produce or commission five separate reports on each client country: a Country Economic Memorandum (CEM)/Development Policy Review (DPR), a Country Financial Accountability Assessment (CFAA), a Country Procurement Assessment Review (CPAR), a Poverty Assessment (PA), and a Public Expenditure Review (PER). Four other reports are identified as "important in advancing the Bank's corporate priorities," while twelve other sector reports are mentioned in management guidelines but are mercifully optional.

The fear of PR fiascos is so extreme that some aid officials reportedly refuse to do whole classes of projects, like roads and dams, even when the benefits may greatly outweigh the costs on a particular project.

SPIN CONTROL

The increased scrutiny of foreign aid bureaucracies causes them to engage in a mixture of obfuscation and advertising. Carefully hedged diplomatic language is an art form in aid agencies. A war is a "conflict-related reallocation of resources" (World Bank Ethiopia report, 2001). Rich country aid efforts to anarchic warlords like in Liberia are "difficult partnerships" (OECD 2001). Countries with homicidal rulers are known as "low income countries under stress" (World Bank 2002). Countries whose presidents loot the treasury experience "governance issues." Bad performance is "progress [that] has not been as fast and comprehensive as envisioned in the PRSP" (World Bank PRSP Sourcebook 2001). Other aid community jargon, like "good investment climate," simply lacks any meaning that economic science can discover. You might as well say "the investment climate will be stormy in the morning, gradually clearing by afternoon with scattered expropriations."[16]

Spin control glosses over the contradictions in the different efforts of the aid agencies. Thus, the contradiction between "country ownership" and the requirement that countries meet arbitrary Millennium Development Goals goes unremarked. The tradeoffs between targets set out in the Comprehensive Development Framework and the Millennium Development Goals—say between faster poverty reduction and greater environmental protection—also escape mention. Nor is there acknowledgment that different societies may have different priorities, or that policy instruments may have different effects in different countries. The implied philosophy is simply, "Do everything."

Like laundry detergent, aid is now sold as "new and improved." One instrument for conveying this spin is the "reorganization" of the aid agency. World Bank President James Wolfensohn has carried out a large-scale reorganization since he took office in 1995. The U.S. foreign aid effort was reorganized in 1999 (when USAID was moved back into the State Department). President George W. Bush in 2002 proposed an important new reorganization of the U.S. aid effort with his Millennium Challenge Account.[17]

A related recent spin is increased emphasis on desirable "new" goals. For example, one hallmark of donor policy in the new millennium (enshrined in 2002's so-called "Monterrey Consensus") has been the new emphasis on "selectivity" of foreign aid, because "aid has a big effect on growth and poverty reduction" only in countries with good policies (World Bank, *Assessing Aid*, 1998). The World Bank in a recent report on aid effectiveness (World Bank 2002) stated that, indeed, "during the 1990s, overall aid allocation shifted in favor of countries with good policies." One's enthusiasm at the sinners' religious conversion is tempered only by the history of many previous conversions. Indeed, every successive aid document over the decades has called for increased "selectivity," beginning 39 years ago: "Objective No. 1: To apply stricter standards of selectivity . . . in aiding developing countries" (President John F. Kennedy 1963).

The current "new" emphasis on poverty in the aid agencies is another classic example of nearly content-free spin. Way back in 1960, the creation of the International Development Association (IDA) for the poorest countries reflected an early concern with poverty. World Bank President McNamara came along in 1973 to "to place far greater emphasis on policies and projects which will begin to attack the problems of absolute poverty" (McNamara 1973, IDA-4). Each new round of replenishment of the IDA called for a renewed focus on poverty: ". . . a growing proportion of lending is directed to combating poverty" (1980, IDA-6). ". . .The Deputies encouraged an even stronger emphasis on poverty reduction in IDA's programs" (Stern 1990, IDA-9). "The poverty focus of CASs [Country Assistance Strategies] should be enhanced" (IDA-12, 1998).

A similar story applies to another "new direction" in foreign aid policy, which is home-grown development, known by such vivid bureaucratese as "country ownership," "partnership," "beneficiary participation," "community-driven development (CDD)," "empowering the poor," "consultation of stakeholders," and "bottom-up development." The process of the country preparing a Poverty Reduction Strategy Paper (PRSP) is described as a means to this goal by the World Bank and IMF in 2001: "the PRSP . . . was a crucial step towards greater national ownership of development programs which is essential for increased effectiveness of external assistance" (World Bank 2001, IDA-13).

Yet despite the current rhetoric, donors often violate national sovereignty with their own rapidly proliferating agendas.[18] Moreover, pressure to "move the money" still causes donors to substitute their own institutions for those of the recipient country, despite the supposed emphasis on fostering self-reliance. Since the international financial institutions (IFIs) decided the preparation of a PRSP was necessary to receive debt relief under the HIPC program, most countries had little time for the "consultation with civil society" that was supposed to be included. Surveys turned up reports of PRSPs being prepared in English in non–English-speaking countries, and even "in some cases, the rush was such that the IFIs simply took over the task of writing the PRSPs in a way that it would meet the approval of the Boards in Washington" (Jubilee South 2001).

However, even if the PRSP were prepared with participation by everyone and their cousins, how a document can redistribute power remains unexplained. The donors might as well say, "May the force be with you." For example, the World Bank and IMF awarded a second round of debt relief to Burkina Faso in April, 2002 based upon the satisfactory completion of a participatory PRSP.[19] It would be interesting to know how fully the poor have been empowered in a one-party state which was in the worst fifth of the world in corruption in 2001, and which supported rebel warlords that perpetrated tragic atrocities in Sierra Leone, Liberia, and Angola.

Similarly, the poor in Tajikstan must have wondered about the "participatory" process by which the government of Emomali Rakhmonov created its Interim PRSP in the fall of 2000. Since 1992, President Rakhmonov has presided over an authoritarian government whose rule has featured years of civil war, ethnic conflict, and favoritism, political repression, continuing violence, extrajudicial killings, disappearances, torture, arbitrary arrests by the security forces, and trafficking in women and children.[20] Nonetheless, the World Bank and IMF praised Tajikstan's government in 2002 for a "more open dialogue" (IDA and IMF 2002).

Of course, in the language of foreign aid spin control, there is "participation," but no politics. The IFIs assume away the political combat between polarized classes, regions, or ethnic groups that is the stuff of everyday life in both rich and poor nations. The IFIs assume that political strongmen like President Rakhmonov will cheerfully give some of their power away to the poor, doing what the poor want instead of what President Rakhmonov wants, all through a bureaucratic exercise—the crafting of a Poverty Reduction Strategy Paper. If only the world worked like that.

AID AMNESIA

The examples above of "new" initiatives that simply mirror the past reflect the lack of historical memory in the aid community. Today's increased levels of critical scrutiny make the aid community even less willing than before to critically examine the past. Doing so might lead to negative publicity and revelations of past failures, threatening the ability to raise new aid revenue. No wonder the eminent authors of a well-received two-volume history of the World Bank in 1997 (commissioned by the World Bank at considerable expense for its 50th anniversary) were never invited to give a lecture on their findings within the World Bank (Kapur et al. 1997). Unfortunately, the unwillingness to shine light on past failures makes new failures more likely.

A comparison with the academic community is illuminating. Generally speaking, academic papers are published only if they generate new findings. Papers subject to the competitive academic publishing process cite previous studies and make clear what they have to add that is fresh. By contrast, studies produced within the aid cartel often duplicate and repeat one another without citation (sometimes due to simple ignorance of past research). A USAID consultant recently gave me the example of a large mission that had produced a report on corruption in Uganda in 2001 without knowing that a British team had produced a report on the same topic six months earlier.

World Bank reports continue to repeat particular policy recommendations without analyzing the past failures of those same recommendations. World Bank reports recommended restructuring or privatizing Kenya Railways in 1983, 1989, 1995, 1996, and 2000. They recommended increased funding for road maintenance in 1979, 1983, 1989, 1994, 1996, and 2000. In 1998, the World Bank reported that, in Kenya, "the World Bank provided aid to support identical agricultural policy reforms five separate times." The sheer repetition of adjustment loans to countries with poor track records, like Kenya's 21 World Bank and IMF adjustment loans as of the year 2000, reflects the pervasive historical amnesia.

Aid agencies make little effort to collect case studies of adjustment programs, projects, and sectoral programs, or to use case studies to inform current management and staff about mistakes to avoid and successes to emulate. Under Wolfensohn, the World Bank inaugurated an expensive program of sending managers for six-week intensive training at the Harvard Business School. They would have done better to send their managers to the World Bank's own library and document archives, where they could read case studies of projects failing and (sometimes) succeeding.

When the aid agencies do report on the past, they focus on success stories for which they can claim some credit. For example, the World Bank (2002) offers six aid success stories: China, India, Mozambique, Poland, Uganda, and Vietnam. This is a somewhat surprising list, since China and India receive little aid relative to their GDP (0.4 % and 0.7% of GDP respectively in the 1980s and 1990s, which is the period the World Bank study mentions). Poland and Vietnam are also below-average recipients of foreign aid, even if we ignore the periods before recent reforms when they got no aid at all. And there is more than a little irony in highlighting two of the world's few remaining Communist party dictatorships (China and Vietnam) as a triumph of aid from Western capitalists![21]

Of course, the reason for selecting these countries is no mystery. China, India, Mozambique, Uganda, and Vietnam were the fastest growing low-income

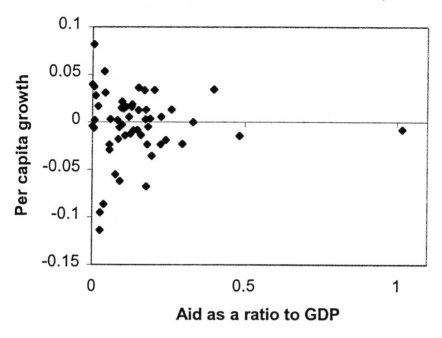

FIGURE 7.3   *Aid and growth in low-income countries in the 1990s*

countries in the 1990s, except for Sudan (ranked third), which the World Bank apparently didn't want to celebrate. Poland is the fastest-growing transition country. Inconvenient facts are ignored in the report: for example, that as many aid-receiving low income countries had negative per capita growth as positive, or that most aid-receiving transition countries were a disaster in the 1990s. In fact, among all low-income countries, there is no clear relationship between aid and growth (figure 7.3).

CONCLUSIONS

Foreign aid today demands the most from bureaucracy under the conditions in which bureaucracy functions worst. Operating with little effective feedback and with severe skill shortages in the recipient countries, the aid bureaucracy tries to manage aid through a hierarchical, top-heavy, top-down process.[22] It seems obvious that this is a recipe for failure.

Given the multiple goals and procedures that exist in foreign aid, consistent with the urge to produce visible outputs and avoid visible fiascos, the center has become the chokepoint for aid. Frontline staff in aid agencies can barely keep up with the flood of mandates, political pressures, procedural requirements, and authorizations required to keep the aid money flowing. In the recipient governments, the relative burden on the management is even greater, given the scarcity of skills, the extreme political pressures in factionalized societies, and the prevalence of red tape and corruption.[23] The mighty river of aid must pass through a very small administrative funnel. No wonder so little help ever reaches the intended beneficiaries.

The aid community has responded to the difficult current environment by organizing itself into The Cartel of Good Intentions, suppressing critical feed-back, ignoring the lessons of the past, and limiting competitive pressures to deliver results. The result is that foreign aid continues to lose support in the rich countries just as liberal political and economic ideals lose support in the poor countries. Until this system undergoes a fundamental reform, the talent, energy, resources, and good will of the aid community will continue to be wasted.

ENDNOTES

1. Calculated by applying the 1999 PPP per capita income of Ethiopia and multiplying it by an estimate of the rural/urban income ratio.
2. http://www.imf.org/external/np/prsp/2000/eth/01/113000.pdf; http://poverty.world-bank.org/files/country_timelines.pdf.
3. Poverty Reduction Strategy Paper Sourcebook.
4. There is a large literature that makes these common sense points. See especially Wilson 1989. The World Bank's World Development Report on Institutions (2001a) presented evidence that direct election of individual politicians, more political competition, and a free and independent media reduced bureaucratic corruption and improved public service delivery. Djankov et al. 2001 similarly finds that government domination of the media worsens social service delivery. La Porta et al. 1998 found that more democratic governments were more efficient and delivered more public goods, as were governments bound by common law rather than civil or socialist law (arguing that common law gives more voice to citizens). Kaufmann et al. 2001 and Kaufmann et al. 2002 show how bureaucracies in Bolivia with more citizen voice and more transparency deliver a higher quality and quantity of pub-lic services. Isham, Kaufmann, and Pritchett 1995 found that countries with civil liberties had higher returns on aid projects. Pritchett and Woolcock 2002 describe the failure of the bureaucratic model in public service delivery under unfavorable conditions in poor countries.
5. For a review, see Dixit 1996 and 2000.
6. For a general treatment of the incentive problems that afflict organizations, see Milgrom and Roberts 1992 and Prendergast 1999.
7. This argument is inspired by Pritchett's (2001) model of why "it pays to be ignorant."
8. There is a large economics literature on the theory of bureaucracy, principally started by Niskanen (1968, 1971), with good recent surveys by Niskanen (2001),

Moe (1997) and Wintrobe (1997). There is also a rich literature on bureaucracy from other social scientists, of which the outstanding example is Wilson (1989).

9. The report of the Meltzer Commission in March 2000 summarized many of the complaints about aid ineffectiveness.

10. To make this calculation, the World Bank technical study in 2002 was still using the Harrod-Domar growth model 44 years after its demolition by Solow.

11. http://global.finland.fi/english/publications/annual/2001/annual_02appendices.pdf.

12. Bureaucracies in rich countries where clients don't have much voice could be equally oppressive, like Customs or Immigration in the United States. The U.S. government during the Clinton Administration tried to make various agencies more client-friendly. According to an anecdote by John Nellis, the response of Customs officials to this initiative was "we don't have clients; we have suspects."

13. World Bank2001b.

14. UNDP.

15. http://www.worldbank.org/cdf/cdf-text.htm.

16. The President of the World Bank, April 2002.

17. http://www.usaid.gov/about/chronology.html.

18. To put this in perspective, think of whether the United States would have been willing to have international agencies or foreign governments dictate its policies or institutions at any point in American history. The most famous case of "foreign aid" to the United States happened early in American history with French military support to the American revolution—but remember George Washington was in command.

19. http://lnweb18.worldbank.org/news/pressrelease.nsf/673fa6c5a2d50a67852565e200692a79/6b834179b3fd616b85256b990077a8a7?OpenDocument.

20. Freedom House rated Tajikstan as "not free" from 1992 to 2000. The U.S. State Department Human Rights Report 2001 mentions the human rights violations cited here.

21. Milanovic points this out.

22. See the excellent description by Morton 1994.

23. Tendler 1975 has a very good description of this process, which remains timely today.

REFERENCES

Alesina and Dollar. 2000.

Alesina Alberto, Edward Glaeser, Bruce Sacerdote. 2001. "Why Doesn't The U.S. Have a European-Style Welfare System?" NBER Working Paper 8524

Arndt, H. W. 1987. *Economic Development: The History of an Idea*. Chicago: University of Chicago Press.

Birdsall, Nancy and John Williamson, with Brian Deese. 2002. *Delivering on Debt: From IMF Gold to a New Aid Architecture*, Center for Global Development and Institute for International Economics.

Blank, Rebecca. 1997. *It Takes a Nation: A New Agenda For Fighting Poverty*. Princeton: Russell Sage Foundation.

Blank, Rebecca and David Ellwood. 2001. "The Clinton Legacy for America's Poor." NBER Working Paper 8437, August.

Boote, Anthony, Fred Kilby, Kamau Thugge, and Axel Van Trotsenburg. 1997. "Debt Relief for Low-Income Countries and the HIPC Debt Initiative." In Z. Iqbal and R. Kanbur, eds. *External Finance for Low-Income Countries.* International Monetary Fund.

Cassen, Robert. *Does Aid Work?* Oxford: Oxford University Press, 1985.

Catholic Relief Services. 2001. Review of the Poverty Reduction Strategy Paper Initiative, Based upon the Experiences and Comments of CRS Partners in Bolivia, Honduras, Zambia and Cameroon, December.

Dixit, Avinash. 1996. *The Making of Economic Policy: A Transaction-Cost Politics Perspective.* Cambridge: MIT Press.

———. 2000. "Incentives and Organizations in the Public Sector: An Interpretive Review." Photocopy: Princeton University.

Djankov, Simeon, Caralee McLiesh, Tatiana Nenova, and Andrei Shleifer. 2001. "Who Owns the Media?" NBER Working Paper No.w8288, May.

Easterly, William. 1999. "The Ghost of Financing Gap: Testing the Growth Model of the International Financial Institutions." *Journal of Development Economics,* (60)2 (December): 423–38

———. 2001. *The Elusive Quest for Growth: Economists' Adventures and Misadventures in the Tropics.* Cambridge: MIT Press.

———. 2002. "What Did Structural Adjustment Adjust? The Association of Policies and Growth with Repeated IMF And World Bank Adjustment Loans." Photocpy, Center for Global Development.

Ellerman, David. 2001. "Generic Problems with Social Funds." DECVP, World Bank, Photocopy, October.

European Union. 2001. Ethiopia—European Union Country Strategy Paper and Indicative Program 2002–2007, December. http://europa.eu.int/comm/development/strat_papers/docs/et_csp.pdf.

Ferguson, James. 1994. *The Anti-Politics Machine: "Development," Depoliticization and Bureaucratic Power in Lesotho.* Minneapolis: University of Minnesota Press.

———. 1999. *Expectations of Modernity: Myths and Meanings of Urban life on the Zambian Uopperbelt.* Berkeley: University of California Press.

Filmer, Deon and Lant Pritchett. 1997. "What Education Production Functions Really Show: A Positive Theory of Education Expenditures." World Bank Working Paper.

———, Jeffrey Hammer, and Lant Pritchett. 1997. "Health Policy in Poor Countries: Weak Links in the Chain." World Bank Working Paper.

Fleming, Alexander and Mary Oakes Smith. 1987. "Raising Resources for IDA: the Eighth Replenishment." *Finance and Development* (September): 23–16.

Fox, James. 2000. "Applying the Comprehensive Development Framework to USAID Experiences." OED Working Paper Series No. 15. World Bank.

Goldwin, Robert A. ed. 1963. *Why Foreign Aid?* Rand McNally Public Affairs Series.

Grusky et al. 2000, Globalization Challenge Initiative

Hanushek Eric A. and Steven G. Rivkin. 2001. *"Does Public School Competition Affect Teacher Quality?"* Paper prepared for NBER Economics of School Choice Conference Islamorada, Florida. February 22–24, revised May 2001

Her Majesty's Treasury and Department for International Development, 2002, *The Case for Aid to the Poorest Countries*, United Kingdom.

Hotz, Joseph and John Karl Scholz. 2001. "The Earned Income Tax Credit." NBER Working Paper 8078, January.

Hoxby, Caroline M. 2001. "School Choice and School Productivity (or Could School Choice be a Tide that Lifts All Boats?)." Paper prepared for NBER Conference on The Economics of School Choice. Cheeca Lodge, February 23–24, 2001.

Hsieh Chang-Tai and Miguel Urquiola. 2002. When Schools Compete, How Do They Compete? An Assessment of Chile's Nationwide School Voucher Program." Princeton University and Cornell University Photocopy.

International Development Association. 1970. *IDA: 50 Questions and Answers*, May.

———. 1980. Sixth Replenishment of IDA Resources: Report of the Executive Directors to the Board of Governors.

IDA9.

———. 1998. Additions to IDA Resources: Twelfth Replenishment A Partnership for Poverty Reduction.

———. 2001.Thirteenth Replenishment Supporting Poverty Reduction Strategies.

——— and International Monetary Fund, 2002, "Review of the Poverty Reduction Strategy Paper (PRSP) Approach: Early Experience with Interim PRSPs and Full PRSPs." March 26.

International Food Policy Research Institute (IFPRI). 2000. "Is PROGRESA Working: Summary of the Results of an Evaluation by IFPRI." Washington: IFPRI, Photocopy.

International Monetary Fund, Description of the Poverty Reduction and Growth Facility, http://www.imf.org/external/np/exr/facts/prgf.htm

——— and the International Development Association. 2001. Federal Democratic Republic of Ethiopia, Interim Poverty Reduction Strategy Paper, Joint Staff Assessment.

Isham, Jonathan, Daniel Kaufmann, and Lant Pritchett. 1995. "Governance and Returns on Investment: An Empirical Investigation." World Bank Policy Research Working Paper 1550. (November).

Jubilee South. 2001. Focus on the Global South, AWEPON, and the Centro de Estudios Internacionales with the support of the World Council of Churches. "The World Bank and the PRSP: Flawed Thinking and Failing Experiences."

Kanbur, Ravi. "Aid, Conditionality and Debt in Africa." In Finn Tarp, ed. *Foreign Aid and Development: Lessons Learnt and Directions for the Future.* City: Routledge, 2000.

——— and Todd Sandler, with Kevin Morrison. 1999. "The Future of Development Assistance: Common Pools and International Public Goods." ODC Working Paper No. 25.

Kapur, Devesh, John P. Lewis, and Richard Webb. 1997. *The World Bank: Its First Half Century*, Volume 1: History. Washington DC: Brookings Institution Press.

Kapur, Devesh. 2002. "Do As I Say Not As I Do: A Critique of G-7 Proposals on Reforming the MDBs." Photocopy, Harvard University Department of Government.

Kaufmann, Daniel, Massimo Mastruzzi and Diego Zavaleta. 2001."Sustained Macroeconomic Reforms, Tepid Growth: A Governance Puzzle in Bolivia?" The World Bank (September) 2001

———, Gil Mehrez and Tugrul Gurgur. 2002. "Voice or Public Sector Management?: Determinants of Public Sector Performance based on a Survey of Public Officials in Bolivia—Theory and Evidence," World Bank and IMF Photocopy.

Kennedy, John F. 1961.

Kennedy, John F. 1963.

Klitgaard, Robert. 1990. *Tropical Gangsters*. New York: Basic Books.

Lancaster, Carol. 1999. *Aid to Africa: So Much to Do, So Little Done.* Chicago: University of Chicago Press.

La Porta, Rafael, Florencio Lopez-de-Silane, Andrei Shleifer, Robert Vishny. 1998. "The Quality of Government." *Journal of Law Economics and Organization* 15 (April): 222–79.

McNamara, Robert S. 1973. Address to the Board of Governors, Nairobi Kenya, September 24. Speech made during 4th replenishment of IDA negotiations.

Meltzer Commission Report, March 2000, http://www.house.gov/jec/imf/meltzer.pdf

Milgrom, Paul and John Roberts. 1992. *Economics, Organization, and Management.* Upper Saddle River, NJ: Prentice Hall.

Millikan Max F. and W. W. Rostow with the collaboration of P.N. Rosenstein-Rodan and others at the Center for International Studies, MIT. 1957. *A Proposal: Key to an Effective Aid Policy*, With the collaboration of P.N. Rosenstein-Rodan. New York: Harper, 1957.

Milanovic cite (note 22).

Moe, Terry. 1997. "The Positive Theory of Public Bureaucracy." In Dennis Mueller, ed., *Perspectives on Public Choice: A Handbook*. Cambridge, Cambridge University Press, pp. 455–80.

Morley Samuel and David Coady. 2002. "Reducing Poverty Through Subsidized Human Capital Accumulation." Photocopy. Washington, DC: Center for Global Development.

Morton, James. 1994. *The Poverty of Nations: The Aid Dilemma at the Heart of Africa.* London: I. B. Tauris.

Moynihan, Daniel Patrick. 1969. *Maximum Feasible Misunderstanding: Community Action in the War on Poverty*. New York: The Free Press, 1969.

Neumark, David and William Wascher. 2000. "Using the EITC to Help Poor Families: New Evidence and a Comparison with the Minimum Wage." NBER Working Paper No. 7599 March.

Niskanen, William. 1968. "The Peculiar Economics of Bureaucracy." *American Economic Review Papers and Proceedings* 58: 293–305.

———. 1971. *Bureaucracy and Representative Government*. Chicago: Aldine-Atherton.

———. 2001. "Bureaucracy." In William F. Shughart II and Laura Razzolini, eds. *The Elgar Companion to Public Choice*. Cheltenham, UK: Edward Elgar.

OECD Development Assistance Committee. 2001. "Poor Performers: Basic Approaches for Supporting Development in Difficult Partnerships," November.

Pearson, Lester B. 1969. *Partners in Development: Report of the Commission on International Development*, New York: Praeger.

Peterson, Paul E. with William G. Howell Patrick J. Wolf and David E. Campbell. 2001. "School Vouchers: Results from Randomized Experiments." Paper prepared for the Conference on School Choice, sponsored by the National Bureau of Economic Research, Florida Keys, Florida, February.

Prendergast, Canice. 1999. *The Provision of Incentives in Firms. The Journal of Economic Literature* 37 no. 1 (March): 7–63.

———. 2001. "Selection and Oversight in the Public Sector, with the Los Angeles Police Department as an Example." NBER Working Paper 8664.

Preparatory Committee for the International Conference on Financing for Development. 2001. Resumed Third Session, October 15–19. Statement by Mr. Lennart Båge, President of the International Fund for Agricultural Development, Delivered on behalf of the three Rome-based UN Agencies, FAO, IFAD, and WFP, United Nations, New York, October 17.

Pressman, Jeffrey and Aaron Wildavsky. 1984. *Implementation*, 3rd Edition. Berkeley: University of California Press.

Pritchett, Lant. 2001. "Why It Pays To Be Ignorant." Photocopy. Harvard Kennedy School.

——— and Michael Woolcock, "Solutions When the Solution Is the Problem: Arraying the Disarray in Development." Harvard University Center for Global Development and World Bank. Photocopy, March 19.

Ravallion, Martín and Quentin Wodon. 1999. "Does Child Labor Displace Schooling? Evidence on Behavioral Responses to an Enrollment Subsidy." World Bank working paper 2116.

Rostow, W. W. Stages of Economic Growth, a Non-Communist Manifesto. Cambridge: Cambridge University Press, 1960.d

Scott, James C. 1998. *Seeing Like a State: How Certain Schemes to Improve the Human Condition Have Failed*. New Haven: Yale University Press.

Skoufias, Emmanuel, Benjamin Davis and Sergio de la Vega. 2001. "Targeting the Poor in Mexico: An Evaluation of the Selection of Households for Progresa." Washington-FCND # 103.

Soros, George. 2002. *George Soros on Globalization*. New York: Public Affairs.

Stern, Ernest. 1990. "Mobilizing Resources for IDA: The Ninth Replenishment." *Finance and Development* (June): 20–23

Svensson, Jakob. 2002. "Why Conditional Aid Doesn't Work and What Can Be Done About It?" *Journal of Development Economics*. (Forthcoming.)

Tendler, Judith. 1975. *Inside Foreign Aid*. Baltimore: The Johns Hopkins University Press.

———. 1997. *Good Government in the Tropics*. Baltimore: The Johns Hopkins University Press.

———. 2000. "Why Are Social Funds So Popular?" In Shahid Yusuf and S. Evenett, eds. *Local Dynamics in an Era of Globalization*. Oxford: Oxford University Press: 114–29.

Tirole, Jean. 1994. "The Internal Organization of Government." *Oxford Economic Papers* 46: 1–29.

Truman, Harry S. 1949. Inaugural Address January 20.

UN Expert Group 1951. Measures for the Economic Development of Under-developed Countries. New York: United Nations, Department of Economic Affairs, May.

UNDP. 2001. Review of the Poverty Reduction Strategy Paper (PRSP).

———. 2001 Progress Report.

Van de Walle, Nicolas. 2001. *African Economies and the Politics of Permanent Crisis, 1979–99.* Cambridge: Cambridge University Press.

Voices of the Poor. 2000.

Wade. Robert 2001. "The U.S. Role in the Malaise at the World Bank: Get Up Gulliver," G-24. September.

Wapenhans Report. 1992. "Effective Implementation: Key to Development Impact." World Bank.

Wilson, James Q. 1989. *Bureaucracy.* New York: Basic Books.

Wintrobe, Ronald. 1997. "Modern Bureaucratic Theory." In Dennis Mueller, *Perspectives on Public Choice: A Handbook.* Cambridge: Cambridge University Press, 429–454.

Wolfensohn, James D. 1999. "A Proposal for a Comprehensive Development Framework." World Bank, January 21.

World Bank. 1981. *Accelerated Development in Sub-Saharan Africa: An Agenda for Action,* 1981.

———. 1983. *Sub-Saharan Africa: Progress Report on Development Prospects and Programs.*

———. 1984. *Toward Sustained Development in Sub-Saharan African: A Joint Program of Action.*

———. 1985. *World Development Report.*

———. 1986. *Financing Adjustment with Growth in Sub-Saharan Africa, 1986–90,* Washington DC 1986.

———. 1987. *World Development Report.*

———. 1988. *World Development Report.*

———. 1989. *World Development Report.*

———. 1989. *Sub-Saharan Africa: From Crisis to Sustainable Growth – A Long Term Perspective Study.*

———. 1990. *World Development Report.*

———. 1991. *The African Capacity Building Initiative (ACBI).*

———. 1994. *Adjustment in Africa: Reforms, Results, and the Road Ahead.*

———. 1995. *A Continent in Transition: Sub-Saharan Africa in the Mid-1990s, Africa Region.*

———. 1997. *IDA in Action 1993–1996:The Pursuit of Sustained Poverty Reduction.*

———. 1998. *Assessing Aid: What Works, What Doesn't, and Why.*

———. 2000a. *Can Africa claim the 21st Century?*

———. 2000b. *Voices of the Poor.*

———. 2001. Private Sector Development Strategy: Directions for the World Bank Group, December 3.

————. 2001a. *World Development Report 2002: Building Institutions for Markets.*

————. 2001b. *Ten Things You Never Knew About the World Bank.*

————. 2001c. *Poverty Reduction Strategy Paper Sourcebook.*

————. 2001d. Goals for Development: History, Prospects, and Costs, preliminary draft, December 21.

———— 2002a. *The Role and Effectiveness of Development Assistance: Lessons from the World Bank Experience*

———— 2002b. *African Development Indicators.* Press Release April 11.

———— 2002c. Social Development Department. *Participation in Poverty Reduction Strategy Papers: A Retrospective Study*, January.

World Development Movement. 2001. "Policies to Roll-back the State and Privatize? Poverty Reduction Strategy Papers Investigated."

8

Feasible Globalizations

DANI RODRIK

W E WANT ECONOMIC INTEGRATION to help boost living standards. We want democratic politics so that public policy decisions are made by those that are directly affected by them. And we want self-determination, which comes with the nation-state. This chapter explains why we cannot have all three things simultaneously. The political "trilemma" of the global economy is that the nation-state system, democratic politics, and full economic integration are mutually incompatible. We can have at most two out of the three. Because global policymakers have yet to face up to this trilemma, we are headed in an untenable direction: global markets without global governance.

I argue instead for a renewed "Bretton-Woods compromise": preserving some limits on integration, as built into the original Bretton Woods arrangements, along with more global rules to handle the integration that can be achieved. Those who would make a different choice—toward tighter economic integration—must face up to the inevitable choice: either tighter world government or less democracy.

The strategy pursued by the leaders of the world economy underwent a subtle but important shift sometime in the 1980s. During the first four decades after the Second World War, international policymakers had kept their ambitions in check. They pursued a limited form of economic internationalization, leaving lots of room for national economic management. Successive rounds of multilateral trade negotiations made great strides, but focused only on the most egregious of national barriers and excluded large chunks of the economy (e.g., agriculture, services, and "sensitive" manufactures such as garments). In capital markets, restrictions on currency transactions and financial flows remained the norm rather than the exception. This Bretton Woods/GATT regime was successful because its architects subjugated international economic integration to the demands of national economic management and democratic politics.

This has changed drastically during the last two decades. Global policy is now driven by an aggressive agenda of "deep" integration: elimination of *all* barriers to trade and capital flows. The results have been problematic in terms of both economic performance (relative to the earlier postwar decades) and political legitimacy. The simple reason is that deep economic integration is unattainable in a world where nation states and democratic politics still exert considerable force.

Thus, the title of this essay—"feasible globalizations"—suggests two ideas. First, that there are inherent limitations to how far we can push global economic integration. It is not feasible (nor is it desirable) to maximize what Keynes called "economic entanglements between nations."[1] Second, that within the array of feasible globalizations, there are many different models to choose from. Each of these models has different implications for whom we empower and whom we don't, and for who gains and who loses.

We need to recognize these two facts in order to make progress in the globalization debate. One implication is that we need to scale down our ambitions with respect to global economic integration. Another is that we need to do a better job of writing the rules for a "thinner" (that is, less ambitious) version of globalization.

My argument about the limits to globalization isn't self-evident. It rests on several building blocks. First, markets need to be embedded in a range of non-market institutions in order to work well. These institutions create, regulate, stabilize, and legitimize markets, all functions that are crucial to the performance of markets..

The second and much widely less appreciated point is that there is no simple or unique correspondence between these functions and the form of the institutional infrastructure. American-style capitalism differs greatly from Japanese-style capitalism; there is tremendous variety in labor-market and welfare-state institutions even within Europe; and low-income countries often require heterodox institutional arrangements if they are to succeed at development.

Third, this institutional diversity is a significant impediment to full economic integration. Indeed, now that formal restrictions on trade and investment have mostly disappeared, regulatory and jurisdictional discontinuities created by heterogeneous national institutions constitute the most important barriers to international commerce. Deep integration would require removing these transaction costs through institutional harmonization—an agenda on which the World Trade Organization has already embarked. However, because institutional diversity performs a valuable economic (as well as social) role, this is a path full of dangers.

Fortunately, there are feasible models of globalization that would generate significantly more benefits than our current version—and a much more equitable distribution of those benefits. Toward the end of this chapter, I'll discuss a modification of global rules that would produce particularly powerful results: a multilaterally negotiated temporary visa scheme that would allow a broader mix of skilled and unskilled workers from developing nations to enter the developed world. Such a scheme would create income gains greater than all of the items on the WTO negotiating agenda taken together, even if the increase in cross-border labor flows was relatively small.

Markets and Nonmarket Institutions

The paradox of markets is that they thrive best not under *laissez-faire* but under the watchful eye of the state. Here is how historian Jacques Barzun describes the extensive regulatory apparatus in place in Venice at the height of its wealth and power around 1650:

> There were inspectors of weights and measures and of the Mint; arbitrators of commercial disputes and of servants and apprentices' grievances; censors of shop signs and taverns and of poor workmanship; wage setters and tax leviers; consuls to help creditors collect their due; and a congeries of marine officials. The population, being host to sailors from all over the Mediterranean, required a vigilant board of health, as did the houses of resort, for the excellence of which Venice became noted. All the bureaucrats were trained as carefully as the senators and councilors and every act was checked and rechecked as by a firm of accountants (Barzun 2000: 172).

What made Venice the epicenter of international trade and finance in seventeenth-century Europe was the quality of its public institutions. The same can be said of London in the nineteenth century and New York in the second half of the twentieth.

It is generally well understood that markets require nonmarket institutions—at the very least, a legal regime that enforces property rights and contracts. Without such a regime, markets cannot exist in any but the most rudimentary fashion. But the dependence of markets on public institutions runs deeper. Markets are not self-regulating, self-stabilizing, or self-legitimizing. As Adam Smith complained, businessmen seldom meet together without the conversation ending up in a "conspiracy against the public." In the absence of regulations pertaining to antitrust, information disclosure, prudential limits, public health and safety, and environmental and other externalities, markets can hardly do their job correctly. Without a lender-of-last-resort and a public fisc, markets are prone to wild gyrations and periodic bouts of underemployment. And without safety nets and social insurance to temper risks and inequalities, markets cannot retain their legitimacy for long.

The genius of capitalism, where it works, is that it has managed to continually reinvent its institutional underpinnings, with innovations that include central banking, stabilizing fiscal policy, antitrust and regulation, social insurance, and political democracy.

However, creating, regulating, stabilizing, or legitimizing markets are *functions* that need not map into specific institutional *forms*. Consider property rights, for example. What is relevant from an economic standpoint is whether current and prospective investors have the assurance that they can retain the fruits of their investments, not the precise legal form that this assurance takes. China is an extreme but illustrative example. It has managed to provide investors with this assurance despite the complete absence of private property rights. It turns out that institutional innovations in the form of the Household Responsibility System and the Township and Village Enterprises have served as functional equivalents of a private-enterprise economy. How else can we explain the tremendous burst in entrepreneurial activity that has taken place in China since the reforms of the late 1970s?

By contrast, many countries, such as Russia during the 1990s, fail to provide investors with effective control rights over cash flow, even though private property rights are nominally protected.

The variety of legal and social forms among today's advanced 3countries underscores the point. The United States, Europe, and Japan are all successful societies. Each has enjoyed a period of vogue among economists and social scientists: Scandinavia was everyone's favorite in the 1970s; Japan became the model to emulate in the 1980s; and the United States was the undisputed king of the 1990s. Yet none of these models can be deemed a clear winner in the contest of "capitalisms"; each has produced comparable amounts of wealth over the long term.

Nonetheless, their institutions in labor markets, corporate governance, regulation, social protection, and banking and finance all differ greatly. Furthermore, despite much talk about convergence in recent years, there have been few real signs of it. Financial systems (and to a much lesser extent corporate governance regimes) have tended to move toward an Anglo-American model. But labor marker arrangements (as measured by union membership or collective bargaining coverage rates) have actually diverged.[2]

There are good reasons for the resistance of national institutions to convergence. For one thing, societies differ in the values and norms that shape their institutional choices. To take an obvious example, Americans and Europeans tend to have different views as regards the determinants of economic outcomes;

compared to Americans, Europeans put greater weight on luck and smaller weight on individual effort.[3] Europeans correspondingly favor extensive redistribution and social protection schemes. Americans, for their part, tend to focus on equality of opportunity and tolerate much larger amounts of inequality.

There is a second, subtler reason for the absence of convergence in institutional arrangements: Different elements of a society's institutional configuration tend to be mutually reinforcing. Consider, for example, how Japanese society provides its citizens with social protection. Unlike Europe, the Japanese government does not maintain an expensive welfare state financed by transfers from taxpayers. Instead, social insurance has been provided in the postwar period through a combination of elements unique to Japanese-style capitalism: lifetime employment in large enterprises, protection of agriculture and small-scale services ("mom-and-pop" stores), government-organized cartels, and regulation of product markets.

All of these affect other parts of the institutional landscape. One implication of these arrangements is that they strengthen "insiders" (managers and employees) relative to "outsiders" (shareholders). This necessitates a particular corporate governance model. In Japan, "insiders" have traditionally been monitored and disciplined not by shareholders but by banks (Aoki 1997). In the United States, by contrast, the prevailing model of shareholder-value maximization privileges profits over the interests of insiders and other stakeholders. But the flip side is that profit-seeking behavior is constrained by the toughest antitrust regime in the world. It is difficult to imagine governments in Europe or Japan humiliating their premier high-tech company as the United States has done with Microsoft.

With such mutual dependence among the different parts of the institutional landscape, anything short of comprehensive change can be quite disruptive and is therefore difficult to contemplate in normal times. The result is what economists call "path dependence" or "hysteresis": if the institutional setup performs reasonably successfully (and often even when it does not), it gets locked in.

The last major category of reasons for institutional diversity has to do with the special needs of developing nations. Sparking and maintaining economic growth often requires institutional innovations that can depart significantly from American or Western ideals of best practice. Consider China again, the most spectacular case of success in the developing world in the last quarter century. A western-trained economist advising China in 1978 would have advocated a complete overhaul of the socialist economic regime: private property rights in land, corporatization of state enterprises, deregulation and price liberalization, currency unification, tax reform, reduction of import tariffs and elimination of quantitative restrictions on imports. China undertook few of these, and those that it did take on (such as currency unification and trade liberalization) were delayed for a decade or two after the onset of high growth. Instead, the Chinese leadership devised highly effective institutional shortcuts. The Household Responsibility System, Township and Village Enterprises, Special Economic Zones, and Two-Tier Pricing, among many other innovations, enabled the Chinese government to stimulate incentives for production and investment without a wholesale restructuring of the existing legal, social, and political regime.[4]

The Chinese experience represents not the exception, but the rule. Transitions to high growth are typically sparked not by comprehensive transformations that mimic best-practice institutions from the West but by a relatively narrow range of reforms that mix orthodoxy with domestic institutional innovations. South Korea and Taiwan since the early 1960s, Mauritius since the early 1970s, India since the early 1980s, and Chile since the mid-1980s are all examples of this strategy.[5]

INSTITUTIONAL DIVERSITY VERSUS DEEP INTEGRATION

When economists talk about obstacles to global economic integration, they typically have in mind things like import tariffs, quantitative restrictions on trade, multiple currency practices, restrictive regulations on foreign borrowing and lending, and limitations on foreign ownership. The past few decades have witnessed unparalleled reduction in such barriers; all have been eliminated or slashed across the globe. With these textbook impediments gone, one would have expected national economies to become seamlessly integrated with each other. But, to their surprise, economists have discovered that economic integration remains seriously incomplete.

To be sure, the volume of cross-border trade and investment flows has increased enormously in recent decades. Yet when measured against the benchmark of *national* markets, international markets remain highly fragmented. A well-known study calculated that the volume of trade between two Canadian provinces is twenty times larger than that between a province and an adjacent United States (McCallum 1995: 615–23). While later academic studies have reduced this large differential, they all confirm that national borders strongly depress economic exchange (Anderson and van Wincoop 2001).

A different strand of the literature has focused on a related phenomenon trade economists call "missing trade." It seems that the flow of "factors" (such as labor and capital) embodied in trade falls far short of what standard theories of comparative advantage predict. In other words, given the very large differences in relative factor endowments across countries and the apparent absence of formal trade barriers, there is much less trade in "factor services" than there should be.[6]

From an economic standpoint, what matters is not the volume of trade as much as the degree of price convergence across national markets. Here, too, the results have been disappointing. Prices of tradable commodities often diverge substantially across national markets, even after the effects of indirect taxes and retail costs are eliminated from the comparison. Moreover, when prices do converge to a common level, it happens slowly, over several years.[7] All of these pieces of evidence point to the same conclusion: National borders continue to act as serious impediments to economic exchange, even though formal trade barriers have all but disappeared.

Surprisingly, much the same is true in capital markets. In a world of free capital mobility, households would invest in internationally diversified portfolios, and the location of enterprises would not affect their access to financing. In reality, financial markets are subject to a large amount of "home bias." Investments in plant and equipment are constrained by the availability of domestic savings, and portfolios remain remarkably parochial (Tesar and Werner 1998). Even in periods of exuberance, *net* capital flows between rich and poor nations fall considerably short of what theoretical models would predict. And in periods of panic, which occur with alarming frequency, capital flows from North to South can dry up in an instant. Global foreign exchange markets may turn over $1.5 trillion in a single day, but any investor who acts on the assumption that it's all one big capital market out there and that national borders don't matter would be in for a big surprise—sooner rather than later.

How do these border barriers arise? We are now in a position to link this discussion with the concept of institutional diversity. Institutional and jurisdictional discontinuities serve to segment markets just as transport costs or import taxes do. In effect, national borders, and the institutional boundaries that they define, impose a wide array of transaction costs.

These transaction costs arise from various sources. Most obviously, contract enforcement is more problematic across national boundaries than it is domestically. Domestic courts may be unwilling—and international courts may be unable—to enforce a contract signed between residents of two different countries. This problem is particularly severe in the case of capital flows, as financial contracts inevitably involve a *promise* to repay. Thus, a key reason why more capital does not flow to poorer countries is that there is no good way such a promise can be rendered binding across national jurisdictions (short of resorting to the gunboat diplomacy of old).

Often, contracts are implicit rather than explicit, in which case they require either repeated interaction between the parties or side constraints to make them sustainable. Within a country, implicit contracts are often embedded in social networks which provide sanctions against opportunistic behavior. One of the things that keep businessmen honest is fear of social ostracism. The role played by ethnic networks in fostering cross-border trade and investment linkages (for example, among the Chinese in Southeast Asia) suggests the importance of group ties in facilitating economic exchange (Casella and Rauch 1997). But such ties are hard to set up across national borders in the absence of fortuitous ethnic and other social linkages.

Transaction costs also result from national differences in regulatory regimes and in the rules of doing business—informal as well as legal. That such differences raise the cost of buying, selling, and investing across national boundaries is one of the most frequent complaints heard from businessmen around the world. Indeed, these differences are increasingly to blame for trade conflicts. When the United States blames Japan's retail distribution practices for keeping Kodak out of the Japanese market, or when it lodges a complaint against the EU in the WTO because of Europe's ban on hormone-treated beef, the issue is the impact that different styles of regulation have on international trade. Conversely, developing nations have won WTO judgments against the United States, centering on gasoline standards and fishing regulations enacted pursuant to the U.S. Clean Air Act and the U.S. Endangered Species Act, on the grounds that these regulations were harmful to their sales of gasoline and shrimp, respectively.

Conflicts like these have forced trade negotiators to focus on harmonizing such regulatory differences away. A major victory in the Uruguay Round of GATT was the Agreement on Trade Related Aspects of Intellectual Property Rights (TRIPs), which established a minimum patent length requirement. In the area of international finance, a similar push is under way through the promulgation of a series of codes and standards on corporate governance, capital adequacy, bank regulation, accounting, auditing, and insurance.

Many economists have concluded that the way forward is to offset the centrifugal forces created by institutional boundaries through international agreements, harmonization, and standard setting. But as I have argued earlier, diversity in national institutions serves a real and useful purpose. It is rooted in national preferences, sustains social compacts, and allows developing nations to find their way out of poverty. Eliminating this diversity might not be beneficial even if it were possible.

THE POLITICAL TRILEMMA OF THE GLOBAL ECONOMY

The discussion of this trilemma draws heavily on Rodrik 2000. The inevitable tradeoffs are illustrated in figure 8.1, which shows what I call The Political Trilemma of the Global Economy. The key point is that the nation-state system, deep economic integration, and democracy are mutually incompatible. We can have a full measure of, at most, two out of these three. If we want to push global economic integration much further, we will have to give up either the nation state or democracy (that is, mass politics). If we want to maintain and deepen democracy, we will have to choose between the nation state and international economic integration. And if we want to keep the nation state, we will have to choose between democracy and international economic integration.

Why is this so? Consider a hypothetical perfectly integrated world economy in which national borders do not interfere with exchange in goods, services, or capital. Transaction costs and tax differentials would be minor; convergence in commodity prices and factor returns would be almost complete. Is such a world compatible with the nation-state system? Can we maintain the nation-state system while ensuring that national jurisdictions—and the differences among them—do not hamper economic transactions? Possibly, if nation states were to focus above all on becoming attractive to international markets. In that case, national jurisdictions would be geared toward maximizing international commerce and capital mobility. Domestic regulations and tax policies would be either harmonized according to international standards, or structured to minimize any hindrance to international economic integration. And the only public goods provided would be those compatible with integrated markets.

It is possible to envisage a world of this sort. In fact, many commentators believe we actually live in it. Many governments today do compete in pursuing policies that they believe will earn them market confidence and attract trade and capital inflows: tight money, small government, low taxes, flexible labor legislation, deregulation, privatization, and general openness. These are the policies that make up what Thomas Friedman (1999) has aptly termed the Golden

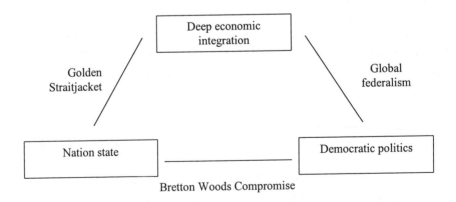

FIGURE 8.1 *The political trilemma of the world economy*

Straitjacket. However, the price of maintaining national sovereignty while markets become international is that politics has to be exercised over a much narrower domain. Friedman writes (1999: 87):

As your country puts on the Golden Straitjacket, two things tend to happen: your economy grows and your politics shrinks. . . . [The] Golden Straitjacket narrows the political and economic policy choices of those in power to relatively tight parameters. That is why it is increasingly difficult these days to find any real differences between ruling and opposition parties in those countries that have put on the Golden Straitjacket. Once your country puts on the Golden Straitjacket, its political choices get reduced to Pepsi or Coke—to slight nuances of tastes, slight nuances of policy, slight alterations in design to account for local traditions, some loosening here or there, but never any major deviation from the core golden rules.

The crowding out of democratic politics is reflected in the insulation of economic policymaking bodies (central banks, fiscal authorities, and so on); the disappearance or privatization of social insurance; and the replacement of developmental goals with the need to maintain market confidence. Once the rules of the game are set by the requirements of the global economy, domestic groups' access to, and their control over, national economic policymaking is necessarily restricted.

No country went farther down this path in the 1990s than Argentina, which looked for a while like the perfect illustration of Friedman's point. Thus, Argentina's ultimate collapse carries an important lesson for this discussion.

Argentina undertook more trade liberalization, tax reform, privatization, and financial reform than virtually any other country in Latin America. It did everything possible to endear itself to international capital markets. Obtaining an investment-grade rating—the ultimate mark of approval by international markets—became the Argentine government's first priority.[8] Why did international investors nonetheless abruptly abandon the country as the decade was coming to a close?

The financial markets did not fear any lack of commitment by the political leadership to repay foreign debt. Indeed, during the course of 2001 President de la Rúa and economy minister Cavallo abrogated their contracts with virtually all domestic constituencies—public employees, pensioners, provincial governments, bank depositors—to ensure their ability to pay 100 percent of their obligations to foreign creditors. What ultimately sealed Argentina's fate in the eyes of financial markets was not what Cavallo and de la Rúa were doing, but what the Argentine people were willing to accept. Markets grew skeptical that the Argentine congress, provinces, and common people would continue to tolerate the policy of putting foreign obligations before domestic ones. And in the end, the markets were proven correct. After a couple of days of mass protests and riots just before Christmas, Cavallo and de la Rúa had to resign.

So Argentina's lesson has proved to be a different one than Friedman intended. Mass politics casts a long shadow on international capital flows, even when political leaders single-mindedly pursue the agenda of deep integration. In democracies, when the demands of foreign creditors collide with the needs of domestic constituencies, the former eventually yield to the latter. In time of crisis, democracy escapes from the Golden Straitjacket.

A conceivable alternative would be to drop nation states rather than democratic politics. This is the solution dubbed "global federalism" in figure 8.1. Global federalism would align jurisdictions with markets and remove border effects. In this scenario, politics would not wither: instead, it would relocate to the global level.

This is the United States model expanded on a global scale. Although there are some differences in regulatory and taxation practices among the American states, the presence of a national constitution, national government, and federal judiciary ensures that U.S. markets are truly national. The European Union, while very far from a federal system at present, is headed broadly in the same direction. Under global federalism, national governments would not necessarily disappear, but their powers would be severely circumscribed by supranational legislative, executive, and judicial authorities.

If this sounds unlikely, it is. The historical experience of the U.S. shows how tricky it is to establish and maintain a political union among states that have major differences in their institutional arrangements. One such difference—slavery—came close to destroying the United States. Today, the uncertain development of political institutions within the EU and the persistent complaints about their democratic deficits reflect the same kinds of difficulties, which persist even though the EU encompasses nations at similar income levels and with similar historical trajectories. Thus, global federalism is at least a century away.

The third and final option is to sacrifice the goal of deep economic integration. I term this the Bretton Woods compromise. The essence of the Bretton Woods-GATT regime was that countries were free to dance to their own regulatory tune so long as they removed a number of border restrictions on trade and generally did not discriminate among trade partners.[9] They were allowed (indeed encouraged) to maintain restrictions on capital flows, since Keynes and the other architects of the postwar economic order regarded a system of free capital flows as incompatible with domestic economic stability.

Under this regime, although impressive trade liberalization was undertaken during successive rounds of GATT negotiations, many barriers remained in place. Services, agriculture, and textiles were effectively left out of the negotiations. Various clauses in the GATT (on anti-dumping and safeguards, in particular) permitted countries to erect trade barriers when their industries came under severe competition from imports. And developing country policies were effectively left outside the scope of international discipline.

Until the 1980s, these loose rules left enough space for countries to follow divergent paths of development. Western Europe chose to integrate separately and to erect an extensive system of social insurance. Japan developed its own distinctive brand of capitalism, combining a dynamic export machine with large doses of inefficiency in services and agriculture. China grew by leaps and bounds once it recognized the importance of private initiative, even though it flouted every other rule in the guidebook. Much of the rest of East Asia relied on industrial policies that have since been banned by the WTO. And until the late 1970s, scores of countries in Latin America, the Middle East, and Africa generated unprecedented economic growth rates by following import-substitution policies that insulated their economies from the world economy.

The Bretton Woods compromise was largely abandoned in the 1980s as the liberalization of capital flows gathered speed and trade agreements began to break through national borders. We have since been trapped in an uncomfortable and unsustainable zone somewhere between the three nodes of figure 8.1. Neither of the alternatives to the Bretton Woods compromise provides a real way forward. The Golden Straitjacket may be feasible, but it is not truly desirable. Global federalism may be desirable, but it is not feasible.

Therefore, if the principal locus of democratic politics is to remain the nation state, we have no choice but to settle for a thin version of globalization—to reinvent the Bretton Woods compromise for a different era.

Alternative Globalizations: The Case of Labor Mobility

Global economic rules are not written by Platonic philosopher-kings, or even by the present-day pretenders to that status, the academic economists. If WTO agreements were truly about "free trade," they could all be replaced with a single sentence: "Trade shall be free." The reality, of course, is that politics plays a role in WTO agenda setting and rule making, and those with power get more out of the system than those without it. Nonetheless, advocates of globalization often present their position with an air of inevitability, as if it has a natural logic that only economic illiterates would reject. Recognizing that there is a multiplicity of feasible globalizations—as there is a multiplicity of institutional underpinnings for capitalist economies—would have an important liberating effect on our policy discussions.

So what kind of globalization should we strive for? There are important choices to be made. Consider the following thought experiment. Imagine that the negotiators who recently met in Doha to hammer out an agenda for world trade talks really meant it when they said that the new round of GATT would be a "development round," that is, one designed to bring maximum benefit to poor countries. What would they have focused on? Increasing market access for developing country exports? Reform of the agricultural regime in Europe and other advanced countries? Intellectual property rights and public health in developing nations? Rules on government procurement, competition policy, environment, or trade facilitation?

The answer is none of the above. In all these areas, the benefits to developing countries are slim at best. The biggest bang by far would lie in something that was not even on the agenda at Doha: relaxing restrictions on the international movement of workers. This would produce the largest possible gains for the world economy, and for poor countries in particular.

We know this because of a basic principle of economics: *The income gains that derive from international trade rise with the square of the price differentials across national markets.* What does this mean? Compare the treatment of markets in goods and financial assets, on the one hand, with that of markets for labor services on the other. The removal of restrictions on markets for goods and financial assets has narrowed (though it has not eliminated) the price differentials in these markets. Remaining price differences rarely exceed 2 to 1. By contrast, markets for cross-border labor services are still very restricted. Consequently, wages of similarly qualified individuals in the advanced and low-income countries often differ by a factor of 10 or more. Applying the economics principle enunciated above, liberalizing cross-border labor movements could be expected to yield benefits that are roughly 25 times larger than those that accrue from liberalizing the flow of goods and capital!

It follows that even a minor liberalization of international labor flows would create gains for the world economy that are much larger than the combined effect of all the post-Doha initiatives under consideration. Consider, for example, a *temporary* work visa scheme that would allow skilled and unskilled workers from poor nations to work in the rich countries for three to five years, to be replaced by a new wave of inflows upon return to their home countries. Even if the workers involved amounted to no more than 3 percent of the rich countries' labor force, a back-of-the-envelope calculation indicates that such a system would easily yield $200 billion annually for the citizens of developing nations. That is vastly more than the existing estimates of the gains from the current trade agenda. The positive spillovers that the returnees would generate for their home countries—the experience, entrepreneurship, investment, and work ethic they would bring back with them and put to work—would increase these gains even further. Equally important, the economic benefits would accrue directly to workers from developing nations. We would not need to wait for trickle-down to do its job.

So relaxing restrictions on cross-border flows through temporary work contracts and other schemes has a compelling economic logic. But is it politically feasible? Probably not. Such flows might hurt workers in advanced countries, especially low-skill workers. Worries about crime and other social problems (as well as racism) have made immigration unpopular in many rich countries. And some might fear that increased labor flows could enhance the threat of terrorism in our post–September 11 world.

Yet the political factors at work are subtler than is commonly supposed. Imports from developing countries—which are, in economic terms, nothing other than inflows of embodied labor services—create the same downward pressure on rich country wages as immigration, and that has not stopped policymakers from bringing trade barriers down. The bias toward trade and investment liberalization (and against increased labor flow) is certainly not due to domestic politics. The typical voter in the advanced countries is against both immigration *and* imports: less than 20 percent of Americans and Britons favor unrestricted imports, about the same as the fraction that believe immigration is good for the economy. In any case, a well-designed scheme of labor inflows could address many of the social and economic worries among citizens in the host countries. For example, we can imagine aligning the skill mix of guest workers with that of the natives, allowing in no more than one construction worker or fruit picker, say, for every physician or software engineer.

Thus, substantial liberalization of trade and investment has taken place not because it is popular among voters, but because the beneficiaries (mainly multinational firms and financial enterprises) have organized successfully and become politically effective. By contrast, increased labor flows have no well-defined constituency in the advanced countries. When a Turkish worker enters the European Union or a Mexican worker enters the United States, the ultimate local beneficiaries can't be identified in advance. Only after the worker lands a job does his employer develop a direct stake in keeping him in the country. This explains why, for example, the U.S. federal government devotes a large amount of resources to border controls to prevent *hypothetical* immigrants from coming in, while it does little to deport employed illegals or fine their employers once they are actually inside the country. The same principle also explains why the rare relaxations on labor restrictions come about only in response to pressure from well-organized interest groups such as agricultural producers or Silicon Valley firms.

The lesson? Political constraints can be malleable. Economists have remained excessively tolerant of the political realities that underpin restrictions on international labor mobility, even as they continually decry the protectionist forces that block further liberalization of an already very open trading system.[10]

To ensure that labor mobility produces benefits for developing nations, it is imperative that the regime be designed in a way that generates incentives for return to home countries. While remittances can be an important source of income support for poor families, they are generally unable to spark and sustain long-term economic development. Designing contract labor schemes that are truly temporary is tricky, but it can be done. There need to be clear incentives for all parties—workers, employees, and home and host governments—to live up to their commitments. One possibility would be to withhold a portion of workers' earnings until return takes place. This forced saving scheme would ensure that workers would come back home with a sizeable pool of resources to invest. In addition, there could be penalties for home governments whose nationals failed to comply with return requirements. For example, sending countries' quotas could be reduced in proportion to the numbers that fail to return. That would increase incentives for sending government to do their utmost to create a hospitable economic and political climate at home and to encourage their nationals' return.

In the end, it is inevitable that the return rate will fall short of 100 percent. But even with less than full compliance, the gains from reorienting our priorities toward the labor mobility agenda would remain significant.

CONCLUSION

I have highlighted two shortcomings of current discussions of globalization. First, there's too little appreciation of the fact that economic globalization is necessarily limited by the scope of desirable institutional diversity at the national level. Under current political configurations and economic realities, deep integration is impossible.

Second, there are many models of feasible globalization, each with different economic implications. As my discussion of labor mobility illustrates, we are not focusing currently on the areas of economic integration with the biggest potential gains.

The hopeful message is that it is possible to squeeze much additional mileage out of globalization, while still remaining within the boundaries of feasibility I have identified

ACKNOWLEDGMENT

The author is grateful to Michael Weinstein for very helpful suggestions.

ENDNOTES

1. Keynes 1933 used this phrase in an essay written in the midst of the Great Depression, in which he appeared to have given up on free trade altogether: "I sympathize with those who would minimize, rather than those who would maximize economic entanglements between nations. Ideas, art, knowledge, hospitality and travel should be international. But let goods be homespun whenever it is reasonable and conveniently possible, and above all let finance be primarily national."

.2. On the limited convergence in effective patterns of corporate governance, see Mayer 2000; Khanna, Kogan, and Palepu 2001. On divergence in labor market institutions, see Freeman 2000.

3. For an analysis of differences in attitudes toward inequality, see Alesina, di Tella, and MacCulloch 2001.

4. See the discussion of "transitional institutions" in Yingyi Qian (forthcoming).

5. This is why studies such as Dollar and Kraay 2001, which purport to show that "globalizers" grow faster than "non-globalizers," are so misleading. The countries used as exemplars of "globalizers" in these studies (China, India, Vietnam) have all employed heterodox strategies, and the last conclusion that can derived from their experience is that trade liberalization, adherence to WTO strictures, and adoption of the "Washington Consensus" are the best way to generate economic growth. China (until recently) and Vietnam were not even members of the WTO, and together with India, these countries remain among the most protectionist in the world.

6. The standard reference on this is Trefler (1995: 1029–1046).

7. For example, Bradford (2000: table 2) estimates that domestic prices of motorcycles and bicycles exceed world prices by 100% in the U.K., 76% in Belgium, and 60% in Germany. See also the survey by Rogoff(1996: 647–68).

8. The much-maligned currency board system, originally aimed at stopping inflation, eventually became part of this same strategy. A government that was prevented from printing money, it was felt, would be more attractive to foreign investors.

9. John Ruggie has written insightfully on this, describing the system that emerged as "embedded liberalism." See especially Ruggie 1983.

10. Characteristically, two recent books by prominent academic defenders of free trade pass over the question of labor mobility entirely. See Bhagwati 2002 and Irwin 2002.

REFERENCES

Alesina, Alberto, Rafael di Tella, and Robert MacCulloch. 2001. "Inequality and Happiness: Are Europeans and Americans Different?" National Bureau of Economic Research Working Paper 8198, Cambridge, MA (April).

Anderson, James E. and Eric van Wincoop. 2001. "Gravity with Gravitas: A Solution to the Border Puzzle." National Bureau of Economic Research Working Paper 8079, Cambridge, MA (January).

Aoki, Masahiko. 1997. "Unintended Fit: Organizational Evolution and Government Design of Institutions in Japan." In M. Aoki et al., eds. *The Role of Government in East Asian Economic Development: Comparative Institutional Analysis*. Oxford: Clarendon Press.

Barzun, Jacques. 2000. *From Dawn to Decadence: 500 Years of Western Cultural Life.* New York: Perennial.

Bhagwati, Jagdish. 2002. *Free Trade Today*. Princeton: Princeton University Press.

Bradford, Scott. 2000. "Paying the Price: The Welfare and Employment Effects of Protection in OECD Countries." Economics Department, Brigham Young University. Unpublished paper (December).

Casella, Alessandra and James Rauch. 1997. "Anonymous Market and Group Ties in International Trade," National Bureau of Economic Research Working Paper W6186 (September).

Dollar, David and Aaart Kraay. 2001."Trade, Growth, and Poverty" (Development Research Group, The World Bank), unpublished paper (March).

Freeman, Richard. 2000. "Single Peaked vs. Diversified Capitalism: The Relation Between Economic Institutions and Outcomes," National Bureau of Economic Research Working Paper 7556, Cambridge, MA, February 2000.

Friedman, Thomas L. 1999. *The Lexus and the Olive Tree*. New York: Farrar Strauss Giroux.

Irwin, Douglas A. 2002. *Free Trade Under Fire*, Princeton: Princeton University Press.

Keynes, John Maynard. 1933. "National Self-Sufficiency." *Yale Review*.

Khanna, Tarun. Joe Kogan, and Krishna Palepu. 2001. "Globalization and Corporate Governance Convergence? A Cross-Country Analysis." Harvard Business School, unpublished paper (October).

Mayer, Colin. 2002. "Corporate Cultures and Governance: Ownership, Control, and Governance of European and US Corporations." Said Business School, Oxford University, unpublished paper (March). 2002.

McCallum, John. 1995. "National Borders Matter: Canada-U.S. Regional Trade Patterns." *The American Economic Review* 85, no. 3. (June): 615–23.

Qian Yingyi. Forthcoming. "How Reform Worked in China." In Dani Rodrik, ed. *In Search of Prosperity: Analytic Narratives on Economic Growth*. Princeton: Princeton University Press.

Rodrik, Dani. 2000. "How Far Will International Economic Integration Go?" *Journal of Economic Perspectives* (Winter).

Rogoff, Kenneth S. 1996. "The Purchasing Power Parity Puzzle." *Journal of Economic Literature* 34, no. 2 (June).

Ruggie, John. G. 1983. "International Regimes, Transactions, and Change: Embedded Liberalism in the Postwar Economic Order." In Stephen D. Krasner, ed. *International Regimes*, Ithaca: Cornell University Press.

Tesar, Linda and Ingrid Werner. 1998. "The Internationalization of Securities Markets Since the 1987 Crash." In R. Litan and A. Santomero, eds. *Brookings-Wharton Papers on Financial Services*. Washington DC: The Brookings Institution.

Trefler, Daniel. 1995. "The Case of the Missing Trade and Other Mysteries." *The American Economic Review* 85, no. 5. (December).

9

Globalization and Patterns of Economic Growth

JEFFREY D. SACHS

THIS CHAPTER EXPLORES cross-country patterns of growth in the era of globalization—specifically, during 1980–98, a period in which world trade and financial flows increased enormously, more rapidly than economic output. I'll argue that the world economy is divided between a "core" that is characterized by self-driven (or *endogenous*) economic growth, and the rest of the world, whose long-term growth depends on the economic linkages with the core. These linkages are influenced not only by institutional characteristics that economists have long studied (such as openness of trade and protection of property rights) but also by physical endowments and geography.

In studying the growth of the non-core economies during 1980–98, I've found that rapid growth was associated with some simple population patterns, including a large population, a high proportion of the population near the coast, and a low proportion of the population in regions of malaria transmission. I've also found that non-core economies have benefited from government policies aimed specifically at promoting science and technology. I conclude with a brief description of the policy implications of these findings, and some suggestions as to what the developed nations can do to help more developing nations benefit from stronger economic growth in the years to come.

WHY GROWTH RATES DIFFER

During the past two decades, globalization has been fueled by technology (especially the falling costs of transportation, communication, and information processing) as well as by the political and economic choices of national governments (notably through liberalization of trade policy, the dismantling of socialist development models, and the growth of international institutions such as the World Trade Organization). As a result, most of the world is increasingly integrated in a global market system. But economic performance has varied greatly from country to country, with developing countries struggling in particular.

Mainstream economists have long held that a core set of economic institutions is crucial to high rates of economic growth. That core set includes the rule of law, protection of private property, macroeconomic stability, and openness of trade. The central goal of the so-called Washington consensus, which has guided the policy advice of the Bretton Woods institutions during the past two decades, has been to encourage economic reforms to create such institutions. Recently, several economists have even argued that such institutions are *all* that is needed to promote rapid growth, claiming that other factors influence growth only by influencing these economic institutions (Acemoglu, Johnson and Robinson 2001; Easterly and Levine 2002).

I favor an alternative hypothesis, which my co-authors and I have advocated in a series of recent studies (for example, Gallup, Mellinger and Sachs 2000 and Sachs 2003b). We contend that growth is a function of economic institutions and physical endowments as well as geography. In this view, different parts of the world have preferred paths to growth, by dint of their specific structural— and especially geographic—characteristics. Moreover, I suggest that the Washington consensus gives short shrift to the importance of science and technology policies in the design of national economic policy (Sachs 2003a).

THE CORE AND THE PERIPHERY IN THE GLOBAL ECONOMY

Theoretical models of economic growth typically study a "representative" economy, which implies that all economies follow a shared path of economic development. Models of endogenous growth, in which long-term growth is fueled by technological innovation, have become particularly popular in the past decade, following the path-breaking work of Paul Romer (1986, 1990). The endogenous growth framework, which stresses the virtuous circle of rising incomes and increasing incentives to innovate, no doubt has great relevance for the world's richest economies. And since these countries carry so much weight in global GNP, this model is important for understanding overall world economic growth.

Empirical evidence also supports the endogenous growth framework. After decades of growth accounting (following Robert Solow 1957), it's clear that the long-term fuel of economic growth in the leading economies has been technological advance spurred by the growth of incomes.

Often overlooked, however, is that endogenous growth is not a general pattern that characterizes growth in all economies. Instead, it is found in countries with only about one-sixth of the world's population.

Most economies produce little if any technological innovation. Instead, the poorer countries tend to achieve technological advancement through the diffusion of technologies originally developed in the high-income, endogenous growth economies. This diffusion takes place through many channels, including foreign direct investment in technologically lagging economies, importation of capital and consumer goods from the advanced economies, flows of knowledge among scientists and engineers, and joint ventures and other strategic relations between enterprises from high-income and low-income economies.

Patent statistics make this point abundantly clear. The U.S. Patent Office records the country of residence of the lead inventor on all utility patents granted in the United States (a utility patent is graned for a new "process, machine, article of manufacture, or composition of matter, or any new and useful improvement thereof" as defined by the U.S. Patent and Trademark Office). In the *Global Competitiveness Report 2001–2002*, McArthur and Sachs (2002) identified the core economies as the 24 economies, mainly from North America, Western Europe, and East Asia, which produce 15 or more U.S. utility patents per year per million population.[1] There were 18 such economies in 1980, and six more countries joined the core between 1980 and 2000.[2] Since I am studying growth from 1980 to 1998, I define the core economies as of 1980, the base year of the empirical analysis. In that year, the 18 core economies had 16 percent of the word's population and 99 percent of all utility patents awarded in the United States.

These figures make it obvious that the non-core economies rely almost entirely on the core economies for new technologies (although, with concerted policies, they may also graduate from the ranks of technology adapters to technology producers and thereby join the core). The non-core economies absorb technologies from the core through trade, imports of capital goods, foreign direct investment, and flows of ideas and skilled workers. The rate of absorption is affected by geography, as well as by social and ethnic networking (for example, national diasporas that transmit technologies across borders), strategic/military relations, geopolitical linkages, and patterns of foreign assistance.

At least four key factors influence geographical diffusion of technologies and eventual upgrading to membership in the core:

- *Low-cost transporting to major markets.* For bulk commodities, shipping by sea is much cheaper than shipping by land or air. Coastal access thereby affords a significant cost advantage. Similarly, proximity to major markets (contiguity by land, or short shipping distances by sea) reduces transportation costs and shipping times, and facilitates cross-border management.

- *Shared ecology.* Many technologies—in health, agriculture, construction, energy use, and other areas—are ecologically specific. Diffusion is therefore faster within rather than across ecological zones. In practice, temperate regions outside of the core areas are often the first to be able to utilize new technologies from the core.[3]

- *Supportive economic and political institutions.* Technology diffuses faster to regions that protect financial, physical, and intellectual property, and that harmonize their institutions with those of the core. Core economies often give special market privileges to such states, especially when they are geographic neighbors.

- *Development strategy oriented toward science and technology.* The capacity to upgrade technology is enhanced by government sponsorship of research and development, support for higher education, and use of industrial policies such as aggressive tax holidays to promote inflows of foreign direct investment in high-technology industries.

A Growth Equation for the Non-Core Economies

To test the importance of these factors, and to compare the growth of the core and non-core economies, I examined the growth rates of 111 countries with available data for 1980 to 1998. I defined economic growth as the average annual percentage change in per capita GNP adjusted for purchasing power parity (PPP), using the GNP estimates of Angus Maddison (2001) for this purpose. (See the "Technical Note" at the end of this chapter for details.)

I examined the growth of the core and non-core economies separately, as they are likely to have different underlying determinants. The growth of the 18 core economies was remarkably uniform, as shown in the map in figure 9.1. All 18 core countries achieved positive growth during the period, varying from a low of 0.7 percent per year in Switzerland to 2.5 percent per year in Norway (where the growth rate was obviously bumped up by the discovery and exploitation of Norway's North Sea oil). Another relatively fast-growing core economy, Japan, slowed dramatically in the 1990s. Otherwise, the growth rates among the core economies are so uniform that there are no clear and robust determinants of the cross-country differences in growth among these economies.

The growth rates of the 93 non-core economies in our sample vary from a low of minus 9.6 percent per year (Iraq) to a high of 6.0 percent per year (Korea). A significant number of the economies (43) experienced negative growth during

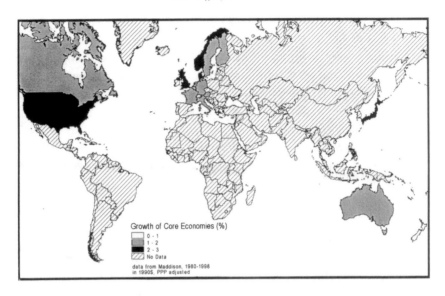

Growth of Core Economies (%)
- 0 - 1
- 1 - 2
- 2 - 3
- No Data

data from Maddison, 1980-1998
in 1990$, PPP adjusted

FIGURE 9.1   *Growth of core economies (%)*

this interval—that is, an absolute decline in measured PPP GNP per capita from 1980 to 1998—while 50 experienced positive growth. A map of the growth rates of the non-core economies is shown in figure 9.2. (Countries that do not appear either in figure 9.1 or 9.2 are not covered by the Maddison data).

I then tested that proposition that the growth rates of the non-core economies depend on five variables described below:[4] For statistical purposes, the variables are defined in table 9.1, which appears at the end of the chapter, as does a technical note on the statistical analysis.

Governance. The main growth prescription of most mainstream economists is institutional reform, instilling the rule of law, the sanctity of contracts, open trade, and protection of private property into a particular economy. Following the standard in growth models, I measured governance with an index that averaged country ratings across several dimensions, and then averaged the index over the years 1985–90. In addition, I separated out countries (Haiti, Iraq, South Africa, and Yugoslavia) subject to an international regime of sanctions for some portion of the period 1980–98.

Size of the Domestic Economy. Even in a world of open trade, relatively small economies may suffer a shortfall in growth for lack of adequate domestic market scale.[5] This is less likely to be true for small economies tightly integrated with their immediate rich neighbors (such as Luxembourg and Switzerland), but is much more likely to be the case for small developing countries far away

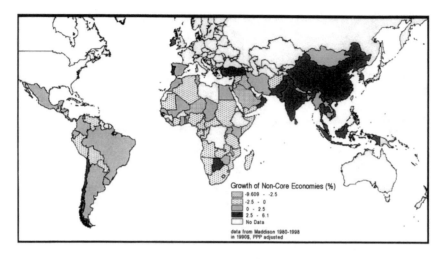

FIGURE 9.2 *Growth of non-core economies (%)*

from major markets. Therefore, in addition to controlling for the level of per capita income in 1980 in the statistical analysis, I used a measure of the total size of the country's market in 1980.

Proximity to Core Markets. Proximity to core markets should also matter, since foreign investment and trade flows are inversely correlated with distance. A country is deemed proximate to core markets if it has either a land border with a core economy or lies within close shipping distance and with at least 80 percent of the population living within 100 kilometers of the coastline (and thus strongly impacted by sea-based trade). For these noncontiguous economies, I deemed a country within close shipping distance as follows: Central America and the Caribbean (close to the United States); Mediterranean coastal economy (close to Europe); and the ASEAN Countries, China, Hong Kong, Taiwan, and Korea (close to Japan). Applying the criteria of coastal population, the countries that are proximate to the core economies are shown in figure 9.3.

Ecological Characteristics. Earlier research has shown that tropical ecological zones have a growth deficit relative to temperate ecological zones. This may relate to intrinsic differences in productivity, or to the fact that the core economies are located in the temperate zone so that global innovative activity is highly oriented to the specific problems of temperate-zone economies (regarding disease, agriculture, building materials, construction techniques, and so forth).

Perhaps the greatest difference between ecozones lies in disease ecology, with malaria by far the most significant tropical disease. I therefore separate out regions in which underlying disease ecology favors the high level of transmission

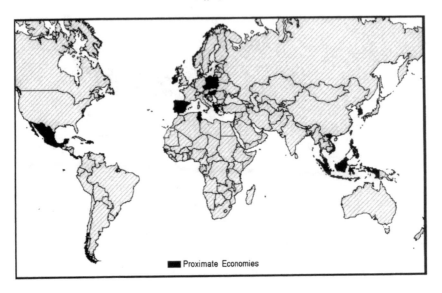

FIGURE 9.3   *Proximate economies*

of falciparum malaria. Around 90 percent of annual malaria deaths in the world occur in that region.[6] The level of effort of malaria control exhibited by each country was not considered in assigning this variable.

Science and Technology Orientation. The governance indicators regarding rule of law, property rights, and so forth, do not measure a government's commitment to technological upgrading. I have observed elsewhere that a few developing countries, notably Israel, Korea, Singapore, and Taiwan, put a great stress on investments in science and technology, while most developing countries do not (Sachs 2003a).

Unfortunately, it is not easy to measure these inputs of government policy. As an imperfect alternative, I include in the statistical analysis a measure of a country's actual patenting performance during the first half of the period of observation. Specifically, I use the average annual number of utility patents per million population granted to lead inventors residing in each country by the U.S. Patent Office during 1985–90.

The basic results of the statistical analysis are shown in the first column of table 9.1. They provide overwhelming evidence that three kinds of factors play a role in economic success or failure during the period of globalization:

- *Initial per-capita income.* As expected, poorer countries grow more rapidly than richer economies (other things being equal).

- *Governance and policy.* Well-governed countries outgrow poorly governed countries, while countries facing sanctions from the international community severely under-perform the rest by nearly 5 percentage points of growth per year on average. (The latter fact may, of course, reflect both the direct effects of sanctions and the underlying factors of civil strife and poor governance that led to the imposition of sanctions.)
- *Structural characteristics and physical geography.* Malarious regions underperform non-malarious regions. Regions that are located within easy shipping distance of core countries grow faster than countries that are geographically separated from developed countries. Large economies outperform small economies.

GROWTH REGRESSION ESTIMATES

Thus, the proposition that only institutions affect economic growth is simply false. Countries may be severely disadvantaged by their underlying geographical conditions. According to the estimates, a non-proximate, malarious country will under-perform a proximate non-malarious country by fully three percentage points of growth per year (with two percentage points due to the vulnerability to high malaria transmission, and one percentage point due to the lack of proximity to the core markets).

The finding that a malarious ecology impedes economic growth is consistent with the commonplace observation that life expectancy at birth is an important positive predictor of subsequent economic development (holding constant the initial income and other variables), as well as the more recent finding that the total fertility rate is a negative predictor of subsequent growth. This is because malaria transmission tends to reduce life expectancy, while malaria transmission also tends to raise the total fertility rate (while holding per capita income constant in both cases).[7]

There are two very large outliers in the regression. North Korean growth fell 6.1 percentage points per year below the predicted rate, while Botswana's growth was 5.4 percentage points higher than predicted. But even if these two anomalous countries are dropped from the analysis (second column of table 9.1), the economic implications of the analysis remain exactly the same. Indeed, the statistical results are strengthened.

The analysis shows that a country's level of patent activity strongly influences growth. Each ten patents per million population raise the growth rate (other things being equal) by 3.1 percentage points per year. I surmise (without proving it here) that developing countries that pursued intensive investments

TABLE 9.1 *Dependent Variable: Annual Percentage Growth between 1980 and 1998 (t-statistics in parentheses)*

Regression 1	Market Size
Regression 2	(LY80)
Initial Income (LYPC80)	0.32 (2.00)
−1.58 (5.03)	0.41 (2.93)
−1.64 (6.19)	
	Malarious ecology
Governance (GOVERN8590)	(MALHIGH)
6.95 (3.46)	−2.10 (3.24)
6.32 (3.65)	−2.45 (4.44)
International Trade Sanctions	Patents per Capita, 1985–90
(SANCTIONS)	(PAT8590)
−4.75 (4.36)	0.29 (1.95)
−4.97 (5.39)	0.31 (2.45)
Proximity to Core Markets	Constant
(PROXIMATE)	6.63 (2.26)
1.08 (2.06)	6.72 (2.71)
0.97 (2.17)	

*Variables:

GOVERN8590: an index of governance that averaged country ratings across several dimensions, and then averaged the index over the years 1985–90.

SANCTIONS: 1 for Haiti, Iraq, South Africa, and Yugoslavia, which were subject to an international regime of sanctions for some portion of the period 1980–98; 0 otherwise.

LY80: market size, GNP measured according to PPP (Purchasing Power Parity).

PROXIMATE: 1 for a proximate economy and 0 otherwise). Proximity = 1 if country has either a land border with a core economy or lays within close shipping distance and with at least 80 percent of the population living within 100 kilometers of the coastline. Close shipping distance determined as follows: Central America and the Caribbean (close to the United States); Mediterranean coastal economy (close to Europe); and the ASEAN Countries, China, Hong Kong, Taiwan, and Korea (close to Japan). See Figure 9.3. .

MALHIGH. This index was based upon the climatic and mosquito characteristics of each country, set equal to 1 in high-risk regions, and 0 otherwise.

PATPM8590: the average annual number of patents per million population granted to lead inventors residing in each country by the U.S. Patent Office during 1985–90.

Number of countries
80
78

Adjusted R^2
0.51
0.63

in developing science and technology reaped large benefits in subsequent economic growth.

As mentioned earlier, six economies made the transition from non-core to core status between 1980 and 2000, using the criterion of at least 15 patents per million population: Hong Kong, Iceland, Ireland, Korea, Singapore, and Taiwan. (Note that Iceland, with a population smaller than 300,000, is not included in our analysis.) In all of these cases, one can identify specific government policies—investments in higher education, tax breaks for inward foreign investments in high-tech industries, government subsidies for research and development activities—designed to spur the high technology sectors of the economy.

I also stress that even in today's globalized trading system, the size of national economies still matters for growth in a non-core economy. Our sample includes nine core economies with populations over 50 million in 1980, and eight of these experienced positive economic growth (Nigeria was the only exception). There were another 11 non-core economies with populations between 20 million and 50 million, and only two of these experienced negative growth (Philippines and South Africa). Yet of the non-core economies with 1980 population less than 20 million, a remarkable 40 experienced absolute declines in income. Many of these are in sub-Saharan Africa, but of the 43 sub-Saharan countries with 1980 population less than 20 million, fully 20 had a negative growth rate.

The conclusion is inevitable: Size of national economy still matters for developing countries. This strengthens the case for regional economic integration, since the broader market access this creates can serve as a substitute for a large domestic economy. Unfortunately, even free trade areas don't usually achieve the same degree of market integration as national economies.

SOME IMPLICATIONS FOR MANAGING GLOBALIZATION

The standard macroeconomic viewpoint on globalization is that all countries are running the same race. Thus, one strategy fits all: Each country should improve its business environment and economic institutions so as to achieve the highest possible rate of economic growth, consistent of course with other social objectives such as equity, environmental sustainability, and the like. According to this viewpoint, there is no magic to economic development; it's merely a matter of national organization and politics to make the breakthrough to sustained economic growth.

The results described in this chapter, which offer merely a taste of more elaborate arguments that can be found elsewhere, suggest that all countries are *not* in fact running the same race. Some developing countries are blessed by proximity to major markets, a large-scale domestic economy, a malaria-free environment, and so forth, which gives them a significant advantage relative to others in achieving sustained economic growth.

These factor endowments may affect economic growth both in obvious and not-so-obvious ways. Natural resource deposits, for example, may affect the level and growth rates of national economies in unexpected directions. A significant flow of export earnings from a key primary commodity such as oil or diamonds may raise the level of income but also slow its growth as a result of the so-called Dutch-disease phenomenon (commodity exports raise the value of the currency, thus making manufactured goods less competitive relative to other nations and decreasing exports).

However, even when the Dutch disease tends to make natural resource holdings a curse rather than blessing for long-term growth, the discovery and exploitation of new resource deposits is likely to be associated with a burst of economic growth. Thus, Equatorial Guinea was the fastest-growing economy in the world during the 1990s, as the result of the exploitation of newly discovered offshore oil deposits.

Geographical conditions may matter in even more subtle yet important ways. Climate conditions, for instance, may be conducive to high or low crop productivity, or to a high or low incidence of various diseases. Tropical ecological zones are particularly subject to a high prevalence of certain vector-borne diseases, most importantly malaria (Gallup and Sachs 2001), while tropical food production may be plagued by special problems associated with high tropical temperatures.[8] Since most innovations take place in the high-income temperate-zone economies of the United States, Western Europe, and East Asia, developing countries in tropical ecological zones are probably less able than their counterparts in temperate ecological zones to adopt the technological advances of the rich countries.

The findings described in this chapter suggest not only a different view of the patterns of growth (and decline) evident in the world economy since the onset of globalization, but also a different perspective on policy choices and objectives.

If, for example, malaria is truly a major barrier to economic growth, then significant investments in malaria control should become a priority in any integrated strategy for economic development of a malarious region (especially in sub-Saharan Africa).

Countries not proximate to major markets also require special attention, perhaps in the form of improved infrastructure investments in ports and telecoms, or in improved market access to the core economies.

Small countries probably need to focus more attention on regional integration and harmonization. The recent re-launch of African cooperation in the African Union may turn out to be an important step in this regard, if the new Union moves beyond words to true economic integration.

Perhaps most fundamental, however, should be the recognition that the world is divided between a small group of economies that experience robust endogenous growth and a much larger part of the world that relies on technological diffusion from the core economies as its underlying engine of growth.

This division suggests many additional characteristics about the world economy, such as a bias in science and technology toward the needs and wants of people living in temperate-zone economies as opposed to people living in tropical economies. It also probably offers the most important reason for the growing divergence in incomes between the richest and poorest countries. The former are in a virtuous circle of science-led development, while the latter are stuck in a downward Malthusian spiral, in which growing populations are not relieved by improvements in technology.

But the most important implications for global policy are two. First, we should be working much harder than we are now to make sure that the global scientific community addresses the special needs of the poorest countries in health, agriculture, and other ecologically specific areas.

Second, national development strategies, especially of the middle-income countries, should include special efforts to bridge the divide between the users of technologies developed abroad in the core countries. A few countries, such as Korea and Taiwan, have made the transition from non-core to core, but very few other developing countries have pursued science-and-technology policies in the past two decades and thereby prepared themselves for that leap. Many others need to begin to move in this direction if significant improvements in global economic growth are to occur.

TECHNICAL NOTE

In conducting the analysis described in the chapter section entitled "A Growth Equation for the Non-Core Economies," I considered a set of 150 economies with population greater than 1 million in 1980, and then reduced the sample to 80 non-core countries based on the available data.

I defined growth between 1980 and 1998 as

$$GR8098 = (1/18)*\ln(Ypc1998/Ypc1980)*100.$$

As in almost all cross-country growth studies, the basic regression equation was in the following form:

$$GR8098_i = a0 + a1 \ln(YPC80_i) + b[PRIME] Z_i$$

The annual growth rate was regressed on the initial per capita income (in logarithms) and the vector Z of country-specific variables described in the body of the chapter. We expected "conditional convergence" to apply: that is, holding constant the vector of Zs, an initially poorer country should experience faster growth than an initially richer country as it takes advantage of the initial income gap (which presumably also signals a higher marginal productivity of capital, holding constant the Zs).

We estimated the regression for the set of non-core economies for which the relevant right-hand side data are available. This led to a regression estimation for 80 countries.

ACKNOWLEDGMENT

The author wishes to thank Mr. Gordon McCord, Director of the Earth Institute at Columbia University, for excellent research assistance.

ENDNOTES

1. Australia, Austria, Belgium, Canada, Denmark, Finland, France, Germany, Hong Kong, Iceland, Ireland, Israel, Italy, Japan, Korea, Netherlands, New Zealand, Norway, Singapore, Sweden, Switzerland, Taiwan, and United States. Andorra and St. Kitts and Nevis meet the criteria but were not included because of their small size.

2. Italy is on the borderline, with 14.2 patents per million in 1980. We include Italy among the core economies in 1980. The newcomers include Hong Kong, Iceland, Ireland, Italy, Korea, and Singapore.

3. As an important example, new agrobiotechnologies involving genetically modified organisms have diffused from the United States most rapidly to other temperate-zone regions including Argentina, Brazil, and China.

4. The data set used in this study is available from the author.

5. If, as typically supposed, there are fixed costs in setting up off-shore production facilities, then large markets are likely to attract a disproportionate share of foreign direct investment.

6. It is true, therefore, that MALHIGH acts largely as a regional dummy variable for Sub-Saharan Africa, and therefore may be proxying for other characteristics of the region in addition to malaria per se. But for those who argue that governance is the essence of Africa's problem, we note again that the MALHIGH variable is significant even in the presence of direct measures for governance.

7. The effect of malaria on total fertility presumably works through infant and child mortality. Countries in which infant and mortality rates are high tend to exhibit high total fertility rates as parents compensate for the risk of child mortality by having a larger number of children.

8. Such problems include low levels of soil organic matter, high rates of nighttime respiration, high rates of evapotranspiration and therefore water stress, and instability of climate patterns related to El Niño and other tropical climate fluctuations.

REFERENCES

Acemoglu, Daron, Simon Johnson and James Robinson. 2001. "The Colonial Origins of Comparative Development: An Empirical Investigation." *American Economic Review*. Vol. 91, no. 5 (December): 1369–1401.

Barro, Robert J. 1997. *Determinants of Economic Growth: A Cross-Country Empirical Study*. Cambridge: MIT Press.

Easterly, William, and Ross Levine. 2002. "Tropics, Germs, and Crops: How Endowments Influence Economic Development." NBER Working Paper #9106. Cambridge, MA: NBER, August.

Gallup, John, Andrew Mellinger, and Jeffrey Sachs. 2000. "Climate, Coastal Proximity, and Development." in Gordon Clark, et. al. (eds). *Oxford Handbook of Economic Geography*. Oxford: Oxford University Press.

———— and Jeffrey Sachs. 2001. "The Economic Burden of Malaria." Supplement to *The American Journal of Tropical Medicine & Hygiene*. 64, nos. 1, 2 (January/February).

Lee, Jong-Wha and Robert Barro.2002. "IMF Programs: Who is Chosen and What are the Effects?" NBER Working Paper #8951. Cambridge, MA: NBER, May.

Maddison, Angus. 2001. *The World Economy: A Millennial Perspective*. Development Centre of the Organization for Economic Cooperation and Development. Paris: OECD.

McArthur, John and Jeffrey Sachs 2002. "The Growth Competitiveness Index." In *World Economic Forum, The Global Competitiveness Report 2001–2002*. Oxford: Oxford University Press, 2002.

Romer, Paul M. 1986. "Increasing Returns and Long-Run Growth." *Journal of Political Economy* 94 (October): 1002–1037.

————. 1990. "Endogenous Technological Change." *Journal of Political Economy* 98 (October): S71–S102.

Sachs, Jeffrey D. 2003a. "The Global Innovation Divide." In Adam B. Jaffe, Josh Lerner and Scott Stern, eds. *Innovation Policy and the Economy, Vol. 3*. Cambridge: MIT Press.

————. 2003b. "Institutions Don't Rule: Direct Effects of Geography on Per Capita Income." NBER Working Paper 9490 (February).

Solow, Robert. 1957. "Technical Change and the Aggregate Production Function." *Review of Economics and Statistics* 39 (August): 312–20.

10

The Overselling of Globalization

JOSEPH E. STIGLITZ

GLOBALIZATION HAS BEEN SOLD as bringing unprecedented prosperity to the billions of people who have remained mired in poverty for centuries. Yet, globalization faces enormous resistance especially in the Third World. Why so?

I argue that globalization today has been oversold. I use the term to refer not only to closer integration of the countries and peoples of the world that has resulted from the lowering of transportation and communication costs and manmade barriers but also to the particular policies, the so-called "Washington Consensus," that have been commonly associated with globalization and pushed on developing countries by the international economic institutions. The Washington Consensus emphasizes deregulated markets over government provision, balanced budgets and open borders across which goods and capital freely flow and flexible exchange rates. Many critics of globalization, like myself, are opposed not so much to globalization per se but to the particular set of policies that the International Monetary Fund (IMF) and the United States have imposed on developing countries in recent decades. During this period, many countries have suffered rising poverty, a degraded environment, and destroyed indigenous culture. Right or wrong, critics blame globalization. Moreover, there is widespread feeling that globalization, as practiced, has undermined democratic processes.

Managing globalization well, so that its potential benefits emerge, will not be easy. But unless we understand how globalization came to be misshapen we will not succeed in reforming globalization. In the discussion below (and in my recent book *Globalization and Its Discontents*), I argue that the failures are related to governance of globalization. By and large, the rules of globalization have been determined by the advanced industrial countries, for their interests, or more precisely for the interests of special interests, often to the marked disadvantage of the developing world. Within the democracies of the advanced industrial countries, there is a natural set of checks and balances. Financial and commercial interests loom large, but other groups—like labor and consumers and environmentalists—have a seat at the table. In the international arena this is not so. At the IMF, it is only finance ministers and central bankers whose voices are heard; in trade negotiations, it is the trade ministers, often with close links to commercial and financial interests, who set the agenda. In the last section of the chapter, I make recommendations how to right the governance structure for globalization.

THE ADVOCATES' CASE FOR GLOBALIZATION

Advocates of globalization cite studies which show that globalization, with increased trade and investment, has brought increased growth. According to this line of argument, countries that have remained removed from the world economy, like Myanmar, do worse than countries that have become integrated. True. And as I shall explain shortly, the most successful countries in the world, those in East Asia, had development strategies based on globalization, absorbing technology from more advanced countries and basing growth on exports. But these countries did not follow the prescriptions of the IMF or United States Treasury. They governed globalization in their own way. By contrast, the countries that followed the IMF's "Washington Consensus" policies performed worse. It is this observation which supports the conclusion that the problem is not with globalization per se, but with the way it has been managed.

Finally, the advocates of globalization, when confronted with its glaring failures, try to shift the blame to the developing countries themselves, to their corruption, to their lack of transparency, to their lack of resolve in making the needed reforms. There is little doubt that such problems exist in developing countries, just as they do in developed ones, and that had they addressed their problems, the countries would be better off. But recognizing these problems does not really answer the critics of globalization. With or without corruption, globalization, in the way that it has been carried out, has worsened the plight of many developing countries. I believe that Argentina would have had its crisis, given its fixed exchange rate, given the fall in the value of the currency of its trading partners, especially that of Brazil, even if there had been absolutely no corruption. The crisis might have happened a little later (or a little sooner), and it might have been a little less severe. But there would have been a crisis. And indeed, I have argued elsewhere that the policies, including the privatizations, that the IMF imposed on Argentina made the crisis worse. In many countries around the world, the privatizations that the IMF pushed increased corruption. In short, the failures of globalization cannot really be blamed on the policies of the developing world.

Some Unsung Successes of Globalization

Certain aspects of globalization have been undersold. Globalization of knowledge has, especially where governments have undertaken active technology policies, narrowed the knowledge gap between developed and less developed countries, a gap that is every bit as important in explaining disparities in income as the gaps in resources.[1] The rapid spread of knowledge across boundaries has led to improved health, contributed to the global reduction and in some cases even elimination of diseases. Global civil society—of which the global protest movements against globalization is but one manifestation—has had some notable successes: The Land Mines' Treaty was adopted, over the strong opposition of the U.S. Defense Department; the Jubilee 2000 movement succeed in pushing through debt relief for 27 of the poorest countries in the world, after years of foot dragging on the part of the IMF (during which only seven countries[2] succeeded in getting debt relief.) The global environmental movement succeeded in putting a halt to most large dam projects. Globalization of ideas, such as democracy and transparency and women's rights, has had enormous impacts on political processes throughout the world. These all represent dimensions of globalization which are too seldom noted.

East Asia

Moreover, China and many of the other countries in East Asia succeeded in rapid growth—accompanied by large reductions in poverty—largely as a result of globalization: their economic strategies, in which government played a key role, was based on the expansion of exports, taking advantage of international markets. But these countries did not follow the full array of Washington Consensus policies. They liberalized gradually (rather than quickly), they had government-managed industrial policies, and used government , rather than the private sector, create new state enterprises[3] They did not open themselves up to short-term capital flows early in their development; some, like China, still have not done so; others, such as Malaysia, re-imposed controls during the global financial crisis. In short, the countries of East Asia grew because of globalization, but they managed it, shaped it, in ways that worked to their own advantage. It was only when they succumbed to outside pressures, only when they went faster and further with liberalization, that globalization no longer served them well.

Reconsidering the Economic Theory of Globalization

The economist's case for globalization is straightforward: it increases a country's economic well-being because it increases the country's opportunities. Countries have more markets in which to sell their goods, more sources of funds with which to finance their development, and access to new technologies to enhance productivity. Increasing opportunities, almost by definition, enhance well-being.

But there are serious flaws in this textbook conclusion. For starters, even if globalization improved average living standards, it would hurt some sectors badly. Second, the notion that free trade and investment promote growth relies on the assumption that private markets are competitive and well functioning. When that is not the case—a circumstance rampant in the world—then, as my work and that of other economists makes clear, trade can actually make an economy worse-off. Economists have recently explored the consequences of imperfect markets. Take the issue of imperfect contracting—so-called agency problems, when one person (a manager) acts on behalf of another person (an owner) though their incentives are not perfectly aligned.

Take as a second example reputation problems—for example when buyers must rely on the reputation of the seller to gauge the quality of products. In both cases, the fact that buyers and sellers do not share the same information may worsen as the size of the market increases, and the ability of mechanisms, like reputation, to control markets may be weakened. Because globalization increases the size of markets it can, under circumstances of imperfect markets, devastate innocent economies.[4] Take Latin America. When the United States Federal Reserve Bank hiked interest rates to unprecedented levels in the early 1980s, it threw Latin America into a decade-long tailspin.

Third, with globalization comes new rules, often imposed by industrialized countries, that can strip countries of the economic tools they could previously use to manage economic crises.

Fourth, globalization, as implemented, has driven down the price of products that poor countries export relative to the price of goods they import. Agricultural subsidies in the North increase production, thereby lowering the price of products grown in the South.

As shown below, globalization has been hijacked by the special interests in the North, often at the expense of the poor in developing countries. For example, the

1994 international trade accord, known as the Uruguay Round, has been hailed in the North as a major achievement. But a recent report says it made the poorest region of the world, Sub-Saharan Africa, worse off (by some 2 percent), largely as a result of the worldwide effects cited earlier.

CULTURAL AND OTHER NONECONOMIC MATTERS

The critics of globalization do not limit themselves to purely economic benefits and costs. While my main focus is on those economic costs and benefits, I want to say a few words about the democracy and culture.

Democratization

Advocates claim that globalization has led to an increased number of democracies. And certainly, the globalization of ideas has been an important impetus. But critics argue that globalization, as practiced, has undermined effective and stable democracy. The economic instability associated with globalization (which I describe more fully below) has brought with it political instability: democratically elected governments have been toppled in Ecuador and Argentina.

A key component of the Washington Consensus has been to open developing countries to short-term speculative capital flows. But that hands foreign investors enormous sway over political processes within these countries. If foreign investors dislike a political candidate, for example, they can withhold loans, driving up interest rates and toppling the economy into depression. In other words, foreign investors can increase the cost of electing someone they dislike.[5] While the recent election of Lula in Brazil shows that capital markets do not yet have a full veto, the episode nonetheless demonstrates that capital markets enter into the political process in an important way. Advocates of globalization say that this is all to the good—foreign investors provide a check against populism and help push good economic policies. But critics point out that the financial markets are myopic; they are not concerned with long-term economic growth, let alone broader social values. They feel happier if an economy has a smaller fiscal deficit, even if that leaves larger unmet education or infrastructure needs.

While the virtues of democracy have been lauded, countries have been told to cede the most important economic decisions, those concerning monetary policy, to independent central banks, focusing exclusively on inflation.

International trade agreements have ceded further authority, e.g. about a wide range of issues, the full impact of which remains uncertain.

For countries that have to turn to the international financial institutions in times of crisis there has been an even greater derogation of economic sovereignty. The conditions imposed go well beyond those which an ordinary bank would impose to ensure repayment. The internationally imposed settlements go deep into areas which, in countries like the United States, would be viewed as quintessentially political. Even when countries might have undertaken policies on their own, there is something unseemly in today's world of having those policies forced on a country, particularly given yesteryear's colonialism. To those in the developing world, the image of the cross-armed Michel Camdessus, the IMF's Managing director, standing over Indonesia's Suharto, as he put his signature on a piece of paper, seemingly signing away that country's economic sovereignty, will never be forgotten.[6]

Issues which are of intense political debate in the United States and Europe—whether to privatize Social Security or whether the central bank should worry about unemployment and growth along with inflation—are taken off the political agenda. The IMF tells the country what to do. I thought it was wrong for the IMF to tell crisis-stricken countries in Asia what to do in 1997 and 1998. The role of the economic adviser is to describe the consequences of alternatives, including the risks, and who benefits and who loses. The political process—not some international bureaucrat lacking any political accountability—should make the decision. But another reason I reacted so strongly to what the IMF and Washington told Asian countries to do is that the advice was not, in many cases, based on economic science.

Globalization and Collective Action

International institutions and agreements should focus on areas where global collective action is desired. Private markets sometimes fail, and for well-understood reasons. Two stand out. First, externalities—transactions between country A and country B can affect an innocent third part, country C. Second, public goods. Take public health. Country A's ability to control the spread of AIDS can affect the well being of the population of its neighbors. Or take the reasons why the IMF was created. Economic crisis in one country can drag down another (an externality) and foreign investors, because of imperfections in the way that international capital markets work, cannot be counted on to supply funds to expand fiscal policy even if the country would almost certainly repay its loans. There is, then, a need for global collective action to overcome financial crises.[7]

In recent years, the United States has refused even to discuss issues of global collective action in these terms. The worry is that both the American government, and the special interests which seem to have such influence over its international economic policy, see international agreements as instruments for advancing their particular interests. Consider the way the United States handled negotiations over the rules governing the protection of patents over pharmaceutical drugs. The United States did not ask what would be the intellectual property arrangement which will best balance the interests of buyers and sellers of drugs or which rules would best promote the advancement of science and provide needed medicines at affordable prices to those in developing countries. From the perspective of the U.S. Trade Representative, negotiating the intellectual property agreement, the question was what kind of protection would best advance the interests of American pharmaceutical companies. Even many in America's scientific community thought that the agreement may have impeded advances in science; and while both the Council of Economic Advisers and the Office of Science and Technology Policy raised strong objections to the positions of the U.S. Trade Representative seemed to be taking in the recently completed round of international trade talks, special interests prevailed.

Ceding Sovereignty

Thus, democratic processes even in countries with strong democracies, like the United States, have been undermined by globalization, in the manner in which it has proceeded. Of course, any international agreement can be thought of as ceding some sovereignty. There are gains from global collective action, and these gains may well exceed the costs, including the costs associated with ceding sovereignty. But when international agreements are more designed to advance particular interests, and are not motivated at all by considerations of global public goods or externalities, it is more likely that the costs exceed the benefits.

In some areas, recent trade treaties have raised the issue in a stark form. In the 1993 NAFTA trade agreement among the United States, Canada, and Mexico, a foreign firm that believes that a domestic regulation impairs its profitability can directly sue for compensation. The backdrop for that provision is the fact that regulations can reduce the value of corporate assets, just as a tax can, and such reductions are referred to as regulatory takings. In the United States, conservatives have repeatedly attempted to enact legislation to make government pay whenever there is such a taking, arguing that such takings represent a deprivation of basic property rights. The courts, however, have almost always said that there is no right to compensation, and legislators, both at the federal and state levels, have ignored these pleadings. Yet in some recent international trade agreements, foreign firms seem to have been able to extract for themselves what firms inside the economy could not. Critics worry that if this becomes widespread, it will impair the ability of government to enact regulations, for instance, concerning health or safety or the preservation of the environment or natural resources. Unknowingly, citizens seem to have given up important rights, hidden away inside a trade bill that was supposed to open up economic opportunities.

Much of the fine print in the 1994 (Uruguay round) international trade accord has yet to be fully interpreted, let alone adjudicated in courts. Some of the provisions—such as the requirement that preference should be given to measures that have "the least disruptive effect on trade" (Understanding on the Balance-of-Payments Provisions of the General Agreement on Tariffs and Trade 1994, article no.2)—threaten the autonomy of countries to set prudent rules. Will the United States, for example, be able to set new accounting rules, in the wake of the Enron scandal, without fear of retaliation if foreign firms cannot meet its tighter standards?

Weakening of the Nation State

For the past two centuries or so, the center of political power in most of the successful countries has been at the level of the nation state. Globalization has entailed a loss of national sovereignty. International organizations, imposing international agreements, have seized power. So have international capital markets as they have been deregulated. And there are a variety of indirect ways in which globalization has impaired the effectiveness of the nation state, including the erosion of national cultures (to be discussed shortly). In early stages of development, the United States and most other countries relied heavily on tariffs, because they were easy to collect. But under the World Trade Organization (WTO) and especially under pressure from the IMF, countries are restricted in their ability to raise revenues through tariffs, and without good sources of revenue, the state is weakened. Some claim that this may be one of the purposes of these restrictions.

So though globalization may not be the cause of the failed states, it has in some instances contributed to them.

Lack of Democracy at the Global Level

One of the arguments for devolution and decentralization is that real democracy is more effective at the local level. More voices can be heard. There are greater incentives for democratic participation. The converse argument presumably also holds: democratic processes would be expected to be weaker at the global level, and there is ample evidence supporting this conclusion. The international economic organizations are organized, and behave, in ways which are troubling. Voting at the IMF is not based on one-person-one-vote, or one-country-one vote, or even one dollar-one-vote. Voting power is partly related to historical accident, mostly the size of the economy fifty years ago, with some adjustments since. China enjoys less voting power than its economic and political size deserve. The United States, in effect, wields a veto. And while the IMF makes decisions which affect every aspect of society, only the voices of finance ministers and central bank governors are heard.

Other protections that we have come to expect of democratic institutions are missing. The organizations are not transparent—there is no freedom of information act. Some of the critical protections against conflicts of interest are missing.

Similarly, dispute-resolution mechanisms at the WTO, lack the openness that we have come to expect in judicial processes in the United States and the United Kingdom. And there is a fear that the judges, while they might be experts in trade law, may not give enough weight to other concerns, whether they are good corporate governance, health and safety, or the environment.

Of course, none of this would make a difference if there were technocratic solutions to the problems confronting globalization; that is, if the were a set of international rules of the game such that everyone were better off with that set of rules than any other But that is not the case. The lack of democracy means that the rules that get promulgated are not necessarily those that would have emerged had there been a more open, democratic process.

Weakening Social Cohesion and Weakening Local Culture

Finally, the critics of globalization worry about the impact on social cohesion, on traditional values, on culture. But advocates of globalization either pay little attention to these concerns, or see this as another attempt to intrude on consumer sovereignty: just as there should be competition for goods, there should be competition for "cultures"; and if McDonald's triumphs, so be it. Critics see society from a more holistic perspective: contrary to Adam Smith's claims, especially in this arena, individual choices may not lead to socially desirable outcomes. Globalization's critics claim that, in focusing on economics, advocates have too narrow a vision of society, and of individual welfare.

The Intertwining of Economics, Politics, and Society

My focus is on economic issues, but I should emphasize that one cannot fully separate out economic issues from a broader context. If the critics are right—

and I believe that they are—there are adverse economic consequences from the failure to pay due attention to the noneconomic factors. For instance, the IMF failed to take into account the predictable (and predicted) consequences during the Asian financial crisis in 1997 and 1998 of combining measures that cracked down on the economy, leading to huge increases in unemployment and reductions in real wages, and measures to eliminate food and fuel subsidies. And all the austerity was imposed at the same time that billions were being provided to bail out international creditors.[8] The political and social turmoil led to the flight of capital and high-skilled individuals, creating adverse economic consequences for years to come. The same story applies to Argentina.

More broadly, there are a large number of social interactions, which have effects on economic relations. Consider the most basic of economic relationships, a simple contract. It takes "trust" to achieve enforcement without recourse to litigation. Such trust results from repeated cooperative relations. But predictable repetition of commercial interactions is undermined by rapid economic change brought on, for example, by sky-high interest rates imposed by the IMF in the aftermath of economic crisis.[9] Social control mechanisms are extremely important in ensuring the efficient use of common resources, including environmental resources.[10]

Critics of globalization argue that social relations are not just means to economic ends. They are ends in themselves and means to ends which have more than economic dimensions. The international community has recognized the importance of preserving biodiversity from the ravages of unrelated markets. Neither can markets be trusted to protect ethnic and cultural diversity.[11]

A century ago, Social Darwinism had its advocates. Those who could not compete in the modern world should be left to wilt on their own. To do otherwise was to interfere with the progress of civilization. Today, within Western democracies, there are few adherents to these extremist views; even conservatives advocate compassion. But in the global arena, some of the more ardent advocates of globalization advance a position not far different from that of social Darwinism: tough luck for the cultures that cannot survive in the face of the forces of globalization; they should be left to die, and the quicker the death the better. Some in the anti-globalization camp take an almost equally extreme position: recognizing the possible fragility of cultures, the possibility that local customs and practices, no less than local firms, will be overridden by the onslaught of globalization, which too often is simply seen as Americanization, they wish to have none of it. In *Globalization and its Discontents*, I support a third way, between these two extremes—one which seeks to control the pace of globalization to give societies time to adapt. It is often the encounter of differing civilizations, the fusion of cultures, that gives rise to the greatest episodes of human creativity. But the pace and manner needs to be controlled so that the process vanquishes neither.

Unbalanced Globalization

Within the narrow realm of economics, critics of globalization have charged that globalization reflects an unbalanced political agenda. I largely agree.

Global Inequities

The inequities are highlighted by the international trade regime. The North has insisted that the South eliminate subsidies and open up their markets, yet the North has maintained protectionist measures and huge agriculture subsides: the United States recently increased these subsidies with a $190 billion farm bill. Agriculture subsidies in the North are so large that they exceed the entire incomes of sub-Saharan Africa. The question naturally arises: how can these poor countries compete?

One of the alleged achievements of the Uruguay Round was the application of free-trade principles to services. But what services? Opening up markets to financial services, to the comparative advantage of the United States, was included. But opening markets to maritime and construction services, of interest to developing countries, was excluded.

The intellectual property regime embedded in the Uruguay Round (the so-called TRIPS agreement) reflected the interests of the pharmaceutical industry and other producers of intellectual property. In pushing for the interests of the drug companies, the 1994 accord might slow the overall pace of innovation. Knowledge itself is one of the most important inputs to the production of knowledge, and the intellectual property regime put into place makes access to knowledge by researchers more difficult. Even at the time the agreement was being negotiated, I and others at the Council of Economic Advisers worried about access to drugs by the very poor in the least developed countries—a concern that subsequent events showed was well justified, as the world watched in horror as AIDS patients in the poorest countries found their access to life-preserving drugs cut off and as the American government rallied behind the drug companies.

An Unbalanced Political Agenda

If the WTO showed most forcefully the inequities of the global regime, the IMF repeatedly showed its lack of balance, as it pursued policies that George Soros and others have labeled "market fundamentalism"—extreme reliance on unregulated private markets. The Clinton Administration, of which I was a part, reflected the imbalance as it pushed international financial institutions to pursue policies that it opposed at home. At the same time that administration was busy implementing tough financial regulations in the wake of the collapse of saving and loan banks in the 1980s, the IMF, largely controlled by the United States, pushed for sweeping deregulation of financial markets in developing countries. Similarly, while successfully opposing an amendment to the United States Constitution that threatened to rule out deficits as a tool to reverse economic contraction, the Clinton Administration backed deficit reduction in crisis-stricken East Asia. And though the administration fought off proposals that would have the United States Federal Reserve Bank focus exclusively on fighting inflation, the IMF, largely controlled by the United States, insistently called on the central banks of developing countries to adopt exactly that single-minded focus. The IMF also called on those countries to provide central banks with more independence, and less direct accountability to democratically elected politicians. While the Clinton Administration attacked the first Bush administration for the seeming belief in trickle-down economics, it supported international financial institutions that argued for policies that could, at best, be described as trickle-down plus.

While the Clinton administration resisted attempts by creditors to push creditor-friendly bankruptcy provisions into law, it backed efforts by the IMF to push bankruptcy reform on developing countries, acting as if bankruptcy law was simply a matter that should be left to technocrats ("best practice"). And, of course, what they thought of as the "best practice" closely reflected the perspectives of the financial community.

Economic science emphasizes the limitations in our knowledge and information, so that there are large risks associated with any policy. The role of the economists is to describe the risks. The role of the political process is to make the choices. Yet, critics of globalization argue that it has been used to force choices on poor countries which reflect special interests. The IMF-imposed contractionary policies on East Asia during its financial crisis hit workers and small businesses the hardest. More fundamental, deregulating capital markets before deregulating labor markets—permitting capital to pick up and leave before permitting laborers to do the same—dramatically change the bargaining strength of investors. They can take their capital and leave if they view taxes or wages as too high. Workers cannot.

THE ECONOMIC FAILURES OF GLOBALIZATION

While East Asia benefited greatly by taking advantage of globalization, elsewhere globalization has fallen far short of the promise. In developing countries, in the race between population growth and improving living standards, population won. Though the percentage of people in poverty fell, the absolute number of poor people rose. And poverty reduction occurred almost entirely in China and India, both of which deviated in central ways from the market fundamentalism of the Washington Consensus.

In Latin America, the statistics for the first full decade under reform and globalization are in. Growth rates during the 1990s were little more than half of what they were in the pre-reform decades of the 1950s, 60s, and 70s, let alone the so-called lost decade of the 1980s.[12] The rapid growth that occurred in the early part of the 1990s was not sustained. Critics of globalization might dismiss the fast growth of the early 1990s as unsustainable—just as advocates of globalization dismiss the high-flying growth during the pre-reform decades after World War II as unsustainable. And even in countries which have succeeded in growing strongly, such as Mexico, much of the gains went to the richest 30 percent of the population, and especially the top 10 percent, with many in the bottom worse off.[13]

Increased Global instability

Meanwhile, globalization has been accompanied by increased instability: close to a hundred countries have had crises in the past three decades.[14] Globalization created economic volatility, and those at the bottom of the income distribution in poor countries often suffer the most. They have no reserves to shield them from economic shocks, and the social safety nets in most developing countries are anemic.[15] With inadequate safety nets, the suffering in these crises of those who lose their jobs is enormous. As the roster of seemingly well managed countries experiencing crises, including those who were given A +'s by the IMF, grows, everyone asks, who will we be next? Among the major emerging markets, only those which have not fully deregulated their capital accounts, like India and China, have been spared. I argue that this is no accident.

INTERPRETING THE RECORD

The defenders of globalization retort that globalization could not, and was not intended to, solve all the world's problems. It could not eliminate poverty, at least overnight. The relevant question is the counterfactual: in the absence of globalization, would growth have been slower? Would poverty have fallen? These questions are always hard to answer: each country globalizes only once.

The Limits of Statistical Studies

To get around this problem, some economists conduct elaborate statistical studies, comparing the records of countries that have opened up their borders to international trade and investment to those that have not. They ask whether, on average, globalization promotes growth. Such statistical studies are fraught with problems, not the least of which is that countries are concerned with particular policies in their particular circumstances. The statistical studies often shed little light on these issues. Indeed, the studies have been part of the general process of overselling globalization. Consider, for instance, the recent World Bank studies[16] which argue that globalizers, the countries that have become more engaged internationally, have done better. The existence of a systematic relationship between engagement with the outside world and growth does not, of course, prove causality: it could be that very poor, subsistence economies have little to trade with the outside world and that they would trade little even if they were to strip away all trade barriers. Said another way, countries aren't poor because they don't trade; they don't trade because they are poor.

Moreover, any look across the performance of the countries around the world will note that East Asia was the most successful region. Its rapid growth was based on exports. In that sense the countries were globalizers. But they violated all other components of the pro-market Washington, consensus. The East Asians were slow to take down import barriers and they invoked active industrial policies. Some welcomed foreign investments. But others, like Korea, did not. Few fully opened up their capital markets to foreign investors. The new big entry into the success cases in the 1990s, India, has not fully opened up its capital markets. There are, to be sure, a few instances of successful liberalization. The frequency with which Chile is cited is evidence of the paucity of examples. But as I shall comment shortly, it is not clear how to interpret the Chilean experience.

Statistical studies that focus on policy differences among countries have ambiguous results. The most widely cited study on the impact of deregulated capital markets—using as a measure of deregulation the extent to which the actual policies pushed by the IMF were adopted—shows no significant effect on growth or investment.[17] While there have been several studies claiming that trade liberalization is systematically related to growth, Rodrik and Rodriguez have provided a devastating criticism of those studies, one to which the advocates of globalization have yet to provide a persuasive response.[18]

CASE STUDIES

What matters, in the end, are not just particular policies but combinations of policies and the circumstances and manner in which the policies are implemented. That is one of the reasons why it is often so difficult to interpret what has happened, and why most of the cross country regressions looking at particular policies (so far) have been so unconvincing.

Given the limitations on the statistical analysis, economists of one persuasion or another have had to rely on case studies, anecdotes, analytical arguments, and more broadly "theory."

Korea, India, and Chile provide examples of how those with different perspectives can look at the same country's experience and come to different conclusions. To some, such as Ann Krueger,[19] second in command at the IMF, Korea's success is a case study in the success of liberalization (the economist's term for deregulation); to others, it proved the opposite. I side far more with the latter interpretation. Its growth was based on the expansion of exports, not the removal of import duties. It did not liberalize financial or capital markets until late. To some, the collapse of Korea proved that its particular variant of a market economy, in which the government plays a central role, was prone to crony capitalism and doomed to failure. To many, the quick recovery of Korea shows that that the Korean model is sound—if its problems were as fundamental as the IMF had argued, then its problems could not have been corrected so quickly. Many market fundamentalists seemed to have wanted Korea and the other East Asia countries to fail, because their success had been based on a different model far different from the one advocated by the Washington Consensus.

Another country often cited as "evidence" of the virtues of the liberalization strategy is India. There has been robust growth since 1991, when it began liberalizing, averaging almost 6 percent per year. But critics respond that (a) it did not fully liberalize—it has yet to open its capital account—and its ability to withstand the global financial crisis, its ability to have sustained growth, rested on the fact that it only partially liberalized; (b) its growth spurt relative to other developing countries began well before the strategy of liberalization[20]; and (c) the one area of widely cited success, its "Silicon Valley" in Bangalore, was not related to its liberalization strategy, but to the traditional stress on education and the strong links between its diaspora, particularly the more well educated recent emigrants, and the home country. In this respect, India may have benefited from globalization, but it is not the part of globalization that is ever stressed. It benefited from the movement of people rather than the movement of capital or goods. Critics of globalization, in the form advocated by the United States and Western Europe, emphasize the asymmetry between free mobility of capital, which has been high on the agenda, a free mobility of labor, which is hardly mentioned (and in fact there have been efforts within the United States to restrict immigration). From the perspective of global economic efficiency, free mobility of labor has the potential to contribute as much, more to growth than free mobility of capital, though, as we note below, the distributive consequences are markedly different.

Chile is the one country that allegedly followed the Washington consensus policies, and succeeded. But even the president of Chile has suggested that it was successful because it was selective in following the advice of outsiders. Chile did some of the things that the IMF recommended, but not others. Also, it did some things that were not stressed by the Washington consensus. Its early flirtation with market-fundamentalist policies, including the deregulation of the financial system, had ended in disaster, and most of the country's debt can be traced to the financial crisis which followed. During the period of their rapid economic growth, they had restrictions on the inflow of capital; they were slow to privatize, and even today government-owned copper mines generate a substantial fraction of export earnings. These government enterprises are just as efficient as the private enterprises, but yield far more revenue to the government. And Chile emphasized education and health, promoting policies of social cohesion that are particularly important in a country with a troubled political history. To be sure, Chile undertook some of the policies that were part of the Washington consensus. It maintained sound macroeconomic policies and kept borders open to imports.

China, India, and Chile provide evidence of the role that globalization can play in enhancing growth. Each involved some form of openness to the outside world. In each case, though, the success lay in the country managing globalization, using policies that deviated in significant ways from the Washington Consensus policies.

The Theory of Capital Market Liberalization

To understand why globalization has so often failed, it is important to look at the arguments for, and against, trade and capital market liberalization. For instance, the standard argument for capital market liberalization is that removing impediments to the free flow of capital increases the efficiency of resource allocation, hence increases incomes, hence contributes to growth. Indeed, even workers benefit, as the additional capital competes for the services of workers, driving up wages. But that assumes that markets, by and large, work well, without the artificial constraint of government. But capital markets in particular are plagued with a host of imperfections, many related to imperfections of information. For example, almost no well-trained economist believes today in unregulated banking. There must be some regulation of banks. (See, e.g. Stiglitz 1993). Given the imperfections that infect capital markets, eliminating controls on short-term capital flows may well lead to greater risk, lower growth, and a less efficient allocation of resources. The empirical evidence that capital market liberalization leads to greater risk is clear.[21] Greater risk leads lenders to insist on higher interest rates, which impede growth. In economies with underdeveloped stock markets, firms that cannot afford to borrow must rely on self-finance. But that in turn means that capital will be allocated less effectively. The implication is clear. Deregulation of capital markets can hurt investment and economic growth. Countries that borrow foreign currencies short term have to put aside more into reserves to reassure investors that they will be able to get their money back when their loans come due. These reserves come at a high cost. This represents another way in which unregulated, short-term foreign investment can dampen investment and growth.[*]

The Theory of Trade Liberalization

There are similar issues associated with the arguments for trade liberalization. The simplistic argument is that any impediment to trade interferes with the efficient allocation of resources, and therefore lowers incomes. But, as economists have recently shown, the conclusion hinges critically on a false assumption, that private markets work perfectly. If it is acknowledged that people cannot buy insurance to protect themselves against financial volatility, then trade liberalization can make the economy worse off. Economic disruption that comes with heightened trade can drive investors to move their money into safe investment, with lower overall benefit to the economy.

But at a practical level, there is an even more important point: liberalization is supposed to move resources—labor in particular—from low productivity

---

[*]Technically, the problem here is that there is an externality; the firm borrowing the funds short term in foreign currency does not take into account the risks to the overall economy which are associated with that borrowing, and the societal costs of the increased reserves. Given the importance of these externalities, no wonder that resources are not well allocated. There is another market failure: countries, and firms and households within the country, cannot insure themselves against the induced risks.

uses into higher productivity uses. But if markets are not working well—perhaps because interest rates are so highs that investment does not occur—then resources idled because of competition from imports simply move from low productivity uses into unemployment. The East Asian countries paced their liberalization measures with macroeconomic policies that ensured that employment remained high. They recognized, too, that they could open up markets to imports of intermediate and capital goods, thereby lowering the costs of production for domestic firms, without incurring the dislocation of opening up markets for consumer goods.

Advocates of trade liberalization are correct that often the protectionist measures have been abused, that often they have done more to enrich a few wealthy "rent-seekers" in the countries than to promote economic development, that the infants that the "infant industry protection" was supposed to give time to grow up never did so. Industrial policies often failed. But they succeeded sometimes. It is no accident that there are few examples of countries that achieved high growth rates without taking an active role in their economy, especially by promoting education and technology and regulating the financial system.

EXPLAINING THE FAILURES

Some of the failures of globalization come from employing "wrong" economic models, in particular models based on over simplistic views of the economy, based on perfect information, perfect competition, well functioning markets, ignoring the second and third best considerations that are central. I have already provided two examples, in the discussion of capital markets and trade liberalization.

Not surprisingly, bad economic analysis leads to wrong prescriptions. What I have found surprising is the frequency with which seemingly incoherent positions have been taken. For instance, the IMF often seems to argue against government intervention in markets (that is the basis for the argument for capital market liberalization). Yet the rationale for some of its massive bailouts (which are themselves a form of massive market intervention) is market failure like contagion—the spread of financial crisis from one trading partner to another. When there is an externality like contagion, private markets do use resources effectively, and there is a possible role for government or international institutions to improve matters. The intervention should presumably not only come after the crisis occurs, but also before, to prevent the crisis. If short-term capital flows are a major cause of crises, then those flows should be regulated.

Similarly, in the East Asia crisis, the IMF recognized the problems posed by weak banks and the unwillingness of lenders to roll over loans. But their models did not include an analysis of the fact that their monetary and fiscal crackdown would throw businesses into default, cutting their demand or goods and workers and triggering a cascading economy-wide contraction. I have argued elsewhere that the IMF relied on sky-high interest rates to stabilize economics in East Asia after the onslaught of financial crises, but that the policy backfired (See Furman and Stiglitz, 1998). The interest rate spikes bankrupted many businesses, driving foreign investors away and sending the economies deeper into depression. The attempts I and others at the World Bank made to engage the IMF in discussions on these issues suggest, however, that something else was going on: they seemed less interested in alternative perspectives than they should have been.

The obvious explanation relates to the role of ideology (or to put it more mildly, "particular perspectives.") There was a belief in markets. To be sure, the IMF has a research department, one which a recent independent review commissioned by its board did not exactly award accolades.[22] But it is no accident that it did not sponsor the research of critics, like Dani Rodrik, suggesting that deregulated capital markets did not promote economic growth. To a large extent, the purpose of the research was to confirm prior beliefs, not to question them.

But that raises the question: why was it possible that this particular ideology, these particular failed models, should dominate? Economic and political analysis begins by asking: whose interests have been served and moves on to ask, why have these interests come to prevail. We thus return to the central theme: governance. The ideology reflected the perspectives of those who govern the financial community. The ideology, broadly, also reflected their interests.

Here, I should be slightly more careful. There are disparate interests within the financial community (even if there is a dominant ideology or perspective). Capital market liberalization, for instance, reflected more the interests of short-term speculators and those who marketed short-term instruments. Many of the long-term investors recognized that capital market liberalization enhanced instability. They only wanted to be sure that the regulations allowed them to take out their money. Just as there is a distinction between Wall Street and Main Street, so too there is a distinction between short-term financial investors and long-term real investors. The IMF reflects more the interests of the former than the latter.

Some counter the argument that the IMF has been pro-lender by pointing out that that lenders in fact lost considerable amounts. Bailouts were only partial. But the important point is that the IMF did not see its objective as doing everything it could to maintain the economies at as close to full employment as it could. It was far more concerned with ensuring the stability of the exchange rate and the repayment of creditors.

REFORMS

To make globalization work better, I will focus on reform of the IMF, though similar reforms could be advanced for other institutions. My proposals fall into six categories.

Basic governance

The basic problem is that we have a system of global institutions, therefore governance, but without global government. Part of the problem flows form the "chimney" structure of regulation. Trade policy is set by trade ministers, financial policy is set by finance ministers, central-bank policy is set by central-bank governors. This would not matter much if the policies set by each had no ramifications for others; no one would care if central bank governors got together and decided on mechanisms to clear checks. But IMF policies have effects that go well beyond financial markets. If the IMF pushes excessively fiscal austerity, education or health may suffer, and joblessness may increase. If it pushes for excessively tight monetary policy, excessively high interest rates, small businesses may go bankrupt and Main Street suffers. If, in another realm, international banking authorities push for rigid rules, banks may become incapable of lending come the next economic downturn—turning downturn into disaster. If the WTO adopts regulations that interfere with environmental protection, then everyone (but a select group of corporations) may suffer. As the WTO adopted an intellectual property regime, the voices of drug companies were heard more loudly than were the academics, or even disinterested public policy analysts who were concerned about impacts on the overall rate of innovation.

In the case of the IMF, there are thus two problems. Each country is represented by finance ministers and central bank governors. And the IMF has pushed for independent central banks. Increasingly, the IMF has become accountable to those who are themselves not directly accountable to voters, even as the fund pushes for policies with far-flung political impacts. Worse, only a select group of the finance ministers and central bank governors—those from the rich countries—wield real power. Indeed, one country, the United States, can veto important IMF decisions. Some argue that rich countries deserve to dominate the IMF because they bear the costs of bailouts. But in fact, IMF loans are almost always repaid and it is the taxpayers in the poor countries that bear the cost.

With senior people in the institution being political appointees, there is a high likelihood they will do their political biddings, a fact that seemed all too apparent in recent years.

I am not optimistic that the IMF and other international institutions will change anytime soon. So we must look for other reforms.

Transparency and Other Democratic Protections

Transparency—making what institutions do public—is the first needed reform. Given the remoteness from direct political accountability, especially at the IMF, where one of the two governors for each country is a central bank governor not directly politically accountable, transparency is all the more important. In the United States, there is the Freedom of Information Act, which severely limits the information that can be withheld from the public. But American citizens wishing to know what is going on in the IMF have no such recourse. Besides, the international financial institutions have been accused of pursuing an agenda that advances the interests of special interests. Knowing more about who benefits from their policies, who exerted influence in shaping their policies, can not only enable us to better assess those claims, but also to curtail such behavior. As the expression goes, sunshine is the best antiseptic.

If decisions are made in public, with appropriate prior notice, at least those who are affected can express their concerns and galvanize public support on their behalf. Transparency can help improve policy directly. When the IMF makes a forecast, it should disclose its model and assumptions so outsiders can second guess the predictions. What were the assumptions?

In addition, committee structures can affect the "voice" of other groups, creating a labor committee that has to vet all major decisions would ensure that labor's concerns are heard, even if labor did not have a formal vote.

There are other changes in the representation system for executive directors that might increase the effective voice of developing countries. Even without changing voting rights, seats could be reapportioned so that Africa gained additional representation.

Accountability

Before the IMF goes into a country with a program, it should forecast the impact not only on economic growth and the balance of trade, but also on employment and poverty. And when there are large discrepancies between what it forecasts and what happens, the institution and its employees should be held accountable. If there is disclosure about the models used, then it will become possible to identify sources of the errors and, over time, improve the models. The evaluation of the forecasts needs to be conducted by an independent agency. Some critics of the IMF have suggested that the problem is the politicization of the institution. For these critics, the appropriate reform is to make it more independent.[23] I think that is fundamentally wrong. To be sure, the charter enjoins the IMF from engaging in political actions, but the boundary between politics and economics is a fine one, and the IMF has, when it suits its purposes, not been shy about crossing that boundary. The issue of corruption was viewed as a political issue, until President James Wolfenson of the World Bank began emphasizing its adverse effect on development, a view substantiated by World Bank and other studies.[24] As I have noted elsewhere, many of the stances of the IMF on privatization, the role of central banks and other policies are as much based on politics as they are on economic analysis. Giving more power to bureaucrats that are not democratically accountable would make matters worse.

Modes of Operating

There are other changes at the IMF that are underway that have to be reinforced. For instance, it is now widely recognized that in the past, IMF imposed conditions for getting bailouts that reached into areas that were political in nature and had little to do with addressing the immediate financial crisis. There is a widespread perception that conditionality, as it has been practiced in the past, by reducing the scope for democratic determination of economic policies, undermined democracy in many of the developing countries. Conditionality went well beyond the kinds of requirements that lenders always impose designed to enhance the likelihood of repayment.

The most important change in the mode of operation would be to reflect the perspectives of economic science noted earlier: the IMF should be giving advice about the alternatives, the tradeoffs, the risks, the incidence of alternative policies. It should encourage the presentation of alternative perspectives, rather than to force through a particular perspective.

Competition

A general principle that I repeatedly observed in the years I was in the administration was that everyone believed in competition, except in their sector, in which case it was more likely that competition was destructive rather than constructive. This parallels two other principles: everyone believed that there should be no subsidies, except in their industry, and everyone believed in openness and transparency, except in their line of business. The IMF is no exception. It suppressed talk of creating an Asian Monetary Fund to handle the Asian financial crisis of the late 1990s, even though Japan had offered to donate generously to such a fund.

Regional institutions may be able to play a useful role in surveillance, providing a welcomed alternative to the staff of the IMF.

Mandate

There is a now a virtual consensus[25] that the IMF should return to focusing on its original mandate, which is helping countries in times of crisis. It should not be involved in long-term development or in transition. There should be a presumption that something is wrong if an IMF program lasts more than a couple of years: such a country has a chronic problem, not a crisis.

Reforms in the Global Economic Architecture

In the aftermath of the East Asian financial crisis, extensive discussion about global economic architecture took place among industrialized countries and major emerging economies. The one concrete step that the discussions generated concerned standards.[26] Within the developing world, there was a concern that this represented another example of the more advanced industrial countries putting new demands on them, designing standards that were insufficiently attentive to the economic situation in their countries. The full impact of these standards is not yet clear.

The recognition that weak banks had played a role in the Asian financial crisis led to a rethinking of bank regulation. It was noted that the regulatory framework in the more advanced industrial countries had contributed to the problem—banks were given an incentive for short-term lending. Excessive reliance on capital adequacy standards and stringent enforcement can backfire, leading to financial instability, since it can cause all banks in an economy to excessively cut back on lending at the same time in case of a macroeconomic shock, leading to a credit crunch.. [27] Proposed international bank reforms remain a subject for debate. .

Bankruptcy and Standstills

The most fundamental set of reforms concerns how to deal with countries which cannot repay their debts, or in which large numbers of their corporations cannot repay debts. It was the refusal of banks to roll over their loans which, for instance, precipitated Korea's crisis, and it was worries about Argentina's ability to repay its sovereign debt which precipitated its crisis.

Early in the East Asia crisis, there were discussions of standstills and bankruptcy mechanisms, but the IMF quickly dismissed these approaches. Senior IMF officials suggested that such approaches would represent a violation of the debt contract, even though bankruptcy is an implicit part of every contract. Had bankruptcies occurred sooner, I believe, the problem of bad loans could have been resolved earlier and capital flows resumed. Indeed, it was only when Korea finally negotiated a suspension of payment to foreign lenders that its exchange rate and economy stabilized. Besides, greater reliance on bankruptcy, rather than bailout, could make lenders more careful from the get go. I argued that what was required were legal reforms to facilitate the speed with which restructuring could occur, that when there are massive defaults (as was the case in the region), there are macroeconomic consequences associated with delay, and accordingly what was needed was a "super chapter 11," by which I mean an international analog to bankruptcy provisions that provide for quick and orderly resolution of debts of private corporations operating in the United States.[28]

The failure of the IMF bailout in Argentina led to a focus on the use of bankruptcy and standstills for government debt. While such discussions were prominent in the years following the 1980s debt crisis,[29] in the enthusiasm for the big bailouts of the 1990s these discussions were put aside. The IMF, in my judgment, rightly argued that there needed to be a more orderly way of resolving these debt crises and restructuring debts, and what was needed was a statutory approach. They recognized that speed was of the essence, and hence the reference to "Chapter 11." But the more relevant analogy is to provisions of United States bankruptcy codes (Chapter 9) that apply to government units and take account of the fact that governments not only have explicit obligations to creditors but also implicit obligations to pensioners and others. Moreover, the IMF, as a large creditor laying claim to preferred status, cannot play a pivotal role at any stage in the bankruptcy proceeding, other than as one of several key creditors.

The Bush Administration has argued against a statutory approach, saying all that was required was for sovereign borrowers to include voluntary clauses—known as collective action clauses—in their debt contracts providing for standstills in the wake of financial crisis. Neither theory nor evidence supports President Bush's position. If collective action clauses were all that is needed, why is it that no country relies on them to resolve bankruptcies within its borders?

In Stiglitz (2002) I provide a more comprehensive discussion of why such an approach is unlikely to work.

The Global Reserve System

There is some reason to believe that underlying much of the observed instability in the global economic system are problems with the global money supply. Every year, countries around the world have to set aside substantial amounts of money into reserves against unexpected external demands for cash—say by foreign lenders who want quick repayment when their loans come due. Because countries have to build reserves, some of their earnings cannot flow back into the system as demand for other country's products. The amounts are substantial. There are roughly $1.6 trillion held in reserves around the world. Countries like to keep reserves growing in tandem with imports and foreign denominated liabilities. If these grow at 10 percent a year, then countries need to set aside $160 billion every year. Today, they hold these reserves in a variety of forms, including gold and U.S. Treasury bills. While the United States may benefit from the increasing demand for its Treasury bills, the cost to the developing countries is high: they receive a return of 2 percent on their Treasury bills even though they could invest that money at much higher return in their own economies. It is the price for developing countries to reassure their creditors that they can cash in their investments upon demand.

Thus, the current system not only creates a downward bias, but also inequity. What has made the system work in the past is the role that the United States plays as the "deficit country of last resort." This has a resulted in the peculiar situation where the richest country spends beyond its means year in and year out. But as the United States has moved from being perhaps the largest creditor country to the largest debtor country, there is a potential for enormous global instability. If, for one reason or the other, foreigners lose temporary confidence in the United States, the dollar will weaken. With lots of international debt denominated in dollars, a falling dollar will trigger economic dislocation.

There is a simple reform that would do much to redress both the instabilities and inequities associated with the current system: the issuance of a global reserve currency, distributed primarily to poor countries. They could exchange the new currency for dollars, euros, or yen. I am proposing, in effect, to raise the world's money supply. Some of extra money would be used to build reserves of poor countries. The rest could be used to pay for education and health programs in poor countries. In the current arrangement, only the United States can print money, in effect buying more than it produces and living beyond its means. But under my proposal, poor countries would gain the same opportunity—supplying the world with money by spending beyond their means. Surely, it makes more sense for the poorest countries to spend more than they produce than it does for the United States to continue to do so. Relative to global income, now about $40 trillion, the injections of new money into the world economy will be minuscule. Worldwide inflation will not rise. But these injections of purchasing power can loom large in poor countries.

Global Public Goods

As globalization has proceeded, it is increasingly recognized that closer integration of the countries and peoples of the world leads to greater needs for global collective action. Global public goods—goods that simultaneously benefit populations of different countries—are becoming increasingly important. Among these global public goods are international security and peace (including freedom from the threat of terrorism), international economic stability and growth, public health, including protection from communicable diseases like AIDS, the global environment and global knowledge. Just as national public goods (like national defense, the benefits of which accrue within a national jurisdiction) are provided by national governments, so too global public goods must be provided by governments. The problem is that there is no assured source of finance for global public goods; currently, finance is largely derived from voluntary contributions of national governments.

The proposal described in the previous section is one way by which such goods can be financed, but there are other ways which will need to be explored.

Revenues from the Sale of Global Natural Resources. There are large bodies of economic resources which do not lie within the national boundaries. These include the minerals under the oceans and the fish within them, the potential resources in Antarctica, and the resources of the atmosphere; and perhaps eventually resources in the moon and planets. These resources rightfully belong to all of the citizens of the planet, and should be shared among them in an equitable manner. The manner and pace of exploitation of the resources should be done in a way that respects the interests and rights of future generations as well as those alive today, and should be done so as to maximize revenues obtained (subject to the above constraint). Among the most important global resources is the atmosphere. Economic activity that has an adverse effect on the quality of the atmosphere (e.g. depleting the ozone layer) has a potentially large global economic cost, and accordingly those who "use" up the atmosphere should be charged for doing so, with prices set so as to ensure the sustainability of atmospheric quality for future generations.

Revenues from Global Taxes. Two major global taxes have recently been the subject of extensive discussions. A "Tobin Tax" would apply to cross-border financial transactions, triggered every time foreign investors buy and sell currencies. A carbon tax would apply to emissions of greenhouse gases into the atmosphere. Both taxes would do double duty—discourage activities that do social harm (in the first case, destabilizing short-term currency trading; in the second case, environmental damage) and generate revenue for valuable public goods.

Concluding Remarks

Some critics of the critics of globalization have argued that globalization is inevitable: to resist it is futile. That, I would argue, is the wrong perspective. Globalization may be inevitable, but how countries respond to it is not. They do not, for instance. have to open up their capital markets to short-term capital flows. Different countries have, in fact, responded to globalization in different ways, and some have managed globalization better than others.

In the introduction, I suggested that globalization had been oversold, that certainly it has not brought to many of the poorest people in the world the benefits that were promised. In many quarters, it has led to the erosion of cultures. In others it has been associated with the degradation of the environment. Many countries have experienced higher levels of instability and insecurity than in the past.

But in the introduction, I also distinguished between globalization and the particular set of policies that have come to be associated with globalization in much of the world, the market fundamentalist policies, urging rapid privatization and liberalization, focusing more on the risks of inflation than the risks of underemployment and lack of growth, ignoring the impacts of policies on social stability. It is these policies that have been oversold, not globalization itself.

The past three decades have seen some phenomenal successes in development—beyond the wildest expectations of most economists; but they have seen some enormous disappointments as well. Globalization played an important role in both the successes and the failures. The critical distinction is how the individual countries go about integrating into the global economy. For those, like in East Asia, the benefits on the whole have far exceeded the costs. Their growth was based on globalization. For the most part, the countries figured out how to make globalization work for them. They were selective in which policies they adopted, in the pacing and sequencing of reforms. In the late 1980s, however, some of the countries succumbed to international pressure for capital market liberalization, the freeing up of markets to the movements of short-term speculative capital in and out of the country, and they paid dearly for this mistake. For this "episode" of globalization, the costs far exceeded the benefits. With savings rates in excess of 25 percent, sometimes even 35 percent, they didn't

TABLE 10.1 *GDP growth rates in Latin America 1951–2000*

COUNTRY	1951–1980		1951–1990		1980–1990		1990–2000		1980–2000	
	GDP pc	GDP	GDP pc	GDP	GPD pc	GDP	GDP pc	GPD	GDP pc	GDP
Argentina	1.81%	3.45%	0.44%	2.05%	-3.10%	-1.62%	3.53%	4.84%	0.51%	1.91%
Bolivia	0.47%	2.78%	-0.19%	2.07%	-2.21%	-0.13%	1.09%	3.48%	-0.64%	1.59%
Brazil	4.65%	7.46%	3.44%	6.05%	0.40%	2.41%	0.86%	2.30%	0.92%	2.65%
Chile	1.79%	3.81%	1.71%	3.63%	1.64%	3.26%	4.62%	6.15%	3.22%	4.78%
Colombia	2.28%	5.07%	2.05%	4.67%	1.40%	3.50%	1.03%	2.96%	1.16%	3.17%
Costa Rica	2.71%	6.25%	1.82%	5.16%	-0.99%	1.79%	1.71%	4.15%	0.34%	2.96%
Dom. Rep.	3.02%	5.99%	2.46%	5.24%	1.06%	3.31%	4.38%	6.08%	3.08%	5.04%
Ecuador	3.41%	6.37%	2.26%	5.11%	-0.74%	1.86%	-0.71%	1.41%	-0.76%	1.60%
Guatemala	2.14%	4.97%	1.31%	4.06%	-0.74%	1.79%	0.82%	3.47%	0.02%	2.61%
Honduras	0.89%	4.16%	0.61%	3.86%	-0.39%	2.81%	-1.02%	1.79%	-0.56%	2.44%
Mexico	3.22%	6.41%	2.32%	5.25%	0.07%	2.31%	1.95%	3.72%	0.93%	2.93%
Nicaragua	1.48%	4.46%	0.42%	3.34%	-3.02%	-0.24%	-1.95%	0.85%	-2.68%	0.14%
Panama	3.48%	6.30%	2.47%	5.11%	1.13%	3.24%	2.06%	3.85%	1.54%	3.49%
Peru	2.38%	5.09%	1.11%	3.69%	-2.34%	-0.09%	1.76%	3.53%	0.00%	2.01%
Paraguay	2.23%	4.88%	1.94%	4.70%	1.20%	4.29%	-0.31%	2.41%	0.38%	3.28%
El Salvador	1.35%	4.25%	0.62%	3.07%	-2.50%	-1.37%	2.05%	4.10%	-0.20%	1.38%
Uruguay	1.52%	2.48%	0.95%	1.83%	-0.25%	0.38%	2.58%	3.32%	1.26%	1.94%
Venezuela	1.11%	4.75%	0.51%	3.89%	-1.76%	0.88%	-0.35%	1.90%	-1.28%	1.14%
Mean	2.22%	4.94%	1.46%	4.04%	-0.62%	1.58%	1.34%	3.35%	0.40%	2.50%

Source: Alan Heston, Robert Summers and Bettina Aten, Penn World Table Version 6.1, Center for International Comparisons at the University of Pennsylvania (CICUP), October 2002

need additional capital. For them, capital market liberalization simply brought increased risk—with little promise of reward.

Elsewhere, the calculus on globalization is far more problematic. Often trade liberalization led not to increased growth, but to increased unemployment; and while many countries outside East Asia desperately needed foreign capital, the increased instability that capital market liberalization brought made their countries less, not more, attractive: money flocked to China, which had not liberalized.

The successes of China and the other countries which managed globalization on their own terms is even more impressive, because it took place in the context of globalization where the rules of the game have, for the most part, been set by the advanced industrial countries in their own interests, or more precisely, in the interests of special interests within these countries.

It is the inequities in the global trade agreements, the lack of balance with which the global economic agenda has been pursued and the economic policies that have often accompanied globalization that are the problem, not globalization itself.

There is, in a sense, a close link between these failures: the economic policies that have accompanied globalization have been driven by market fundamentalist ideologies, while the economic policies that have been pursued in countries that have been successful are those that reflect a balance between government and the market. Just as market fundamentalism has been pushed by special interests, which have taken advantage of the rhetoric to advance their interests at home (though they have not been so foolish as to allow the rhetoric get in the way of using government to advance their interests, even accepting large subsidies, if they can get away with it), so too has the global economic agenda been shaped by the same forces. Indeed, we have suggested that it is partly because the democratic checks and balances work less perfectly at the global level than they do domestically that they have had greater sway in this arena.

Globalization's impact has been oversold. But not its potential. It has the potential of raising living standards, reducing poverty, even enhancing global economic stability. While the potential benefits of globalization have perhaps only been slightly exaggerated, the potential costs of globalization have been vastly underestimated—as have the difficulties in making globalization work for most people in most of the developing countries. Even if globalization had been managed by those who had the interests of the developing countries at heart, there would have been a large risk of failure. But globalization has not been managed with the interests of the developing countries at the center; accordingly, we should not be surprised that it has worked so poorly for the poor.

It is unlikely that globalization will live up to that potential unless there are fundamental reforms in the way that it is managed. Countries need to learn to cope with globalization better. But even if they do so, if the current system, in which not only the rich gain a disproportionate share of the gains, but the poor may actually be worse off, in which the rich can withstand the instability, but the poor are left to cope on their own, prevails, then opposition to globalization will continue to grow.

ENDNOTES

1. More generally, transparency does not inoculate a country against having a crisis: the last set of major crises prior to those in East Asia was in Scandinavia, the countries with perhaps the greatest transparency.
2. See, e.g. World Bank (1998), Stiglitz (1999), Wolfensohn (1996).
3 Under the original HIPC (Highly Indebted Poor Countries) Initiative, launched in 1997, the countries who received relief were in chronological order: Uganda (April 1997), Bolivia (September 1997), Burkina Faso (September 1997), Guyana (December 1997), Côte d'Ivoire (March 1998), Mozambique (April 1998) and Mali (September 1998) (see Andrews *et al.* [1999]). In 1999 the initiative was thoroughly revised leading to the approval of a total of 23 countries in the program (see IMF [2001].) The 27 countries currently in the program are: Benin, Bolivia, Burkina Faso, Cameroon, Chad, the Democratic Republic of Congo, Ethiopia, The Gambia, Ghana, Guinea, Guinea-Bissau, Guyana, Honduras, Madagascar, Malawi, Mali, Mauritania, Mozambique, Nicaragua, Niger, Rwanda, São Tomé and Príncipe, Senegal, Sierra Leone, Tanzania, Uganda, and Zambia (see IMF [2004].)
4 See, e.g. World Bank (1993), Stiglitz (1996), Wade (1992), Amsden (1989).
5. See, in particular, Dixit (2003) and Stiglitz (2000a).
6. Cf. recent experiences in Brazil
7. The defense, that Camdessus was unaware that the picture was being taken, is of little help: the picture encapsulated the body language that said so much, both to those in Indonesia, and to those elsewhere.
8. See Stiglitz (2002) for an elaboration of this perspective.
9. The latter is relevant because social and political turmoil is related to *perceptions* of equitable treatment (see Rodrik [1997] and IMF [1998].) Note that in an "individualistic" analysis, individuals only care about their own treatment, not how they are treated *compares* with how others are.
10. Cooperation is sustained by individuals comparing the benefits of "cheating" in the short run, with the long run gains from cooperation. The present discounted value of those future long run gains is reduced by higher interest rates. Rapid change means the likelihood of future interactions is reduced, so that the value of cooperative behavior is reduced. See Stiglitz (2000c).
11. See also Seabright (1993), Dasgupta and Serageldin (2000).
12. See Sen (2000), Rao and Walton (2004).
13. The growth rate averaged 3.2% between 1990 and 1999 versus the 5.5% recorded between 1950 and 1980 (see Cardoso and Fishlow [1992], Ocampo and Martin [2003].) As always, there is some controversy concerning how to interpret such numbers. Critics of globalization point out that frequently, a period of stagnation

is followed by a catch; the high growth thus gives an exaggerated picture of the economy's sustainable performance. A better picture is provided by averaging the period of stagnation with the subsequent period. Table 10.1 shows that, viewed from this perspective, the decade of reform/globalization looks even more dismal (on this point see also Ocampo [2003].)

On the other hand, many critics of the growth in the earlier decades suggest it was not sustainable—it certainly wasn't sustained, but whether it was because of intrinsic weaknesses in the system, or because the countries were induced, by this earlier period of capital market globalization, to borrow more than was prudent, remains a subject of debate. In any case, in this perspective, one should include the lost decade of the 80s in the calculations of the earlier period—it was part of the price that had to be paid; even in this perspective, the decade of reform/globalization does not shine well.

14. Bouillon et al. (1998); Inter-American Development Bank (1999), Ros and Bouillon (2000).
15. See Caprio and Klingebiel (1997, 1999) and Caprio et al. (2003).
16. This is true even in the United States. See Furman and Stiglitz (1998).
17 See for example World Bank (2002).
18. See Rodrik (1998), Demirguc-Kunt and Detragiache (1999), and Kaminsky and Schmukler (2001).
19. See Rodriguez and Rodrik (1999).
20. See. Krueger (1995).
21. Growth in the decade prior to the start of the reforms averaged 5.8%.
22. See Prasad et al. (2003).
23. See Independent Evaluation Office (2003).
24. See e.g. Eichengreen (1999).
25. For examples, see Bardhan (1997) or Rose-Ackerman (1998).
26. See, for instance, the report of the Meltzer Commission (2000) and my discussion in Stiglitz (2001).
27. See Bonte (1999).
28. See, for instance, Hellman, Murdoch and Stilgitz (1995).
29. See Miller and Stiglitz (1999) and Stigltiz (2000b).
30. See for example Sachs (1984), Cohen and Sachs (1984), and Eaton, Gersovitz, and Stiglitz (1986).

REFERENCES

Amsden, Alice H. 1989. *Asia's Next Giant: South Korea and Late Industrialization*, Oxford University Press, New York.

Andrews, David, Anthony R. Boote, Syied S. Rizavi, and Sukhwinder Singh. 1999. "Debt Relief for Low-Income Countries—The Enhanced HIPC Initiative." IMF Pamphlet Series No.51, IMF, Washington D.C.

Bardhan, P. 1997. "Corruption and Development: A Review of Issues." *Journal of Economic Literature* 53 (September): 1320–1346.

Bonte, R. (Chairman). 1999. "Supervisory lessons to be drawn from the Asian crisis." Basel Committee on Banking Supervision Working Paper No. 2, Bank of International Settlements.

Bouillon, César, Arianna Legovini and Nora Lustig. 1998. "Rising Inequality in Mexico: Returns to Household Characteristics." Prepared for the Latin American and Caribbean Economic Association (LACEA)/Inter-American Development Bank (IADB)/World Bank (WB) Network on Inequality and Poverty's First Meeting, on October 21, 1998 in Buenos Aires.

Caprio, G., Jr., and D. Klingebiel. 1997. "Bank Insolvency: Bad Luck, Bad Policy, or Bad Banking?" In Michael Bruno and Boris Pleskovic, Proceedings of the Annual World Bank Conference on Development Economics 1996, Washington, D.C.: World Bank.

Caprio, G., Jr., and D. Klingebiel. 1999. "Episodes of Systemic and Borderline Financial Crises." World Bank, photocopy.

Caprio, G., Jr., D. Klingebiel, L. Laeven, and G.. Noguera. 2003. "Banking Crises Database." World Bank, photocopy.

Cardoso, Eliana and Albert Fishlow. 1992. "Latin American Economic Development: 1950–1980." Journal of Latin American Studies, 24, Quincentenary Supplement, pp.197–218.

Cohen, D. and J. Sachs. 1986. "Growth and External Debt Under Risk of Debt Repudiation." European Economic Review 30 (June): 529–560.

Dasgupta, Partha, and Ismail Serageldin, eds. 2000. Social Capital: A Multifaceted Perspective, World Bank, Washington D.C.

Dasgupta, P. and J.E. Stiglitz. 1977. "Tariffs Versus Quotas As Revenue Raising Devices Under Uncertainty." American Economic Review 67, no.5 (December): 975–981.

Demirguc-Kunt, A. and E. Detragiache. 1999. "Financial Liberalization and Financial Fragility." IMF Working Paper 98/83.

Dixit, Avinash. 2003. "Trade Expansion and Contract Enforcement." Journal of Political Economy 111, no.6, pp. 1293–1317.

Eaton, J., M. Gersovitz and J. E. Stiglitz. 1986. "Pure Theory of Country Risk." European Economic Review 30, no. 3 (June): 481–513.

Eichengreen, B.J. 1999. "Policymaking in an Integrated World: From Surveillance to. . .?" Federal Reserve Bank of Boston, Conference Series Proceedings, June, pp. 205–241.

Furman, J. and J. E. Stiglitz. 1988. "Economic Consequences of Income Inequality." In Symposium Proceedings—Income Inequality: Issues and Policy Options, Jackson Hole, Wyoming: Federal Reserve Bank of Kansas City, pp. 221–263.

Hellmann, T., K. Murdoch, and J.E. Stiglitz. 1996. "Deposit Mobilization Through Financial Restraint." In N. Hermes and R. Lensink, eds. Financial Development and Economic Growth. London: Routledge, 1996, pp. 219–246.

IMF. 1998. "Issues Paper." Presented at the Conference on Economic Policy and Equity, Washington, DC, June 8–9.

IMF. 2001. "Debt Relief for Poverty Reduction: The Role of the Enhanced HIPC Initiative." IMF, Washington D.C.

IMF. 2004. "Heavily Indebted Poor Countries (HIPC) Initiative—Statistical Update." IMF, Washington D.C.

Independent Evaluation Office (IEO) of the IMF. 2003. "The IMF and Recent Capital Account Crises: Indonesia, Korea, Brazil." Evaluation Report.

Inter-American Development Bank. 1999. "Facing Up to Inequality in Latin America." Economic and Social Progress in Latin America: 1998/1999 Report, IADB, Washington D.C.

Kaminsky, Graciela L. and Sergio L. Schmukler. 2001. "On Booms and Crashes: Financial Liberalization and Stock Market Cycles." World Bank Policy Working Paper No. 2565.

Krueger, A. 1995. "Policy Lessons from Development Experience since the Second World War." In Berhman J. and T. N. Srinivasan, eds., Handbook of Development Economics: Volume IIIB, pp. 2521–2543, New York: North Holland.

Meltzer, Allan H. (Chairman). 2000. "Report of the International Financial Institutions Advisory Commission." Washington: United States Congress.

Miller M. and J. E. Stiglitz. 1999. "Bankruptcy protection against macroeconomic shocks: the case for a 'super chapter 11.'" World Bank Conference on Capital Flows, Financial Crises, and Policies.

Newbery, D. and J. E. Stiglitz. 1984. "Pareto Inferior Trade." *Review of Economic Studies* 51, no. 1 (January): 1–12.

Ocampo, José Antonio. 2003. "Latin America's Growth Frustrations: The Macro and Mesoeconomic Links." Seminar on Management of Volatility, Financial Liberalization and Growth in Emerging Economies, April 24–25 ECLAC Headquarters, Santiago, Chile.

Ocampo, José Antonio and Juan Martín. 2003. *A Decade of Light and Shadow. Latin America and the Caribbean in the 1990s*. Santiago, Chile: ECLAC.

Prasad, E., K. Rogoff, S. Wei and M.A. Kose. 2003. "Effects of Financial Globalization on Developing Countries: Some Empirical Evidence." IMF Occasional Paper.

Rao, Vijavendra and Michael Walton, eds. 2004. *Culture and Public Action*. Stanford University Press.

Rodriguez, F. and D. Rodrik. 1999. "Trade Policy and Economic Growth: A Skeptic's Guide to Cross-National Evidence." NBER Working Paper No. 7081.

Rodrik, Dani. 1997. *Has Globalization Gone too Far?* Washington D.C.:Institute for International Economics.

———. "Who Needs Capital Account Convertibility?" In Should the IMF Pursue Capital-Account Convertibility? Princeton Essays in International Finance No. 207.

Ros, Jaime and César Bouillon. 2000. "Mexico: Trade Liberalization, Growth, Inequality and Poverty." In Enrique Ganuza, Ricardo Paes de Barros, Lance Taylor, Rob Vos, eds. *Liberalización, Desigualdad y Pobreza: América Latina y el Caribe en los 90*, UNDP.

Rose-Ackerman, S. 1998. "Corruption and Development." Annual World Bank Conference on Development Economics, 1997.

Sachs J. 1984. "Theoretical Issues in International Borrowing." Princeton Studies in International Finance No. 54.

Seabright, Paul. 1993. "Managing Local Commons: Theoretical Issues and Incentive Design." *Journal of Economic Perspectives* 7, no. 4 (Autumn): 113–134.

Sen, Amartya. 2000. "Culture and Development." Paper presented at the World Bank Tokyo Meeting, December 13.

Stiglitz, Joseph E. 1993. "The Role of the State in Financial Markets." Proceedings of the World Bank Conference on Development Economics 1993, Washington, D.C.: World Bank, pp. 41–46.

———. 1996. "Some Lessons from the East Asian Miracle." *World Bank Research Observer* 11, no. 2 (August): 151–177.

———. 1999. "Knowledge as a Global Public Good." In Inge Kaul, Isabelle Grunberg, Marc A. Stern, eds. *Global Public Goods: International Cooperation in the 21st Century.* United Nations Development Programme, New York: Oxford University Press, pp. 308–325.

———. 2000a. "Formal and Informal Institutions." In Dasgupta and Serageldin, eds. *Social Capital: A Multifaceted Perspective*, Washington: World Bank, pp. 59–68.

———. 2000b. "Some Elementary Principles of Bankruptcy." In *Governance, Equity and Global Markets: Proceedings from the Annual Bank Conference on Development Economics in Europe, June 1999.* Conseil d'Analyse economique, Paris, 2000, pp. 605–620.

———. 2000c. "Whither Reform? Ten Years of Transition." In B. Pleskovic and J.E. Stiglitz, eds. *Annual World Bank Conference on Economic Development,* Washington: World Bank, pp. 27–56. Also Chapter 4 in Ha-Joon Chang, ed. *The Rebel Within*, London: Wimbledon Publishing Company, 2001, pp. 127–171. Summary in *Transition Economics*, 3 , no. 12 (June 1999). (Originally presented on April 30, 1999.

———. 2001. "Failure of the Fund: Rethinking the IMF Response." *Harvard International Review* 23, no. 2 (Summer 2001): 14–18.

———. 2002. "Globalization and the Logic of International Collective Action: Re-Examining the Bretton Woods Institutions." In Deepak Nayyar ed. *Governing Globalization: Issues and Institutions.* New York: Oxford University Press, pp. 238–253.

Wade, Robert. 1992. *Governing the Market: Economic Theory and the Role of Government in East Asian Industrialization.* Princeton University Press.

Wolfensohn, James D. 1996. "People and Development." Annual Meetings Address, October 1, 1996, www.worldbank.org/president

World Bank. 1993. The East Asian Miracle: Economic Growth and Public Policy. New York: Oxford University Press.

World Bank. 1998. "Knowledge for Development." World Development Report, World Bank, Washington D.C.

World Bank. 2002. "Globalization, Growth and Poverty: Building an Inclusive World Economy." World Bank Policy Research Report, World Bank and Oxford University Press.

GEORGE J. BORJAS is the Robert W. Scrivner Professor of Economics and Social Policy at the John F. Kennedy School of Government, Harvard University. He is also a Research Associate at the National Bureau of Economic Research. Professor Borjas has written extensively on labor market issues. He is the author of several books, including *Wage Policy in the Federal Bureaucracy* (American Enterprise Institute, 1980), *Friends or Strangers: The Impact of Immigrants on the U.S. Economy* (Basic Books, 1990), *Heaven's Door: Immigration Policy and the American Economy* (Princeton University Press, 1999). He has published more than 100 articles in books and scholarly journals, including *The American Economic Review, The Journal of Political Economy,* and *The Quarterly Journal of Economics.* Professor Borjas received his Ph.D. in economics from Columbia University in 1975.

CHARLES W. CALOMIRIS is the Henry Kaufman Professor of Financial Institutions in the Division of Finance and Economics at the Columbia University Graduate School of Business. He is also a Professor of International and Public Affairs at Columbia's School of International and Public Affairs, the Arthur Burns Fellow in International Economics at the American Enterprise Institute, and a Research Associate of the National Bureau of Economics. He is also a member of the U.S. Shadow Financial Regulatory Committee. Since 1995, Professor Calomiris has co-directed the Project on Financial Deregulation at the American Enterprise Institute. In 1999–2000, he served on the International Financial Institutions Advisory Commission, a Congressional Commission established to draft recommendations for the reform of the IMF, World Bank, regional development banks, and BIS. He is the author of numerous books, articles, and book chapters, including, with David Beim, *Emerging Financial Markets* (McGraw-Hill, 2001), *U.S. Bank Deregulation in Historical Perspective*

(Cambridge University Press, 2000), and *A Globalist Manifesto for Public Policy* (Institute for International Economics, 2001). His work is primarily in the areas of financial institutions, corporate finance, monetary economics, and financial history. Professor Calomiris received his Ph.D. in economics from Stanford.

DAVID DOLLAR is the World Bank's country director for China and Mongolia, based in Beijing. From 1995 to 2004 Dollar worked in the Bank's research department. He co-authored (with Lant Pritchett) the World Bank report, "Assessing Aid" (www.worldbank.org/research/aid). His contributions to the aid-effectiveness research covered the impact of aid on growth and poverty, how aid could be reallocated to have a larger effect on poverty reduction, and the impact of structural adjustment lending and conditionality on policy reform. His current work focuses on the impact of different institutions and policies on inequality and poverty. In particular, he is investigating the impact of globalization—openness to trade and capital flows—on growth, inequality, and poverty. Before joining the research department Dollar was spent six years working in Vietnam (1989–95) and headed up the Bank's policy dialogue with that country during a period of intense reform and structural adjustment. Recent publications: "Growth Is Good for the Poor," with Aart Kraay and "Can the World Cut Poverty in Half?" with Paul Collier. He has a Ph.D. in economics from NYU.

WILLIAM EASTERLY is Professor of Economics at New York University, where he is co-director of the Development Research Institute and joint with the Africana Studies Program. He is also Senior Fellow at the Center for Global Development and the Institute for International Economics. He previously worked for 16 years as a research economist at the World Bank. He is author of the book *The Elusive Quest for Growth: Economists' Adventures and Misadventures in the Tropics* (MIT Press, 2001), as well as of numerous academic articles. He has lived and traveled in many places around the world on all continents except Antarctica. His research specializations include economic growth, foreign aid, ethnic conflict, political economy, and macroeconomic policies. He received his Ph.D. in economics from MIT in 1985.

JEFFREY A. FRANKEL is Harpel Professor of Capital Formation and Growth at Harvard University's Kennedy School of Government, a member of the Business Cycle Dating Committee of the National Bureau of Economic Research, and a former member of the President's Council of Economic Advisors (1997–99). Professor Frankel is a specialist in international economics and macroeconomics. His long-term research interests include the globalization of financial markets, the workings of the foreign exchange market, targets and indicators for monetary policy, the term structure of interest rates, monetary determinants of agricultural prices, international macroeconomic policy coordination, regional trading blocs, financial issues in Japan and the Pacific, crises in emerging markets, European Monetary Union, and economics policy regarding the global environment. Subjects of ongoing research include: exchange rate regimes for emerging market countries and the interaction of geography, trade, growth, and noneconomic goals such as pollution. His books include *Regional Trading Blocs* (Institute for International Economics, 1997), *World Trade and Payments*, with Richard Caves and Ronald Jones (9th edition, Addison Wesley Longman, 2002), and *American Economic Policy in the 1990s* (MIT Press, 2002). Academic articles (co-authored) include "Is Trade Good or Bad for the Environment? Sorting Out the Causality," *Review of Economics and Statistics*, 2004. He received his Ph.D. in economics from MIT in 1978.

Douglas A. Irwin is Professor of Economics at Dartmouth College and a Research Associate of the National Bureau of Economic Research. He is author of *Managed Trade: The Case Against Import Targets* (AEI Press, 1994), *Against the Tide: An Intellectual History of Free Trade* (Princeton University Press, 1996), *Free Trade Under Fire* (Princeton University Press, 2002), and many articles on trade policy in books and professional journals. He has previously taught at the University of Chicago and MIT, and has served on the staff of the President's Council of Economic Advisors and the Federal Reserve Board in Washington. He received his Ph.D. in economics from Columbia University in 1988.

Dani Rodrik is professor of international political economy at the John F. Kennedy School of Government, Harvard University. He has published widely in the areas of international economics, economic development, and political economy. What constitutes good economic policy and why some governments are better than others in adopting it are the central questions on which his research focuses. He is affiliated with the National Bureau of Economic Research, Centre for Economic Policy Research (London), Center for Global Development, Institute for International Economics, and Council on Foreign Relations. Among other honors, he was presented the Leontief Award for Advancing the Frontiers of Economic Thought in 2002. He is the author of "Resistance to Reform: Status Quo Bias in the Presence of Individual-Specific Uncertainty" (with R. Fernandez), *American Economic Review*, 1991; "Distributive Politics and Economic Growth" (with A. Alesina), *Quarterly Journal of Economics*, 1994; "Why Do More Open Economies Have Bigger Governments?" *Journal of Political Economy*, October 1998; "Democracies Pay Higher Wages," *Quarterly Journal of Economics*, August 1999; *The New Global Economy and Developing Countries: Making*

Openness Work (Overseas Development Council, Washington DC, 1999); and editor of *In Search of Prosperity: Analytic Narratives on Economic Growth* (Princeton University Press, 2003). He is a co-editor of *The Review of Economics and Statistics*. Professor Rodrik received his Ph.D. in economics from Princeton University in 1985.

JEFFREY D. SACHS is the Director of The Earth Institute, Quetelet Professor of Sustainable Development, and Professor of Health Policy and Management at Columbia University. He is also Special Advisor to United Nations Secretary General Kofi Annan on a group of poverty reduction initiatives called the Millennium Development Goals. Sachs is internationally renowned for advising governments in Latin America, Eastern Europe, the former Soviet Union, Asia, and Africa on economic reforms and for his work with international agencies to promote poverty reduction, disease control, and debt reduction of poor countries. He was recently named among the 100 most influential leaders in the world by *Time* Magazine. He is author of hundreds of scholarly articles and many books. Sachs was recently elected into the Institute of Medicine and is a Research Associate of the National Bureau of Economic Research. Prior to joining Columbia, Sachs spent more than twenty years at Harvard University, most recently as Director of the Center for International Development. A native of Detroit, Michigan, Sachs received his B.A., M.A., and Ph.D. degrees at Harvard University.

JOSEPH E. STIGLITZ is University Professor at Columbia University, teaching in the Economics Department, The School of International and Public Affairs, and its Business School. From 1997 to 2000, he served as the World Bank's Senior Vice President for Development Economics and Chief Economist. From 1993 to 1997, Dr. Stiglitz served as a member and then as the Chairman of the President's Council of Economic Advisors and as a member of the President's cabinet. In 1979, the American Economic Association awarded Dr. Stiglitz its biennial John Bates Clark Award, which is given to the economist under forty who has made the most significant contributions to economics. In 2001, Dr. Stiglitz was awarded the Nobel Prize. Dr. Stiglitz helped create a new branch of economics—"The Economics of Information"—which has been widely applied throughout the economics discipline. He helped pioneer pivotal concepts such as theories of adverse selection and moral hazard, which have now become the standard tools of policy analysts as well as economic theorists. He has been instrumental in developing new macro-economic theories (a strand of what is sometimes called "New Keynesian Economics"), including new theories of monetary economics, emphasizing the role of credit. His reformulation of development theory has had profound effects on practice, particularly at the World Bank, as well as on theory, particularly in the creation of the modern theory of rural organization He has also made major contributions to the theory of income distribution, the theory of corporate finance, the theory of uncertainty, the theory of industrial organization, and the theory of economic growth. Dr. Stiglitz earned his Ph.D. from MIT in 1967.

MICHAEL M. WEINSTEIN is Director of Research, Policy and Planning for The Robin Hood Foundation. He served as chairman of the Department of Economics at Haverford College during the 1980s. He provided economics analysis and commentaries for National Public Radio before joining *The New York Times*, where he served on the editorial board and as the Times' economics columnist during the 1990s. In 2001, he became the first director of the Maurice R. Greenberg Center for Geoeconomic Studies at the Council on Foreign Relations, also holding the Paul A. Volcker Chair in international economics at the Council. Weinstein directs the Institutes for Journalists at The New York Times Company Foundation (which trains veteran journalists from around the country in complicated subjects about to hit the headlines) and is president and founder of W.A.D. Financial Counseling, Inc., a nonprofit foundation which provides free financial counseling to poor families. In addition to editing this volume he is co-author with Morton Halperin and Joseph Siegle of The Democracy Advantage (forthcoming, Routledge and the Council on Foreign Relations), author of Recovery and Redistribution Under the N.I.R.A. (Amsterdam, North-Holland, 1980), journal articles, and about 1,500 columns, editorials, news analysis articles, and magazine pieces for *The New York Times* about welfare, inequality, poverty, health care, energy, social security, tax, budget, trade, environment, regulation, antitrust, telecommunications, education, banking and many other public policy issues. He received his Ph.D. in economics from MIT in 1979.

INDEX